TWENTIETH-CENTURY HISTORIES

The Hungarian Revolution

David Pryce-Jones

LONDON · ERNEST BENN LIMITED · 1969

First published 1969 by Ernest Benn Limited
Bouverie House, Fleet Street, London, E.C.4
© David Pryce-Jones 1969
Distributed in Canada by
The General Publishing Company Limited, Toronto
Maps drawn by Marc Sale
Book designed by Kenneth Day
Printed in Great Britain
510–18110–4

*The illustration on the title page shows the
burning of propaganda material outside the
Secret Police Building in Budapest*

CONTENTS

PRINCIPAL BOOKS CONSULTED

The Revolt of the Mind, by Tamas Aczel and Tibor Meray (Thames and Hudson, 1961)

The Soviet Bloc, by Zbigniew Brzezinski (Oxford University Press, 1967)

Behind the Rape of Hungary, by François Fejto (New York, David McKay, 1957)

Hungarian Tragedy, by Peter Fryer (Dobson, 1956)

The Cold War as History, by Louis J. Halle (Chatto and Windus, 1967)

Political Prisoner, by Pal Ignotus (Routledge and Kegan Paul, 1959)

The Unexpected Revolution, by Paul Kecskemeti (California, Stanford University Press, 1961)

The Hungarian Revolution, edited by Melvin J. Lasky (Secker and Warburg, 1957)

Thirteen Days That Shook the Kremlin, by Tibor Meray (Thames and Hudson, 1959)

October Fifteenth, A History of Modern Hungary 1929–45, by C. A. Macartney. Parts I and II (Edinburgh University Press, 1961)

The Struggle Behind the Iron Curtain, by Ferenc Nagy (New York, Macmillan, 1948)

On Communism, by Imre Nagy (Thames and Hudson, 1957)

Window onto Hungary, by Dora Scarlett (Bradford, Broadacre Books, 1958)

The East European Revolution, by Hugh Seton-Watson (Methuen, 1956)

United Nations Report of the Special Committee on the Problem of Hungary. *General Assembly Official Records* (New York, 1957)

The Nineteen Days, by George Urban (Heinemann, 1957)

Rift and Revolt in Hungary, by Ferenc Vali (Cambridge, Mass., Harvard University Press, 1961)

Revolution in Hungary, by Paul E. Zinner (New York, Columbia University Press, 1962)

The books were published in London unless otherwise stated.

MAPS

1 From March to August 1919, Bela Kun headed a Communist regime. His policies at home and abroad were a failure and he was forced to flee the country. Finding asylum in Russia, he was executed there in 1937 on Stalin's orders

1 Hungary between Germans and Russians

UNTIL THE END OF 1943 the Second World War did not weigh too heavily on Hungary. Beyond the Carpathian mountains a Hungarian army had been taking heavy losses from the Russians, but it had been withdrawn after a serious defeat that January at Voronezh. In Budapest the famous horse-races were still held, women dressed elegantly, restaurants were full, and German soldiers on leave from the drawn-out fight against the Soviet army on the Eastern Front could hardly believe their temporary luck. On the streets in every town, it was true, roamed bands of local fascists, members of the Arrow Cross in their green uniforms; their organisation and their thoughts taken from the Nazis. But Parliament continued to meet and opposition was not yet wholly suppressed. To many Hungarians their country, even with the Germans in it, seemed like a forgotten corner of ravaged Europe, and a corner which by a mixture of fortune and skill might be overlooked when the Great Powers came to a final reckoning. If the war was being fought to preserve the sovereignty of Central European countries, as the Allies said, then Hungary too might expect eventual freedom from foreign domination.

Such false hopes were soon to be exposed. The Allied landings on the Normandy beachheads in June should have spelled out unmistakably that the Germans had lost the war, but Hungary was a long way from the Western Front. That summer of 1944 was excessively hot in Hungary. No rain fell, the fields were parched, and even on main roads cars or peasants' carts threw up dust. This weather, menacing but passive, was like the Hungarian situation. People came to realise at last that their reprieve from war was coming to an end, and that a former way of life was about to be completely destroyed.

The cause of this growing but helpless feeling of uncertain doom was the alliance with Germany. Such an alliance was the outcome of Hungary's recent past. Until the end of the First World War, Hungary had formed an important part of the Austro-Hungarian empire, ruled by the last Habsburg emperor, Kaiser Franz Josef, in Vienna. But the desire for independence had not only survived, it had grown stronger; first throughout the many sterile years of the Turkish occupation, then during the Austrian administration which had been imposed early in the eighteenth century. The Habsburg empire was dissolved in 1918, after defeat in the First World War, and its several nationalities, including Hungary, gained at last their independence. The break-up of the old nineteenth-century societies brought violence and civil disorder. After a few months the liberal government in Hungary of Count Michael Karolyi was overthrown by the only successful Bolshevik revolution to have taken place in Europe outside Russia. Bela Kun and his Communist regime followed closely the model just set up in Moscow by Lenin. He had little popular support and again, after a few months, was forced to flee the country. A more traditional type of strong government was established under Admiral Miklos Horthy, and backed at first by foreign troops. Admiral Horthy had risen to command the Austro-Hungarian navy, a post rarely held by a Hungarian. He was a chauvinistic, God-fearing man with the qualities and limitations of his kind; as such he was to be the permanent unyielding head of his country for some twenty-five

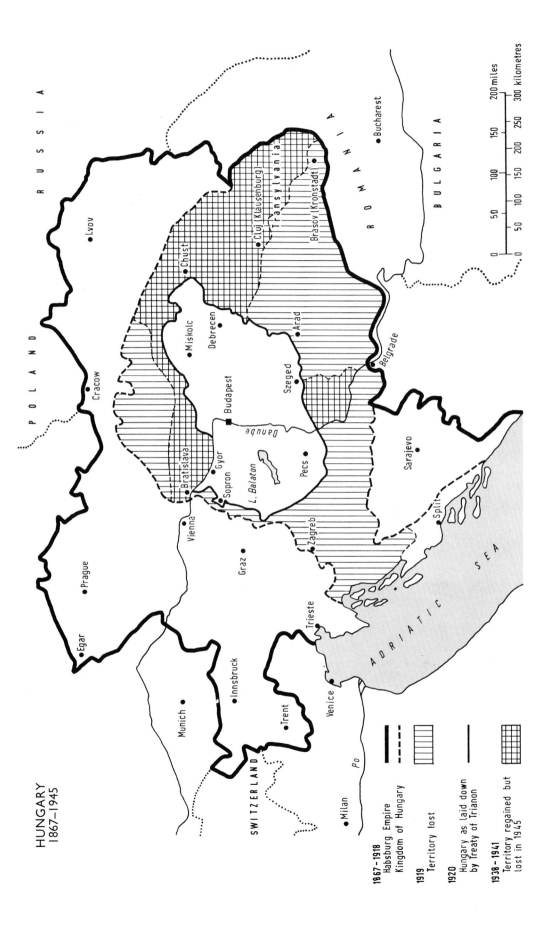

HUNGARY
1867-1945

POLAND

RUSSIA

ROMANIA

BULGARIA

SWITZERLAND

ADRIATIC SEA

• Lvov

• Cracow

• Prague

• Egar

• Munich

• Innsbruck

• Trent

• Venice

• Milan

• Trieste

Vienna •

Graz •

Sopron •

Bratislava •

Gyor •

• Miskolc

Debrecen •

• Budapest

L. Balaton

• Pecs

Szeged •

Zagreb •

Sarajevo •

• Chust

• Cluj (Klausenburg)

Transylvania

Brasov (Kronstadt) •

• Arad

Belgrade •

Split •

• Bucharest

Danube

Po

1867-1918
Habsburg Empire
Kingdom of Hungary

1919
Territory lost

1920
Hungary as laid down
by Treaty of Trianon

1938-1941
Territory regained but
lost in 1945

0   50   100 150 200 miles

0 50 100 150 200 250 300 kilometres

crucial years. Calling himself Regent, for Hungary was in theory still a monarchy with a Habsburg claimant to the throne, Horthy behaved like the uncrowned king that he was. When he took over after the short Communist interlude, he did nothing to stop the ensuing White Terror in which many Communists were killed. Hungarians were to forget neither the Red nor the White atrocities to which independence had given rise, but were prone to find excuses for Horthy's slow dictatorship.

During the 1920s Hungary enjoyed a false stability which came from carrying out no reforms at all. Reforms were urgent if Hungary were to modernise. Its industry was poor and at a primitive stage. The economy was largely agricultural, but dominated by estates of feudal size. Through their vast holdings of land the Hungarian aristocracy played a top-heavy part in the affairs of the country. They were wholly conservative. When Count Karolyi, during his term as Prime Minister, had broken up his estates of 40,000 acres and given them out in lots to the peasants, his action inspired nobody else to do the same. Yet several families owned more than 100,000 acres, and the Catholic Church over a million acres.

Hungary between the wars, as Pal Ignotus, one of its distinguished writers, says, 'was a corrupt and happy-go-lucky society, vulgar in some respects, sophisticated, often astoundingly naïve'. The night-clubs and cafés of Budapest were the best in Europe, and as it turned out, there were growing up many hundreds of writers, musicians, scientists, and fortune-hunters who as émigrés were to be successful in most countries of the world. It was always Hungary's handicap to be too small to contain its native talent. Such a society, however, was unlikely to respond in a healthy way to the rise of Hitler. Many Hungarians had, anyhow, an exaggerated spirit of nationalism and saw in their history all sorts of reasons for believing that as Magyars they were better than the surrounding races, Slavs or Germans. These people sympathised readily with the new Nazi doctrines coming from Germany, and they became natural fascists. The growing bourgeois class had been terrified by what they had experienced of Bolshevism and they asked nothing better than to be protected from it by all means. The peasants had little to say, certainly not as much as the police or the country police, the gendarmes whose cocked hats were picturesque in the eyes of visitors to Hungary, but who were in fact busily repressing signs of democracy. The Communist Party, small as it was, was outlawed. All these factors helped the rising fascist agitation.

Hitler played cleverly on Hungarian weaknesses. Links between Germany and Hungary were emphasised. More essentially Hitler made use of historic quarrels which Hungary had maintained over the centuries with her neighbours. In particular Hungary claimed Transylvania where a large part of the population were indeed Magyar. Romania also claimed the area and had been awarded it by the Treaty of Trianon after the First World War, at a time when peace treaties had been drawn up with a bias which left grudges not only in Hungarian minds. Hitler's startling success at the outset of his career could not be overlooked by a weak country like Hungary which was too close to Germany for comfort. If England and France did not resist such a dictator, what was Hungary to do? Neighbouring Czechoslovakia had also gained her independence in 1918, and when in 1938 that country was divided into separate pieces as a result of Hitler's policy of aggression, and thereby ceased to exist as an independent state, the lesson was not lost on Hungary. Not only might the Hungarians survive by throwing their lot in with the Germans, but they might even profit. This attitude seemed justified when Hitler transferred to them the disputed Transylvania and other

2   The fashionable life of Budapest between the wars was
a by-word in Europe for its ease and elegance

boundary areas by a series of awards. These awards were not recognised by the major
powers, but such powers could do nothing about it, and meanwhile Hungary had
recovered land which Hungarians felt rightfully belonged to them. The means by which
the ends had been achieved could be ignored. At a time when European states seemed
to be returning to the law of the jungle in their dealings with one another, Hungary was
neither more selfish nor more short-sighted than its neighbours.

Admiral Horthy was never wholly convinced by Hitler although he had become a
willing ally and accomplice. Once war was declared between Germany and Russia in
1941, it became obvious that Hungary's geographical position – next to an Austria
now officially part of the Greater German Reich – left her at the German army's mercy.
The fateful moment for Hungary had come in April 1941, when Germany invaded
Yugoslavia. Shortly beforehand Hungary had signed a pact of friendship with Yugoslavia. The Germans insisted on sending their attacking armies through Hungary to
Yugoslavia, and worse, they rewarded Hungary with Yugoslav territory where people
of Hungarian descent had been living. The Hungarian Prime Minister, Count Teleki,
committed suicide, rightly considering that his country, and especially his policy, had
been exploited. Such a gesture could not hide the fact that the Germans were vitally
interested in the strategic and military use of Hungarian railways, and also that they
needed all the food they could get from the rich Hungarian countryside. Supplies were
to be paid for after the war – which has meant in effect that the Germans plundered
Hungary freely for five years.

Once Hitler had carried the war away deeper into Russia, most Hungarians were
easier in their consciences, for anti-communism guided the ruling classes. In 1943 and
1944 Prime Minister Nicholas Kallay made efforts to get out of the war, but he insisted
on surrendering to the Western Allies only. Churchill and Roosevelt could not accept

8

3   Count Pal Teleki (*centre: front row*) was appointed by
the Regent Horthy at the head of his cabinet in
February 1939. He hoped that Hungary would not become
an ally of Germany and committed suicide when his
policy collapsed in 1941

any move leaving out Russia. Throughout the closing years of the war, the two Western Powers were often suspected by Russia of going behind her back. The Western Powers in turn remembered the pact Stalin had signed with Hitler in 1939. To the end, the Germans hoped to benefit from such suspicions and split the Allies. It was therefore unrealistic of Kallay to make secret advances to the West in this way, sending special agents to Istanbul or Lisbon, but by that stage of the war, dread of the Russians was already beginning to loom in Hungary. As the Russians drew closer to Hungary, it became more essential than ever for the Germans to ensure their rear and main lines of communication to the Eastern Front. On 19 March 1944, they took over Hungary, a step which demanded hardly more than driving a Panzer division through Budapest. A former ally had become a satellite. The German minister to Budapest, Veesenmayer, who was Foreign Minister Ribbentrop's expert on Balkan affairs, became the real ruler of the country although he observed the constitutional procedures with Horthy. Kallay fled to the Turkish legation and a collaborator was appointed in his place.

By then Admiral Horthy had also come to realise that the outcome of the war was virtually settled and that he must come to terms with the victorious Russians as well as with the Western Powers. He opened negotiations with left-wing leaders of the Hungarian underground. But in his narrow gentlemanly way, he wished to do the right thing by his former allies, and could not bring himself to double-cross the Germans, however much they had duped him. The British Foreign Secretary, Anthony Eden, has been quoted as saying at the time, 'I expect the Russians will want to be very hard on the Hungarians.' The day was approaching when the Hungarian alliance with Germany would rebound.

9

A few observers, and they included Churchill, had begun to be worried by the thrust of the Russians into Eastern, and now Central, Europe. When the Russians had first been invaded in 1941, the survival of their country was at stake. At tremendous cost, they had pushed back the Germans, and what had been a military situation took on political colouring. Russia's intentions towards her neighbour Poland were the test case. Russia had ruled Poland, completely or partially, for much of her history, although Russia's momentary weakness after the 1917 Bolshevik revolution allowed Poland a short-lived advantage. But the government of the independent Poland which existed from 1918 until Hitler's invasion was anti-Russian and anti-Communist. Stalin who had succeeded Lenin in the foremost position of power in Russia and who had presided over a military revival, was determined that this would not happen again. When he said that he wanted a strong Poland, what he meant was a Poland which Russia could control. Stalin broke off relations with the official Polish government in exile in London and set up a handful of Polish Communists in a body known as the Lublin Committee, and who were to be the future Communist leaders. Over all the Big Three discussions towards the end of the war, between America, England, and Russia, the Polish question and the good faith of the Russians towards the Poles hung like a black cloud. When in August and September 1944, the Russians reached the suburbs of Warsaw, the Polish freedom-fighters rose in revolt to drive the Germans from their capital. While the Poles fought with the courage of despair, the Russian army held off and gave them no help, so that the Germans were able to suppress the rising, inflicting heavy casualties. It became plain that the Russians were as much of a danger to Polish independence as Germany had been. The future of the eastern provinces of Poland, to which the Russians could indeed lay claim, was hardly to be discussed. The land was soon incorporated into Russia.

Romania had been in the same plight as Hungary, but because the Russians had

4   Hitler and his Foreign Minister Ribbentrop (*left*) needed control of Hungary to pursue the war against Russia, of which Admiral Horthy approved. When Horthy sought to break the alliance, the German army occupied Hungary outright.

reached her frontier sooner, she was the first of the German satellites to be able to break away from the Axis. King Michael arrested in his palace the local dictator, Marshal Antonescu, an act for which he received the Order of Stalin, although this did not save his throne four years later. When the Russians occupied Romania, they annexed into the Soviet Union the provinces of Bessarabia and Bukovina. It was a repetition of what they had done in Poland. They also arranged for a government which would serve their ends. The American and British representatives in Romania reserved their right to protest until a proper peace treaty would be signed. This, with the Polish experience, gave some idea of the new order that might emerge in Europe. In a minute to Eden, in May 1944, Churchill had expressed himself bluntly:

> Broadly speaking, the issue is this, Are we going to acquiesce in the Communisation of the Balkans. . . ? I am of opinion on the whole that we ought to come to a definite conclusion about it, and that if our conclusion is that we resist the Communist infusion and invasion, we should put it to them pretty plainly at the best moment that military events permit.

In Churchill's mind there had taken shape a plan to launch an invasion through the Balkans, to capture Vienna and Hungary, and so forestall the Russians in Central Europe. Time and again he was to return to the idea, but it was not accepted by the Americans, principally on the grounds that nothing must be done to arouse Stalin's fears of devious Western motives. Nor were these fears imaginary. Stalin, for instance, suspected that the invasion of Normandy had been deliberately delayed while the Russians and the Germans were encouraged to bleed to death in Eastern Europe. If Roosevelt and Churchill were haunted by the thought that Stalin might make a sudden alliance with Hitler, as dramatically as he had done just before the war, so Stalin was anxious to protect himself against some anti-Communist alliance of Hitler and the Western Powers. Besides, President Roosevelt liked to think of 'bringing home the boys'

5   Churchill and Roosevelt had insisted that their war-aims were the same as those of Stalin – the political future of Europe was not to be allowed to jeopardise victory over Germany

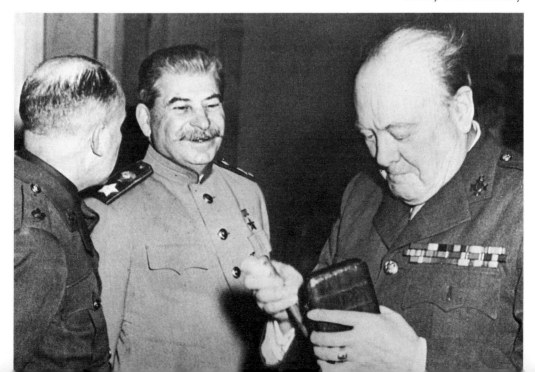

as he did not plan that America should keep troops in Europe longer than was necessary. The Balkans were far away and of no concern to America.

Both Churchill and Roosevelt have been criticised for their conduct as heads of the two most powerful democratic states, the former for having ideas which were impractical, even dangerous, the latter for being idealistic about Russian intentions and therefore deceived by them. In fact, both men finally decided that winning the war was the topmost priority. They realised that this would leave Russia in a strong political position after the war, but they shelved that problem to another day. The communisation of the Balkans was to be observed with regret but not resisted.

Early in September 1944, the Russians moved on from Romania to Bulgaria.

6 Budapest with Parliament in background viewed from Buda (the Fisherman's Bastion), in contrast to the war scene opposite taken from the other bank

7 (*opposite*) Desolation and war damage seen from the Pest side of the Danube, with the old Royal Palace on Buda Hill in the background

Bulgaria, never very happy to belong to the German Axis, had previously declared her neutrality. Nevertheless the Russians occupied the country and dictated their wishes to another government of their choice. Excluding the dismembered Czechoslovakia, Hungary was now the last of the satellites. On 22 September, a Hungarian aeroplane carrying General Naday of the Hungarian First Army arrived at the Allied Headquarters in Caserta, Italy, to ask for an armistice. Another Hungarian general, Bela Miklos, headed a delegation to Moscow with a similar demand. These were Admiral Horthy's final efforts to shake off German overlordship. By then, too, Red army units, accompanied by their brand-new allies, the Romanians, who had hopes of regaining Transylvania as their reward, had crossed into Hungary in a fierce attack. The Germans were going to defend every inch of their retreat, and had moved crack reserve divisions into the line. The beautiful summer was indeed over, there was to be no more lull in the war, no more delusion that Hungary could escape the consequences of her policy. Hungary was to prove a terrible example of a small nation caught in the great struggle of fascism and communism.

As her agony was beginning on the ground, a vital part of the drama had taken place in Moscow. On 9 October, Churchill met Stalin, with their Foreign Ministers, Molotov and Eden, present. Reluctantly accepting that there would be no Allied armies sweeping up through the Balkans, Churchill wanted to salvage what he could for the future of Central Europe. He described the scene in his memoirs.

> The moment was apt for business, so I said, 'Let us settle our affairs in the Balkans. Your armies are in Roumania and Bulgaria. We have interests, missions, and agents there. Don't let us get at cross-purposes in small ways. So far as Britain and Russia are concerned, how would it do for you to have ninety per cent predominance in Roumania, for us to have ninety per cent of the say in Greece, and go fifty-fifty about Yugoslavia?

He then wrote out on a half-sheet of paper the table of percentages which he had proposed. Hungary was another country to be split fifty-fifty. 'Casting an eye over the paper, Stalin took his blue pencil and made a large tick upon it, and passed it back to us. It was all settled in no more time than it takes to set down.' Churchill goes on,

> After this there was a long silence. The pencilled paper lay in the centre of the table. At length I said, 'Might it not be thought rather cynical if it seemed we had disposed of these issues, so fateful to millions of people, in such an offhand manner? Let us burn the paper.' 'No, you keep it,' said Stalin.

The very next day the Russians reached the provincial city of Debrecen in eastern Hungary and called on the Hungarian government to break off relations with the Germans and to join in the fighting against them. At last Admiral Horthy did what he should have done, although it was far too late, now that a pistol was almost literally pointed at his head. Following the dispatch of the armistice delegations, he prepared a *coup* which would take Hungary out of the war altogether. On 15 October, when Marshal

13

8   Hungarian Jews, wearing the star of David badge, were
herded into Auschwitz after transport by cattle-trucks

Malinowski's army had swept across the Tisza River and was within forty-five miles of
Budapest, Horthy announced over the wireless that Hungary had surrendered.
Inefficiently planned – the workers of Budapest were not even given weapons – the
plot was a fiasco. Very few Hungarians heard the broadcast, even fewer reacted.
Immediately a squad of picked commandos under Otto Skorzeny, Hitler's trouble-
shooter and the man who once had daringly rescued Mussolini from detention, arrived
in Budapest, kidnapped Horthy's only surviving son, and deported the Regent himself
to Germany. Veesenmayer then installed as head of state the leader of the Arrow Cross
movement, Ferenc Szalasi, a home-grown fascist with the rank of major, no less dangerous for being somewhat ridiculous. Hungary was caught fast in the German vice, and
now the screws would be turned. Many Hungarians had feared that resistance to
Germany would inevitably lead to such a reprisal. So it did, and at a disastrous moment
which bound Hungary's fate finally to the declining Reich.

Some people felt that this was as it should be. Harold Nicolson, for instance, a
writer of liberal opinions and a Member of the British Parliament, could write in
November, in his weekly column for the *Spectator:*

> When I learnt that the Russian armies were within cannon-range of Budapest, I was
> conscious of delight which I felt to be neither virtuous nor sane. My reason tells me
> that the Hungarians found themselves in a difficult position, and that it would have
> been hard indeed for them to maintain a stubborn neutrality. They were forced into
> the war by geographical necessity and by a burning resentment against the Treaty of
> Trianon. The fact is that since the day more than a thousand years ago, when Arpad
> first entered Hungary, the Magyars have done much harm and little good to Europe. . . .

14

9   Arrow Cross guards round up Hungarian Jews in the Leopold quarter of Budapest. The more the Russians advanced, the more brutal the Arrow Cross became

My satisfaction may be due to the quite rational feeling that this time the Hungarians will not again be able to disturb the peace.

By this, he really meant that the hour had come for the landowners whose aristocratic habits he disliked.

First of all though, Szalasi's Arrow Cross government was to have a reign of terror which brought anarchy, destruction, and almost civil war to the country. The more outrageous the behaviour of the fascists, the more the Red army was looked upon locally as a liberating force. Throughout Hungary, ordinary people came to wait eagerly for the Russians, not because of a sudden conversion to communism but because their arrival could only be after the German departure and the end of the Arrow Cross. Few people waited more eagerly than the Jews, for whom this was a desperate life-and-death matter. In all, some 800,000 Jews were in Hungary, a good few of them refugees who had already fled from Nazi persecution in neighbouring countries. Discriminatory laws had long since been passed against them in Hungary. They were set apart from the community and forced to wear the yellow star on their clothes as a badge of their race. The Prince-Primate of Hungary, Cardinal Seredy, had declared that Jews converted to Catholicism should be exempt. Most Hungarians hardly cared. As soon as the Germans had taken over Hungary, they had turned their attention to the Jewish question. In their eyes, the anti-Jewish laws of the Horthy years were not strong enough. In March, soon after the Germans had seized power, Adolf Eichmann, who had been the SS organiser of transport to the camps, moved into the Majestic Hotel in Budapest and personally supervised the mass deportations. By the end of June, 400,000

Jews had been loaded in cattle-trucks to be exterminated in the camps at Auschwitz and Birkenau. There followed an offer to the Allies from no less a person than Himmler, at the head of the SS, to exchange Jews for lorries, or alternatively, a large ransom. Nothing came of it, and although more deportations proved impossible to carry out, local brutality continued.

That November in Hungary was marked by an atrocity which came to be remembered as the Death March. Transports to Auschwitz had ceased, but orders came from the SS that slave-labour was urgently required in the war-factories around Vienna. Between 30,000 and 40,000 Jews were marched the 120 miles from Budapest in groups whipped on by guards. A witness from the International Red Cross wrote:

> Endless columns of deported persons were marched along: ragged and starving people, mortally tired, among them old and wizened creatures who could hardly crawl along. Gendarmes were driving them with the butt-end of their rifles, with sticks, and with whips. They had to cover 30 kilometres a day until they came to a 'resting place'. This generally was the marketplace of a town. They were driven into the square and spent the nights in the open, huddled together and shivering with cold in the chill of a November or December night. In the morning following the 'rest' we saw a number of corpses which would never rise again from the frosty ground of the market-squares.

For the next weeks, as the Russians closed the ring around Budapest, the Arrow Cross fascists roamed the city in bands looking for Jews or Communists. They shot them on the spot, or sometimes hanged them. Inhabitants became used to hurrying past street-corner murders, and averting their eyes in case they were accused of helping subversives. In all too many cases they even helped to plunder what they could from Jews. Churches or monasteries in which Jews had found refuge were broken into. Neutral legations, notably the Swedish, Swiss, or Portuguese, protested to the Szalasi government and sometimes provided false papers and a hiding-place. Raoul Wallenberg, belonging to a well-known Swedish family of industrialists, but working for the Red Cross, saved thousands of people by his interventions, risking his own life.

At the beginning of December Hitler promised Szalasi that Budapest would be defended to the end. Two Russian armies were encircling the city, but the Germans were to transfer as many as ten divisions from the Western Front into Hungary. Budapest was the site of a final trial of strength. On Christmas Eve, its long-awaited

10 During the winter of 1944, the German army was heavily reinforced in order to defend Hungary

16

siege began. Several hundred thousand people went down into their cellars or makeshift shelters, and learnt to stay in the dark while the ground shook to artillery fire and bombing. The Szalasi government, however, were not among them. Before the blockade was complete, Szalasi motored out of the city and installed himself in Sopron, a town on the Austrian border whose citizens had once voted to become Hungarian. There, watched by their German masters, Szalasi and his henchmen went through the motions of administration in their offices, which were in deserted hotels and the classrooms of the evacuated university. There they drafted imaginary decrees which were never handed out, let alone obeyed, in this twilight-of-the-gods period. Near Sopron was an infamous concentration camp where orders were obeyed, and where many Hungarians who might have shaped the future of their country were killed. Soon Szalasi gave himself up to his private fantasies, imagining that he was in touch with The Beyond through the services of a Scottish medium. Until he was captured he spent much of his time dictating strange versions of his autobiography.

Street by street, the Russians captured Pest, that part of the capital on the east bank of the Danube. The bridges across the Danube were then dynamited on orders from the Nazis. Explosions shook the whole city. In the cellars water gave out; snow had to be melted. There was neither gas nor electricity, and people improvised lamps by using shoe-laces as wicks in lumps of tallow. A bag of flour was more precious than a human life. The streets were strewn with the bodies of those hit by bullets or shrapnel while out scavenging for food. Whenever a horse was killed, the news spread fast and people from nearby came to hack off what they could as a delicacy after the usual diet of beans and potatoes. Installed in Pest, Russian guns ceaselessly shelled across the river. On Buda Hill, the high point of the west bank, stands a centuries-old fortress. The rock underneath is full of caves and interlinking passages, at some places built down for several stories. Some 30,000 German soldiers, many of them SS veterans, died to hold it. When the Russians at last stormed the fortress, they offered survivors the choice of being shot then and there, or joining forces with them. Many Arrow Cross men became turncoats and fought with vigour against the Germans whose comrades they had so recently been.

Buda citadel fell on 14 February 1945, ending a siege which had lasted fifty-one days. Ferenc Nagy, shortly to be Prime Minister, left his hiding and has described what he saw:

11   The siege of Budapest lasted fifty-one days before the Russians captured the city. Hardly a house was intact and thousands of soldiers and civilians had been killed

17

12 Szeged, in southern Hungary, as the Russian army marches in

Man-high rubble covered the streets. High blockades of concrete, steel girders, lumber, brick, and glass from the collapsed buildings jammed the thoroughfares. The wrecks of thousands of planes, tanks, and motor cars were everywhere. Some planes hung precariously with their unexploded bombs in the crumbling masonry of the shattered houses. Merciful snow covered the uncounted dead: animal carcasses littered the streets, the stark outlines of their frozen bodies sharp against the murky snow. Shop windows were full of the dead, while the wraith-like living ransacked the abandoned stores. Twisted streetcar rails jutted skyward like thin fingers of an imploring hand.

All over Hungary, as the battle passed over them, people had been having their first breath-taking experience of the Russians. Front-line patrols gave way to the army of occupation, demanding food and billets. No sooner had Hungarians recovered from the surprise of seeing Russian women soldiers, than they came to realise that this army had no concern for much beyond its physical needs. A collection of French furniture from a country house might serve as firewood for roasting a peasant's pig or goose.

In Budapest the confrontation was even sharper, coming after the siege. Christine Arnothy, emerging from the cellars like everyone else, wrote in her book *I am fifteen and I do not want to die* what happened to her. It was typical.

> The Russians were advancing in uneven waves, taking up the whole width of the street, their weapons at the ready. Their khaki capes were dirty and in tatters. At each house, a group of soldiers left the main body. This human tide drew closer and closer until at last one detachment entered our house. The man who commanded it, a Mongolian with slant eyes, yelled at us to know if there were any Germans in the house. Several of us nodded in the direction of the staircase. The German was killed on the spot and Ilas, whom they had found close to this wounded man, was raped beside the still warm corpse. From the first instant, we understood that what was happening was very different from what we had hoped.

13 The Germans retreated out of Hungary on 4 April 1945, just before the war ended

18

2 Experiments in Politics 1945–1948

WITH THE RUSSIAN TROOPS came a small group of Hungarian Communists, 'Muscovites' as they were known because of the years they had spent in Moscow. Exiled from Horthy's Hungary, these men had prepared single-mindedly for their return. They knew each other and they knew the Kremlin's methods and tactics, and they had already seen that some of their Polish, Romanian, and Bulgarian colleagues were in office. To take over a country where the Communists were no more than a few thousand would not be easy, even with the Red army present.

Tanks and field-guns stood blackened where they had been hit and the bodies of soldiers lay unburied in the winter, but politics were beginning. In villages, towns, districts, and counties occupied by the Russians, 'national committees' sprang up, run by representatives of left-wing movements or trade unions. A National Council on these lines was installed in Debrecen on 21 December 1944, and it was provided with a list of cabinet Ministers approved in Moscow. General Miklos was appointed to head them, as much as to suggest that the armistice mission which Horthy had given him was being carried through. Another Minister was Count Geza Teleki, son of the Prime Minister who had taken his life when the Germans had invaded across Hungary, and the bearer of a respected name. The coalition government resided in an old-fashioned hotel, the Arany Bika, a relic of Habsburg days, and it met in the former Inland Revenue building where each Minister had one room and an anteroom for his staff. Many of the old administrators and civil servants had fled from Hungary. Those who had not, and who made their way to Debrecen, might or might not be employed. Among the thousands of men then waiting in the town for a suitable job was a young captain, Pal Maleter, who had been captured by the Russians and had afterwards fought for them against the Germans. Like the others, he would have seen at first hand how Communists or careerists were promoted to important posts, and perhaps was conditioned for the part he was to play eleven years later in the revolution.

In the circumstances there was not much that the provisional government at Debrecen could do. In March, however, it carried through a land reform. This was long overdue, in a country where almost half the arable land had belonged to one per cent of the landowners. Four and a half million acres were now distributed among 660,000 peasants. Nobody was allowed to own more than fifty acres. More land was later divided, but there was still a shortage and not all peasants could be given their own holdings. Tremendous posters everywhere claimed this reform as an achievement of the Communist Party. The Minister of Agriculture, Imre Nagy, a 'Muscovite', was personally given the credit by the peasants, earning the reputation and popularity which later came to a head during the revolution.

Meanwhile the British and American Military and Political Missions had arrived in Debrecen to live in the out-buildings of a hospital. They were supposed to take an equal share with the Russians on the Allied Control Commission. Weekly meetings were presided over by Marshal Voroshilov, commanding the Russian forces, and he

14 Raoul Wallenberg, from a prominent Swedish family, had rescued many Jews through the Red Cross. The Russians arrested him, and his fate remains unknown

15 Executions of war-criminals were public. Ferenc Szalasi, the Arrow Cross dictator, kisses a crucifix shortly before he was hanged

would in practice announce what decisions he had taken. People also began to disappear, like Count Bethlen, who for ten years had been a conservative Prime Minister under Horthy's regency. Politicians and intellectuals returning to Hungary from German concentration camps were picked up by the Russians, only to vanish. On 17 January, with the Germans still in Buda, Raoul Wallenberg, a war hero through his Red Cross work, had driven up to the Jewish relief office with Russian soldiers, to explain that he was being conducted to Marshal Malinowski's headquarters at Debrecen. 'I don't know whether I'm going as a prisoner or a guest', were his reported words. He has never been heard of since, although his death in Siberia has been rumoured.

All over Europe this was a time of chaos, a time for endless train journeys away from one inhumanity but often towards another. Bands of deserters from several armies, of SS men or partisans or patriots who would not disarm, of Jews still in striped uniforms from the camps, roamed where they might, searching for what they could

16 Debrecen, December 1944. Banners echo support for democracy and the provisional government

find. To own a handcart was to be rich: a rucksack in which to carry home food fetched from a peasant was a luxury. With the spring in Budapest came swarms of flies over the places where corpses had been quickly buried and the smell of decay lay over the streets. Bodies continued to float down the Danube all summer. Demoralised by so much horror, the population of Central Europe was in a poor position to summon up the strength to revive society from within. The Communists alone had a clear goal, and in the Russians they had the only friends who mattered. Soon agitators could be seen riding about the countryside in Soviet army vehicles. Only the Communist Party had access to transport, loudspeakers, and the weapons of propaganda.

Many scores from the war had to be settled. The newspapers were full of photographs of men being hanged or shot by firing squads. Arrow Cross members often chose to join the Communist Party in order that their past record should not be investigated. They then behaved much as they had done previously. After trials, some 122 prominent men were executed as war criminals, four of them former Prime Ministers. Admiral Horthy was not extradited from Germany and spent the rest of his life in Portugal. These executions were public. There were other, less drastic, Justification Tribunals of three to five men, often presided over by a Communist, who decided if a man's record were good enough to allow him to keep his job. On Citadel Hill in Buda, above the old German bunkers, arose a gigantic new monument as a triumph to the Red army. But the Russian phrase, 'Davai chasi', 'give me your watch', became a national byword, spreading from Hungary throughout Europe.

In April the provisional government moved to Budapest. It was a sign of the times that Communist Party headquarters were established in the former German embassy, and that the Soviet Secret Police took over villas where the Gestapo had done similar work. The Communist Party line for the moment was that Hungary was experiencing a liberal revolution of a rather old-fashioned kind, and that all liberal elements should therefore co-operate. 'Unite All Forces for Reconstruction', was the slogan coined by Matyas Rakosi, First Secretary of the Hungarian Communist Party. As a proof of goodwill, Communists helped to rebuild churches. They also activated the other

17   Workmen begin reconstruction of the old Franz Josef bridge in Budapest

18   The monument to the Soviet army: 'To the memory of the liberating Soviet heroes – the grateful Hungarian people'

political parties permitted by the Allied Control Commission. One of these, the National Peasant Party, was virtually a rural branch of the Communists. Another, the Social Democrats, had a strong faction which shared Marxist doctrines with the Communists. Only the Smallholders Party could be called a real alternative, and it therefore contained a wide range of supporters, many of whom found it the only outlet for their dislike of communism.

The Russians might well have encouraged the Communists to take over power then and there. Some of the more impatient Communists were dissatisfied that this did not happen throughout the Russian-occupied countries. Instead the Russians created Popular Fronts, groupings of progressives who would be friendly to Soviet aims and stay within the framework of the law. At the Big Three Conference which had taken place early in 1945 at Yalta, a Crimean seaside resort, the Russians had committed themselves to this restraint. They had approved a statement of principle called 'The Declaration on Liberated Europe'. Conditions of internal peace were to be restored in countries regaining their freedom. Governments were to be chosen by free elections. Neither Churchill nor Roosevelt was pleased by so vague a statement, but felt that it was the best they could expect. The declaration could not cover some awkward questions. What would happen if a country occupied by Russia chose a government hostile to communism? Or what would happen if a country supposed to be a Western ally, like France, Italy, or Greece, chose a Communist government?

At the Potsdam Conference which had continued the work of Yalta, it had been agreed that Russia was entitled to all German-owned property in Hungary. This was to compensate her for some of the losses incurred at the hands of the Germans. About one-third of all Hungarian industry had been controlled by German capital. Its value was probably in the region of 1,000 million dollars. A part of this industry – 200 complete factories and the machinery of 300 more – was dismantled and sent to Russia. For a long while freight trains loaded with all sorts of industrial equipment were a common sight in the marshalling yards and junctions to the east. Russia took over some industries which were still in operation by setting up companies under joint Russian-Hungarian ownership. In this way Russia was able to run and profit from steel plants, railway construction, Danubian shipping and transport, and electricity, coal, and oil. The Minister of Justice, a socialist, joked to a friend about the Joint Soviet-Hungarian Shipping Company, 'You know the agreement came about on a basis of perfect equality. The Russians have the right to ship up and down the river and we have the right to ship across.' One-third of all the livestock and the gold and silver reserves in the National Bank were also expropriated. Three hundred million dollars had to be paid

19 Tugs and barges began to ply again on the Danube

22

20   The grounds of the old Royal Palace were used for wheat-growing during the post-war period when increase in food supplies was vital

in official war reparations, and goods used for such payments were valued at the 1938 price level. The Hungarian budget for 1946–7 set aside for the reparations eight times the sum allotted for reconstruction. When the Peace Conference at last opened, the total material loss to Hungary of Soviet reparations, occupation, and looting, was estimated by United Nations officials at 40 per cent of the national income.

These handicaps to economic revival were already fixed when it came to carrying out the Yalta pledges of free elections, pledges which had been further announced in hoardings all over the country. Acts of lawlessness frightened the voters away from the Communist Party. In the village of Gyomro, Communist policemen had arrested and shot twenty-six people without trial; the police chief of Kecskemet, also a Communist, had not been punished for a similar crime. Marshal Voroshilov gave his consent to the elections on the condition that no matter what their outcome, the coalition formed through the provisional government of Debrecen should continue. Already the Communists had done badly in the Budapest municipal elections. Now in November they obtained only 17 per cent of the total vote, the same proportion as the Social Democrats. The Smallholders Party won an outright majority with 57 per cent. Even with the Russian conditions, these elections were the most free to have been held after the war in Eastern Europe.

Non-Communist Hungarians felt justified in hoping for a favourable peace treaty which would mark the end of the armistice period and decently settle future relations with the Russians. Hungary was formally declared a republic and Zoltan Tildy, a Smallholder and former Calvinist pastor, became its first president. The one opposing vote to this came from a royalist Catholic nun. The work of rebuilding and reconstruction was intensified. The efforts of the population were remarkable in the face of the catastrophic inflation which followed the penalties laid by the Russians on the economy. The official money, the pengo, had slipped in value until several quadrillion were exchanged for the pound, something of an international record. When the National Bank needed dollars or pounds, it instructed the Economic Police to leave the currency

23

21 The collapse of the pengo. A bun could cost four million

22 Hungry people look at food they cannot buy. Prices could be changed several times a day

black market undisturbed, so that foreign money could accumulate by that means. Attempts were made to pay people with food, and there had been fear of hunger. By August 1946, food supplies were under control, and the currency had been stabilised. A few months later, Hugh Seton-Watson, an English professor, writing as a special correspondent in *The Times*, thought that a visitor to Budapest 'will be surprised by the vigorous intellectual activity displayed both in print and in conversation. In comparison with the mental sterility and haunting fear prevalent in the Balkans, Hungary seems an oasis of culture and liberty.'

Ferenc Nagy, chosen by the victorious Smallholders Party to be the Prime Minister – and not to be confused with the former Minister of Agriculture, Imre Nagy – has described in his autobiography how he would have to refer the decisions of his government to the Russian authorities for approval. If he also told the Americans and the British, he was accused of scheming. The Communists were in his coalition government. Matyas Rakosi was Deputy Prime Minister. Imre Nagy was now appointed Minister of the Interior, but was soon replaced by Laszlo Rajk, the most prominent of the Communists who had lived underground in Hungary during the war. Rakosi later stated that 'there was one single organisation over which our Party demanded full control from the very first moment and refused to accept any coalitionist solution. This was the State Defence Authority.' He meant that the Communists insisted on starting and running the political police. 'We kept this organisation in our hands from the first day of its establishment', Rakosi went on. One of Rajk's closest collaborators was Gyorgy Palffy-Oesterreicher who at the same time was organising a political unit within the army. One of the Communist successes which at the time did not receive much attention was to prevent the formation of even the limited army allowed by the Peace Treaty. The army consisted of scarcely 12,000 men. Had it been larger it might well have taken upon itself the task which the democratic parties could not carry out, of organising resistance to the Communists. The patriotic traditions of the Hungarian army died hard, as the revolution was to show.

Now that they had realised their centuries-old ambition and owned their own land, the peasants were content to support the Smallholders Party. If an alliance of peasants

24

and liberal democrats could have been formed, the Communists would have had no chance of ever claiming to be popular. After the 1945 elections, seeing that they could not be a majority party, they set about making sure that neither could any other party be. Effectively, they had to break the Smallholders, while being careful not to drive its members in a body to another party. The Smallholders came from all walks of life. Some of their deputies were alleged to have reactionary pasts, and the party was obliged to expel them. In February 1947, the Communists began an all-out attack on the Smallholders, announcing with great melodrama that a conspiracy had been uncovered thanks to the police work of Rajk and Palffy-Oesterreicher. Several more Smallholder deputies were supposed to belong to a Hungarian Community Movement, whose purpose was to restore the pre-war regime. They were arrested. After holding secret interrogations, the Communists further implied that Bela Kovacs, Secretary-General of the Smallholders Party, was in the conspiracy. The Assembly tried to protect him, as he had parliamentary immunity. The Soviet Military Command then arrested Kovacs, who disappeared and for many years was presumed to have been murdered. The Communists had been demonstrating in front of Parliament with shouts of 'Death to Kovacs.'

Four months later Prime Minister Ferenc Nagy was accused by the Communists of turning a blind eye to this conspiracy. He was on holiday in Switzerland. His small son was sent out to him in exile on condition that he resign. The Smallholders had indeed been smashed to pieces between its two wings: those who had supported them as a bulwark against the Communists and those who recognised that the Communists would win and that they might as well join the victors while the going was good. The Communists saw to it that those politicians who subsequently accepted office were either fellow-travellers or else too frightened to maintain opposition. A few independent-minded leaders in other parties, including the President of Parliament, resigned and

23 When Prime Minister Ferenc Nagy of the Smallholders Party was on holiday abroad his resignation was demanded by the Communists as a condition for releasing his four-year-old son from Hungary. The family went to New York

25

escaped abroad. The foreign consulates were kept busy with Hungarians wanting to emigrate. Growing in power, the secret police intensified the new atmosphere of panic.

When the Russians had arrested Kovacs, they were intervening in exclusively Hungarian affairs. They were also showing what would happen if they did not get their way. Even so, the Communists might not have blanketed all democratic forces had international relations not been changing. Stalin believed the Marxist thesis that the West, the capitalist countries, would try to delay an inevitable collapse by attacking Russia. For this reason, the war-time alliance was as expedient to him as his earlier alliance with Hitler. If the West were to attack, it would only be prudent of the Russians to make quite sure of Central Europe, the likely battle-ground, by subjecting it. That the United States had largely demobilised made little impression. Churchill, Leader of the Opposition in the House of Commons after his defeat in the 1945 general election, had deplored Russian behaviour in a speech delivered in America in March 1946: 'From Stettin in the Baltic to Trieste in the Adriatic, an iron curtain has descended across the continent.' The meeting of the Great Powers a year later in Paris in order to draw up the Peace Treaty concerning Hungary and other enemy satellites confirmed the difference in most respects of Russian and Western policies. It was one more step in the history of mistrust which was in the process of dividing Europe into two armoured, self-contained camps. The Treaty was greatly to Hungary's disadvantage, for it restored the Trianon frontiers resented after the First World War. Romania once more gained all Transylvania, and Czechoslovakia also benefited at Hungary's expense.

President Truman, who had come to office following the death of Roosevelt, clarified the American attitude in a speech to a special Joint Session of Congress, containing what later came to be known as the Truman Doctrine. 'I believe that it must be the policy of the United States to support free peoples who are resisting attempted subjugation by armed minorities or by outside pressures.' Communism, and in particular what Churchill had referred to as 'the Communisation of the Balkans', was now openly to be resisted. Secretary of State Marshall was shortly to announce a plan for aid to countries in need. Poland and Czechoslovakia were among those willing to receive this aid programme, but in both cases Russia forbade them to accept. As a counterweight the Russians founded the Cominform, an association of Communist parties which aimed at making them not only masters in their own house but docile agents of Soviet policy. In 1947 the positions of Russia and America hardened as they came face to face across the territory of their allies, presenting the world with a contest between rival systems. It was a magnified modern version of the old wars of religion with their Latin tag *cujus regio ejus religio* – in other words, to possess a region was also to dictate its beliefs. In wide political terms, Europe had been made a power vacuum, first by Hitler's redrawing of its boundaries, then by the collapse of Germany. As soon as this happened, the war-time alliance had no further reason to continue. The interests of the separate powers had revived and began to extend into the European vacuum. Such competition might prove deadly, but neither the West nor Russia could permit its rival to gain the upper hand. Taking defensive measures, both sides were also being aggressive to a point which stopped just short of war. Hitler had correctly expected this to happen: only his defeat made it possible.

Once again Hungary was one of the small nations which had to bow before the storm. Since the war the West had sent angry diplomatic notes on her behalf, had returned to her some gold reserves blocked in Western banks. Although at the time

24   President Truman, shown here at Potsdam, later
declared the USA's determination to fight communism
in Europe

America alone had exploded an atom bomb, it has not been argued that such a weapon
should have been used, or its use threatened, in order to influence the future of Central
Europe. But direct negotiations between the West and each country in Central Europe
were doomed because the Russians were already strong enough to block any results
unsatisfactory to them. At the Peace Treaty conference, for instance, the Hungarian
Communist Party had not tried to get Hungary's boundaries revised in her favour. Nor
did it oppose except by rhetoric the expulsion from Czechoslovakia of 600,000 Hungarians, who were in theory to be settled in the homes of Hungarians driven out
because of their German origins, just as the German-Poles or German-Czechs were
driven back to Germany. After 1948, with the Communists in power in both countries,
the Hungarian minority remaining in Slovakia was not deported. Once this vast
migration of peoples was concluded, often with cruelties which were excused simply
because the victims were German, the Russians wished to stop keeping such national
antagonisms alive. 'Internationalism' was to replace it. This Marxist phrase meant that
the proletarian elements in the countries under Soviet rule were now assuming power;
and, because they all belonged in principle to the same class, their interests must neces-
sarily be the same. This was in fact a revolution imposed from above, a revolution
which sealed Russian rule upon unwilling countries, and therefore had no further need
for nationalistic differences. Stalin's answer to the Truman Doctrine and the Marshall
Plan was to transform the countries occupied by his armies into imitations of Soviet
Russia.

Within Hungary, it was no coincidence that the arrest of Bela Kovacs was being
plotted while the Peace Treaty was being drafted. For once the Peace Treaty came into
operation, the Allied Missions were dissolved and democratic politicians lost these links
with the West. The Russians, however, did not also leave. Under an article in the
Treaty, they could use Hungary for access to their zone of occupation in Austria. From

then on, the Communists in Hungary, as in every other country under Russian domination, worked whole-heartedly at the final stages of their revolution.

After Prime Minister Ferenc Nagy had been deposed, more elections were arranged for the end of August. The Smallholders had been broken into various opposition parties, mere splinter groups, by the Communists. Rakosi was later to boast of such 'salami tactics'. None of these groups, whether Catholic or progressive or peasant-led, could get a majority. Every sort of fraud was used on the voters, from restricting the franchise to beating them up. Nevertheless the Communists obtained only 22 per cent of the votes. Making a common list with the parties of the Left they could claim a majority. The few independent politicians remaining in the country now fled abroad. The leader of the Social Democrats was among those who escaped, a man who had spent the war in Mauthausen concentration camp. He was replaced in his party by Anna Kethly who was kept under police supervision, and finally by Arpad Szakasits, a Communist sympathiser. The Catholics were squeezed out of politics, their schools nationalised, their youth organisations dissolved. Relations with the Vatican were forbidden. Every day brought more news of violence and intimidation. Only a man of exceptional courage dared to raise his voice against what was happening. Most people were not prepared to become martyrs and adapted themselves to living with what was becoming inevitable.

The mines had been nationalised first, followed by some industrial concerns which had remained in private hands, and the banks. In March 1948, came the general nationalisation law which covered all factories employing more than one hundred workers, a number to be reduced to ten. Easter Monday was declared a holiday and state officials came to the closed factories and merely took possession of them. Firms owned by foreign capital were included in these measures.

In March too, those Social Democrats who were still left at large agreed in principle to join with the Communists; and as a result they purged their leaders once more. In effect this was political suicide. The crisis was resolved on 12 June, at a congress where the Social Democrats under Szakasits voted to join outright with the Communists,

25   Arpad Szakasits (*left*) signed the agreement with Matyas Rakosi which merged the Social Democrats with the Communists, and thereby lost the socialist Left its independence

combining into the Hungarian Workers Party. The Communists had contrived to swallow the socialists, their main opponents. Szakasits received his reward in July. President Tildy, a Smallholder, was forced to resign because his son-in-law, a diplomat in Egypt, was first charged with treason and then hanged at the end of the year. Szakasits took Tildy's place as President of the Republic. The remaining Social Democrats were purged and the fragments of the dejected parties joined in a People's Front. The year 1948 was rightly called 'the year of the big switch'.

The Communist Party had acquired the monopoly of the country's political life. It was therefore able to refashion all the offices and institutions of the state as it desired. Protest, or even advice, could no longer be organised. There remained the Church to deal with, for it alone had retained moral authority, and so presented an alternative, however remote, to communism. Hungary was traditionally and culturally a Catholic country, with large Lutheran and Calvinist minorities. The Vatican felt itself to be seriously threatened by Communist doctrines, and throughout Central and Eastern Europe cardinals and archbishops and priests had taken a stand which led to their persecution. The Prince-Primate of the Hungarian Church, Cardinal Mindszenty, had succeeded Cardinal Seredy in October 1945. Mindszenty, born Joseph Pehm, of German and peasant stock, was a narrow nationalist and conservative, but of fierce conviction. When the Germans had taken him to a local prison camp, he had gone in full episcopal regalia, mitre on head, staff in hand. He had fought the advances of communism, but showed little understanding of the social issues which had to be solved. When Catholic schools were shut down, he ordered teaching priests to give up their jobs. From the pulpit he reminded his flock that in the past the Tartar and Turkish invasions of Hungary had eventually been driven out. In the centre of Budapest, on Christmas Day 1948, he took a last mass in an open-air chapel on Gellert Hill. Thousands of candles were carried by the crowd, as if already in mourning. Two days later

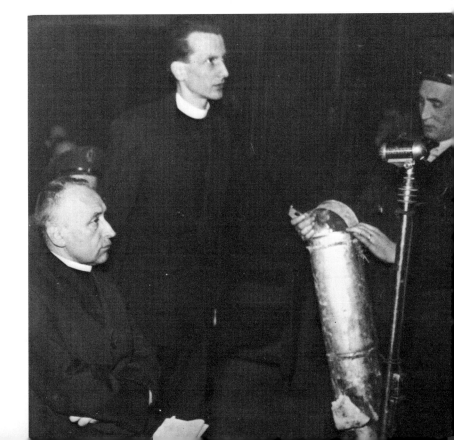

26 Cardinal Mindszenty (*left;* and his secretary, Zalar) astonished the world by pleading guilty at his trial for treason against the new People's Republic

29

the Cardinal was arrested on a charge of conspiracy. Earlier, he had written a caution for just such a possibility:

> If, however, one should read or hear it said that I have made admissions or that I have resigned or even in the case that my signature is used to try to authenticate such admissions or resignations, let these facts be put down to my human weaknesses. I declare them henceforth null and inapplicable.

In the New Year he appeared before a People's Tribunal. There, under bright arc-lamps and before foreign journalists, the Cardinal confessed that his attitudes were mistaken, his outlook reactionary. This caused a sensation and was a widespread victory for the Communists. Because the Cardinal looked broken and ill, rumours spread about the methods used to persuade him to make this confession. The Cardinal was sent to prison for life. Another distinguished leader, Bishop Apor, had been killed in 1945 on the steps of his palace when defending some women against Russian soldiers who were raping them. The Catholic Church was put into the hands of Peace Priests, men who would co-operate with the new regime. Most of the monasteries and convents would be disestablished. A pliant bishop was placed at the head of the Calvinists. The head of the Lutheran Church was arrested on a currency charge.

These events in Hungary were matched in Romania, Czechoslovakia, Poland, Bulgaria. Local conditions did not much vary. Whatever was left of the past in all these countries, was changed with an almost mechanical precision. A clandestine document smuggled out of Hungary after the revolution has this to say about the descent of the Iron Curtain:

> What did it matter that Poland had been a victim of fascism while Bulgaria and Roumania had waged war against fascism, while Hungary had remained at Hitler's side until the end? Some of these countries had strongly rooted democratic traditions, others had not. Czechoslovakia was one of the most industrialised societies in Europe, while Albania was still at the stage of raising goats. So much the worse! All these countries had become 'dictatorships of the proletariat' and on the spot 98% (neither more or less) of the population voted communist with a conviction startlingly illustrated by the Hungarian revolution. In international relations the same system was applied as in a Russian barracks for the recruits: if one man was dark-haired, another fair, or if he had curls, never mind, from now on everybody will be bald. Yes, all bald. On the same day, in the same way, all of you were shaved, with the same degree of enthusiasm.

Formalities remained. In April 1949, the Hungarian Parliament was dissolved, and elections were held for a new Assembly whose task was to proclaim a constitution of the Soviet type: 5.4 million votes were cast for the unified People's Front, 165,283 against. There were no opposition candidates. Hungary, like the other sovereign states of Central and Eastern Europe, was now a Soviet satellite. The text of its new constitution praised the USSR. The Communist *coup* was complete.

3 The Years of Stalinism 1948–1953

THE EASE WITH WHICH CARDINAL MINDSZENTY had been eliminated from the public arena left the country stunned. In the midst of complete social and political upheaval, here had been a great, even classic, conflict of Church and state, held in the open. The state had been able to make a one-sided affair of it. If the Cardinal could be so efficiently pushed aside, nobody was secure. As if to mock nameless fears of totalitarian rule which were settling on Hungary, the weather was again splendid. The Second World Youth Meeting was held in Budapest, and students from many countries wandered about in their heedlessness in the parks beneath budding trees.

On 18 June, the whole of Hungary was horrified to hear news no less sinister than the fate of Cardinal Mindszenty, that the Foreign Minister, Laszlo Rajk, had been arrested in the late hours of the night. That very day, Count Michael Karolyi, former Prime Minister, then ambassador in Paris, had called on Rajk in his office to hand in his resignation as a protest against lack of freedom. Rajk had been distant and had told him to return later. Perhaps he had guessed what might happen to him, but nobody else had an inkling of the violent drama about to burst.

Laszlo Rajk was a picture-book Communist, good-looking, courageous, and dedicated. 'One must have a compass and my compass is the Soviet Union', he was reported

27   Laszlo Rajk (*left*) was Foreign Minister when arrested and executed for conspiracy against the state. General Palffy-Oesterreicher (*right*), hanged with him, had helped him set up the secret police

to have said to an acquaintance. Rajk had fought in the International Brigade during the Spanish Civil War. Staying in Hungary throughout the Second World War, he had worked for the underground. His brothers were distinctly bourgeois and one of them had been powerfully placed in the Arrow Cross. By Communist standards, he was left-wing, in the sense that he believed in the dictatorship of the proletariat, and did not pursue Rakosi's careful class war which had so far only brought in a new set of administrators at the top. Left-wing, too, because he was known to have questioned those decisions of the Communist Party which had given Russia priority in all Hungarian affairs. Born in Transylvania, Rajk could hardly escape being a Hungarian patriot. For this, he was charged with Titoism and 'nationalist deviation'. Instantly the many posters with his portrait were removed. Telegrams were organised by the Party to be sent to authorities demanding 'a rope for the traitor Rajk'.

To understand these accusations, it is necessary to look at the relations between Russia and other Communist states. The international situation of 1948 and 1949 was so tense that no possible crack in Communist solidarity could be permitted in case the Western Powers exploited it. Yet the Russians knew only too well how fragile the new Communist states were, and how resentful their populations were. Repression was the only way to guarantee obedience. There had to be complete conformity for Russia to build the unchallenged basis of her position in the world as an international power. Such conformity was an illusion, for it had to depend on the new Russian-style organisation of the satellites, and also on the Cominform, the recently created agency of the various Communist parties.

One country in this Soviet unified bloc had reached communism through its internal evolution, and that was Yugoslavia. Its history had been particularly shaped by brutality. Yugoslavia is a federation of several small provinces which have clung to their national identities through many dark centuries of struggle. The partisans who rallied under Marshal Tito against the Germans found not only a leader but a cause. They also had to fight rival partisans who feared communism as much as, or more than, Nazism, and who in the last resort were prepared to collaborate with the Germans. Yugoslavia was therefore engaged in a civil war as well as a war of liberation. Tito, a Communist of long standing, took credit for their victory. Russian troops had not driven out the Germans, as elsewhere in the Balkans. In squeezing out the King and stifling opposition, whether royalist or democratic, Tito was apparently a pupil of whom Stalin could be proud. In 1945 only the wisest prophet could have foretold that Yugoslavia would get between Russia and her satellites, the grit in the smooth running of the Soviet machine.

Already when the Cominform started, the two countries had not seen eye to eye, notably over the Greek Civil War in which the Communists were defeated, and over the future of Albania. A Balkan federation proposed by Tito did not find Russian approval. More basically, Russia offended Yugoslavia's sense of independence and acute, war-strengthened nationalism by taking obedience for granted. This was a mistake. The Yugoslav leaders were not like most Communists in power, theoreticians and Party men, but practical men of affairs who had fought their battles for themselves. Tension between the Russians and the Yugoslavs grew. Stalin, a dictator already for some twenty years, was not used to defiance. Controlling all the organs of state through the Communist Party, he had been able to use every kind of pressure, from propaganda to persuasion and terror, in order to carry out his will in his own country. Some opponents had indeed been stubborn, but they were broken at prepared public trials. Some allies, such as the entire Polish Communist leadership in 1938, had been liquidated to suit a new policy. As for the Russian masses, they did what they were ordered to do. Similar procedures could not be arranged in Yugoslavia, even when Stalin had decided that Tito and Titoism amounted to treachery towards the Soviet Union and must be suppressed. The more the Russians demanded of the Yugoslavs, the more the latter resisted. In Communist language this was known as 'nationalist deviation'.

On 28 June, just ten days after Rajk's arrest, a communiqué was published through the Cominform stating that 'Yugoslavia has placed itself and the Yugoslav Party outside the family of fraternal Communist parties'. Khrushchev has recorded a phrase of Stalin's at the time: 'I will shake my little finger and Tito will fall.' Stalin was deluding himself. At the very moment when the Russian empire was extending to its height, when China too was successfully turning Communist, the cause of future trouble was apparent.

All over the world Communist parties were obliged to respond to this attack on Yugoslavia. It came as a shock. Hungary refused to pay her remaining war reparations to Yugoslavia and cancelled some industrial agreements recently signed. Anti-Yugoslav feelings were thought out in detail – in a performance in the National Theatre, *Macbeth* was represented as a play featuring Marshal Tito as the villain-king. The arrest of Rajk on the accusation of being a Titoist was the acknowledgement that Hungary was accepting the role prepared for her in the Communist movement by Russia. Other Communist countries paid a similar tribute. In Poland, Gomulka, First Secretary of the Party, was forced to confess that he, too, was nationalistic in thought, and he was later sent to prison. In Albania, and Bulgaria, and then in Czechoslovakia, leaders were purged and often executed for being accomplices of Yugoslavia, and by implication of the West. The satellites were learning the meaning of the slogan current in these People's Democracies: 'Socialism in one country.'

28   Rakosi, Rajk, and colleagues sit on the steps of Parliament during a Congress of the Communist Democratic Women's League of Health, shortly before Rajk's arrest

In September Rajk and others, including Palffy-Oesterreicher and some Social Democrats and the Yugoslav Lazar Brankov, were put on trial, not in a court but in the Magdolna Street headquarters of the Iron and Steel Workers' Union. The prosecutor had previously presided over Cardinal Mindszenty's trial. The radio broadcast a running commentary, and the whole country, still not properly broken in to this kind of event, was bewildered to hear the accused admit that they had planned a conspiracy with 'the advanced shock troops of international bourgeois reaction'. Rajk had in fact met Tito and Rankovic, the head of the Yugoslav secret police, but only on official business. The accusation against him and his confession stated that he had worked all his life for foreign powers, including Franco's Spain and Hitler's Germany. Because his brother had been in the Arrow Cross, he was also supposed to have been a secret political spy for Horthy, and latterly for the American intelligence services.

Rajk had been replaced in his earlier post as Minister of the Interior by Janos Kadar. Kadar was also one of his closest friends. In the spring Mrs Rajk had given birth to a son and at the Soviet-style name-giving ceremony, Kadar was the godfather. Now Kadar had come to Rajk's prison cell and told him that a confession was in the best interest of the Party and would be the only means of saving his life. So the whole rigmarole of furtive rendezvous and disguises and conspiracies had come to be concocted for Rajk to recite them by memory in a weary voice. All the witnesses against him were also under arrest, and had learnt similar testimonies. When sentence was passed, the court had shown its approval by rhythmic clapping. Rajk and those associated with him were hanged. His wife was imprisoned and her baby taken from her. The man in the street was alarmed that the new princes of his country had turned on one another in this way, but he knew better than to speak out. Party workers toured the factories giving lunch-time lectures about the treacheries and evil designs of imperialists who wished to destroy socialism.

Throughout the People's Democracies, about a thousand men, most of them influential, were purged at this time for the same reasons. They were the more prominent victims of Stalinism, as it has since been called, Stalinism being a shorthand word for the methods decreed by Stalin and put into practice by his colleagues, to further the

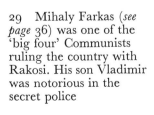

29 Mihaly Farkas (*see page* 36) was one of the 'big four' Communists ruling the country with Rakosi. His son Vladimir was notorious in the secret police

immediate ends of Russia. These ends were thought to justify all means, even if the means were illegal and inhumane. Over the years millions of people died, because some point of ideology had tidied them away into the category of 'enemies of the people', whether they were bourgeois or intellectuals or peasants, or rivals for power. Rajk, and those condemned with him, were thorough Communists whose deaths were not demanded for any wrong they had done, but only as an illustration of doctrine, as a reminder that wrongs were henceforth what it suited the government to call wrong. The new system obliged everyone to be either for it or against it, and if the latter, then punishment was only just and proper. To be against the system was by definition to be against progress, against the future – a way of thinking open to abuse by those in power. What Stalinism reflected was the Russian insecurity in international politics, and the slight hold of the Soviet rulers over so many subjected peoples who had little or no say in their own affairs.

Even so, purges would have been impossible had they not been carried out by Communists who were willing to take their orders from Moscow and had the means of enforcing obedience. It remains a question of curiosity in the history of the human mind that men were eager to govern their countries on behalf of a foreign power in the name of a belief. The Communist leaders of the People's Democracies had been one-time idealists, holding to notions of equality and liberty on their own terms. Yet they signed away the independence of their countries and kept their offices knowing what little popular support they had. Not in the first place cynics, they justified themselves as an élite minority entrusted with the job of showing the majority where its true interests lay. But soon politics became for them a matter of watching closely the tactics of Moscow and adapting themselves to every switch as quickly as possible. The Muscovites have been collectively described by a Hungarian writer, Tibor Meray, as living a life of slogans, and when the slogans changed, of danger.

> A Muscovite's life was never safe, wherever he went – and least of all in the Soviet Union. He learnt that neither his age nor his long Party membership would protect him. He knew that he would not even have to commit a mistake in order to be relieved of his job, or to be arrested or tried. To him, nothing was impossible. After all, he had seen it all in the Soviet Union. His smile, his loyalty, his zeal, served but one purpose, to survive.

The execution of Rajk was a triumph for the Muscovite section of the Hungarian Communist Party. Hungary was in the forefront of the campaign against Yugoslavia and might therefore earn credit in Moscow. With such a move, Rakosi and his close associates emerged as indisputable leaders, their factional rivals eliminated. On a small scale Rakosi could now imitate his master Stalin. Born in 1892 in a southern Hungarian village, the son of a shopkeeper with a large family, Rakosi had come up the hard way. Joining the Social Democrat Party as a young man, he had been influenced by the Bolshevik revolution in 1917 when he was a prisoner of war in Siberia. During the short Bela Kun Soviet republic, Rakosi had been a commissar, until forced to flee to Austria. In 1924 he had been given the task of organising the Communist Party in Hungary, although by then it had been dispersed by the Horthy regime, and declared illegal. Caught, Rakosi was sentenced to fifteen years in prison, which was extended to life, and he was saved from execution before the war by the pleas of Western liberals. In 1940, following the Stalin treaty of friendship with Hitler, Rakosi was sent from prison to Russia in exchange for some Hungarian flags which the Russian army of Tsar Nicholas I had captured in 1849 when suppressing the Hungarian revolution under Kossuth. In Moscow during the war Rakosi married a Russian woman of Kirghiz origins, and he became the most prominent of the Hungarian exiles there. Short and fat and bald (Arsehead and Old Baldy were among his nicknames), he was not pre-possessing. Yet he had a good memory, he took trouble to learn facts and figures by heart, and he had a certain presence which did not fail to make an impression.

By 1945 he was the First Secretary of the Communist Party, and after 1952 also Prime Minister, which meant that all channels of power in the centralised state led to him, the man at the summit, controlling the interwoven bureaucracy both of govern-ment and Party. In the capacity of Prime Minister he guided the decisions of the Central Committee, a body handpicked from the Party. It more or less replaced the elected Parliament as the executive, for Parliament was silent for months on end, and met only to approve what was put before it. The Central Committee had a vast secretariat through which it controlled all the different parts of society. From the Central Commit-tee was elected in turn the Political Committee, or Politburo, usually of only twelve or thirteen members, and this was the highest organ of policy-making. Members of the Central Committee had to be cautious, in spite of their position. Of ninety-two men elected to it at the Party Congresses of 1948 and 1951, forty-six had been removed by 1954.

Rakosi's aides on the Politburo were like himself. Erno Gero was his right-hand man, and known on the streets as 'Moscow's eye'. Gero was a hard-working admini-strator, once a commissar in the International Brigade in the Spanish Civil War. A measure of the man can be found in his comment to Count Karolyi about the Rajk affair.

> We know that he conspired with Tito but we have no proof of it. He must be liquidated, but to tell the entire truth to the public would be madness. They would not understand. They are not politically ripe enough. Whether he was actually a spy or not is irrelevant, for in its essence it comes to the same thing: committing treachery or being a spy. The crudeness of the charge is only the mechanical side of it, and of no importance.

Mihaly Farkas, Minister of Defence, was born in Czechoslovakia and held Soviet citizenship. Although a small man, he liked to strike Napoleonic poses. Soldiers on the march were made to sing, 'We are Mihaly Farkas' men.' All cultural activities were in the hands of Jozsef Revai, whose intelligence and fanaticism were necessary if the busy Hungarian literature were to be suppressed. By 1949 Revai was already confident enough to write about the Communists:

> We were a minority in Parliament and in the country, but at the same time we were the leading force. We had decisive control over the police force. Our force, the force of the Party and the working class, was multiplied by the fact that the Soviet Union and the Soviet army were always there to support us with their assistance.

These four men, Rakosi, Gero, Farkas, and Revai, had in common their Jewish origins. Jews had often become revolutionaries in the hopes of changing their status in a country of traditional anti-Semitism. That the leaders of Hungarian Stalinism proved to be Jewish was something held against them by the masses whose prejudices were not likely to be eradicated by the new government's measures. It did not mend matters that these Jewish leaders adopted the traditional anti-Semitism which had once attacked them. It also helped the Russians to exploit and eventually to discard them.

One 'Muscovite', Imre Nagy, had never got on well with Rakosi. Their quarrel dated back to the days of Moscow exile and was built on differences of personality as well as points of doctrine. Since the Communist Party claims to represent the people, the unity of its doctrine cannot be questioned. The people cannot be seen to be divided among itself. In time, a dispute, even on some technical matter, may come to seem a huge rift involving the national interest, challenging the general will. Stalinist communism had no forum for public discussion, and a man like Rakosi maintained his authority by destroying other opinions before they could come into the open. Imre Nagy might well have been the victim of the Titoist purges instead of Rajk, for his ideas were indeed to prove rather like Tito's. He was a 'rightist deviationist' where Rajk had been 'leftist'. Imre Nagy, that is to say, would have privately agreed with the

30 Jozsef Revai in September 1948, speaking at the
Musical Academy

nationalistic attitudes of Tito while keeping a scrupulous regard for Russia, the source of his Marxist ideals. The 'rightist' accusation was to stick, and after the revolution was used to justify his execution. The more independent Hungary became, ran the charge, the less she adhered to international communism, but lapsed towards her former bourgeois state. A 'rightist' was soon a reactionary. In 1949 Nagy was lucky only to be discredited and given a rubber-stamp job as President of Parliament.

Once Rajk was out of the way, Rakosi set about organising Hungary on truly Stalinist lines. The democratic parties had been reduced to a mere address in the telephone book, and now the Communist Party was brought to heel. From 1949 to 1953 the Party underwent almost continuous purging until its hard core consisted of dependable new recruits. Rakosi is said to have expressed his view of this as the 'law of large numbers', explaining that it meant 'killing some and corrupting the rest'. The Party dismissed about half its membership, those who had joined for safety or for careerism, and who were therefore unreliable. By 1951 its membership was nevertheless one in ten of the whole population. They were closely regimented into cadres. Every citizen had his file with his record on it, and any other information which might prove useful to the authorities. At cadre meetings there were indoctrination classes and lectures and at both work and leisure, obedience and correct thinking could be gauged. Communists might have been expected to be satisfied that the Marxist society was at last a reality. Because they were idealists and often protesters, they were a threat to Rakosi's regime which falsified their hopes. In effect, idealistic communism was as much a casualty of Stalinism as democracy.

Gyorgy Paloczi-Horvath, a writer and at the time a Communist, has described how at the moment of the Rajk trial, he and other writers and scientists were invited to a reception in the once fashionable Gellert Hotel in Budapest. Rakosi

> came over to our table too, stood next to me and asked: How are you unruly characters, you artists and intellectuals? While someone made a noncommittal remark, Rakosi placed his hand on my shoulder and gave me a friendly grin. I had the feeling that he was specially interested in me.

It turned out that Rakosi had already signed the order for the arrest of Paloczi-Horvath, which took place a few days later.

Independence of all kinds had to be destroyed if Rakosi's aims were to be achieved. Centralisation of the bureaucracy was the first step towards industrialising Hungary as rapidly as possible, making it, in Gero's slogan, 'a country of iron and steel'. Industrialisation in itself was necessary and impressive, but its breakneck pace condemned the population to useless suffering and forced planners to take decisions the consequences of which had not been properly considered, and which were therefore often self-defeating. Ambitious projects were started by the 1950 Five Year Plan, projects which had little chance of fulfilment, granted Hungary's shortage of raw materials. Ore had to be imported, for instance, for the large new steel complex at Sztalinvaros. The

31 The mining centre of Komló which was developed rapidly after the war

Budapest underground railway was begun in imitation of Moscow's but without regard to different geological conditions. The tunnels through porous stone always refilled with water and had to be abandoned.

As so often in the past, the peasants had to pay for these expensive plans. Briefly they had owned their land. Now it was taken away from them. Rakosi was to explain that the peasants would have joined forces with the landlords had they been expropriated at the same time. It was easier to deal with them separately. Agriculture was collectivised. By 1952, a quarter of the land was organised into collectives, *kolkhozes* of the Soviet kind, and about half as much land again was given over to state farms. The government was constantly pushing on with the movement to collectivise. Peasants preferred to kill their livestock rather than join co-operatives, but they were punished for such resistance. Sometimes they were moved outright to another district; sometimes the whole family was taken in a lorry and deposited forty miles away, to find that their house had been requisitioned in their absence. Any man who possessed over twenty or thirty acres of land, depending on the soil's quality, was defined as a *kulak*, a Russian term meaning a well-off peasant. To beat up a kulak was a revolutionary deed. Kulak lists were kept and those on who were denounced were sent to forced-labour camps to work without pay. 'Guilt boards' with the names of kulaks were posted on village council houses and those spotlighted in this way were crudely tormented. The more productivity dropped – as it did alarmingly – the more taxes and compulsory deliveries were levied.

As for the industrial workers who were to benefit from such measures, they found that all trade unions had been made subordinate to the Party. In a society run by the workers for the workers, ran the argument, there could be no conflict of labour and management, and therefore the right to strike was pointless, a form of self-injury. The working class soon came to look on the new regime as a more devious form of exploitation.

32 Hungarian peasants had been used to bringing their produce into Budapest to sell in the street

The number of students at university or enjoying higher education rapidly multiplied, and the government hoped that this was the best investment for the future. Half the students lived on grants, often awarded to them because of their working-class background, and hostels were built to house them. There were special Party schools for the clever, and admission there guaranteed bright prospects. On the other hand, indoctrination took up a lot of time and energy. There were active education campaigns against Tito, and against capitalist countries whose teenagers were pictured as deprived and wretched, or else degenerate. Books were rewritten. Youth organisations had an almost religious way of getting together, singing the 'Stalin Cantata', an official work, in choruses.

A revolution had just occurred, so the Party would justify these measures, and therefore class warfare was at its most acute. Class enemies were sniffed everywhere, in the former aristocracy, in the technical and professional layers of society, in the kulaks. Constant trials were held to rub in the message of obedience. The proceedings were published under such titles as 'The Trial of Tito-Fascist Bandits' and in this case the judge would emphasise its purpose: 'The irrefutable evidence shows that, in addition to these robbers and murderers, their exposed instigators from Belgrade and Washington also should be sitting in the dock.'

Intellectuals were specially exposed, for the nature of their work was mostly individual, and each man stood or fell by the attitude towards communism of his book or play or radio script or picture. The press was wholly under the Party's direction. The main daily newspaper, *Szabad Nep*, took the format of the Russian *Pravda*. Literature in all its variety was harnessed to the purposes of the state. A doctrine of 'socialist realism' taught that the arts had to illustrate the struggle of progressive elements against reaction. Artists accused of 'negative' tendencies, in other words of thinking that all might not be for the best in this newest of worlds, were silenced, then arrested. The Five Year Plan, declared the head of the Agitprop Department, had to establish the general line of literature and the choice of subject. The writer, said Jozsef Revai in an attack on Tibor Dery, best known of the Communist novelists, had no right to follow his inspiration.

> He has rights superior to that, because he can freely write the truth but only the truth. We do not grant the writer a free pass, we do not give him 'liberty' to deface the truth of life. . . . The State and the people do not have to conform to his taste and judgement; by work and study, the writer must declare his solidarity with the building of socialism.

The sciences and higher education – including such institutions as the Historical Association and the Academy of Science – came under the control of Party ideologists.

Among the intellectuals, however, the Party also found much support. Many of them came from bourgeois backgrounds which they wanted to escape, so they eagerly joined in the class warfare and cut themselves off from relations and former friends. Some had been shocked by what they had experienced of fascism and were equally convinced that communism would bring about a just society. In return they were given many privileges, so much so that ordinary people could hardly avoid the bitter cynicism of concluding that communism was a way of advancing a few at the expense of the many.

Communist leaders lived in villas taken over from the upper classes. Sentries guarded the gates and saluted as the Party cars drove to and fro, their windows curtained against the public stares. Schools were reserved for the children of the Communist

33   Gabor Peter (seen here voting at the 1947 general election) was at the head of the secret police during the years of the Stalinist terror. He was himself arrested in 1953

élite and shops with Western goods for the parents. At Lake Balaton, the holiday resort of Hungary, this élite had large summer houses screened behind barbed-wire which ran into the waters of the lake. Meanwhile the Hungarian index of real wages for workers and other employees fell by more than 5 per cent between 1949 and 1955. The average Hungarian had been better off before the war.

Such were the visible consequences of the police state which Hungary had become. The secret police were the government's agents for working social transformation. Without the secret police, the Communist Party would have been unable to enforce obedience. In their Russian-type uniforms with blue lapels and black boots, the secret police, known by the initials of its abbreviated name first as the AVO, then as the AVH, had penetrated everywhere, to all levels of society. About 100,000 strong, the AVH enrolled many more to help with its tasks. The clandestine document smuggled out of Hungary reports that 'Almost a million adults, ninety per cent of whom would have been capable of productive work, were employed to record, control, indoctrinate, spy on, and sometimes kill the Hungarians actually accomplishing the productive work.' It is not surprising that production fell if less than forty of every hundred working men really were producers, while the remainder were keeping these in their place. The AVH had eliminated opposition to the Communist Party, it investigated and supervised throughout the country, including the Party which had brought it into existence. It ran the many concentration and labour camps, and prisons. The AVH moved the kulaks into collectives and in May 1951 deported thousands of people out of Budapest, dumping them here and there at abandoned houses or farms in the countryside. These people were deported because of their class backgrounds, or because some incident in their

41

past looked suspicious or because their flat was wanted by someone else, usually the poor and unemployed from the provinces who were to become the industrial workers in the cities. *Csengofrasz*, a Magyar word meaning bell-fever, expressed the dread of everyone that the door-bell might ring in the middle of the night. Once a man was arrested, it might be years before his family heard from him again.

At the head of the AVH was Lt.-Gen. Gabor Peter, who had been trained in the Russian security service and took his orders from Moscow. A collaborator of Rakosi, he would himself conduct interrogations of prominent politicians and intellectuals who had been arrested. Many first-hand accounts have recorded his cruelty and cynicism. One poet, who had spent the war in America, was told by Gabor Peter that he deserved his fate for being stupid enough to return to post-war Hungary. Peter's personal assistant was Colonel Vladimir Farkas, named after Lenin by his father, Mihaly Farkas, the Minister of Defence, and whose sadism has also been described by his victims.

34   Gyorgy Marosan. Originally a Social Democrat, he threw in his lot with the Communists and joined Kadar's government in November 1956

35   Gyula Kallai. He was to return to power under Kadar both as Prime Minister and as a member of the Polit-buro

After Rajk's downfall, the secret police had moved unchecked into their own. Wholesale arrests had begun. Fellow-travellers, mostly socialists or Social Democrats who had voted to merge their parties with the Communists, were not spared. President Szakasits was arrested while at dinner with Rakosi who pulled his guest's prepared confession out of his own pocket. Pal Justus, a Social Democrat leader, had been arrested with Rajk. Now Gyorgy Marosan, Minister of Heavy Industry, and Anna Kethly, both of the same party although opponents within it, were also arrested. The army, at last equipped and uniformed by the Soviet army, was purged, its high command shaken out, the chief of staff shot. In 1951 came a mass arrest of Communists, younger men who had already made a mark as Party functionaries, and who were to play an important part in future events. These included Geza Losonczy, deputy chief editor of *Szabad Nep* and Secretary of State under Revai at the Ministry of People's Culture, and Ferenc Donath, chief of Rakosi's personal secretariat. In May of that year Gyula Kallai and

42

Janos Kadar, among others, were arrested. Kallai had replaced Rajk as Minister of Foreign Affairs and like his predecessor was arrested in office. Kadar had been Minister of the Interior, and shortly before his arrest, had been re-elected to the Politburo. In fact he knew far too much about the Rajk affair. The talk in which he had persuaded Rajk to confess had been secretly taped by Rakosi. Kadar was forced to make a public critique of himself at the Party Congress in 1951, but it did not save him. He is said to have been charged with attempted escape to the West.

There have been many eloquent descriptions of what happened to those arrested. Some, being staunch Communists since long before the war, could only believe that an administrative error was to blame when they found themselves searched and stripped in a police station. The AVH headquarters, Number 60 Stalin Avenue, was notorious. From there, prisoners were taken to various gaols in Budapest, or to camps in the country, Recsk and Kistarcsa having the worst reputations. Charges and trials were a

36 This poster proclaims: 'Long live Matyas Rakosi, liberator of Hungarian Prisoners of War!'

formality, but a formality which was deadly for the prisoner who had to confess to suit the AVH. Not the least part of his anguish was to discover what crime he should admit to, and then to make his admission plausible enough to serve the AVH purposes. The number of political prisoners and people uprooted from their homes is estimated at 150,000, or even as high as 200,000. About 2,000 are thought to have been summarily executed while many more died from torture and prison conditions. One family in five had a member or at least a close friend in prison, so that the terror was impossible to escape. Some of the victims had already been in German concentration camps. These experiences were paralleled in all the countries undergoing Stalinism, the tragic waste of another whole generation.

In Hungarian prisons were foreigners of every nationality, Yugoslavs, Greek Communists who had fled from their civil war, the English Communist Edith Bone, picked up at the airport on her way home to London and sent to solitary confinement for seven years. There were men who confessed to belonging to the intelligence services of the Western Powers, and who claimed in despair that their contacts had been Captain Edgar Allan Poe and Major Walt Whitman, or any other famous names picked at random. There were men who had read out a meteorological report which might be misinterpreted and men who had grumbled in a factory canteen, and men who had reported those who grumbled, and men who had sentenced to imprisonment these very reporters. The Conti Street prison, and the Gyutofoghaz and Marko Street, in Budapest, became household names. Select prisoners ended in the fortress at Vac.

In Vac, as Pal Ignotus has written of his years there, were such topsy-turvy occurrences as the beating-up by a most privileged convict, an ex-SS man, of a former colonel of the International Brigade. Says Ignotus:

> To gauge the proportion of victims who simply had bad luck, as against those who had really shown some spark of patriotism or human feeling, would be difficult. In general, those who survived the purges unharmed were probably more sycophantic and barbarous than others who were murdered, imprisoned, or at least pushed aside until Stalin's death. But some of the executed were chiefly sorry for not being among the executioners. The selection of criminals was based quite openly on assumptions about political deviation, rather than upon anything they had actually said or done.

He goes on,

> We political prisoners under Stalin's rule were a society of frieze-dressed cripples, caricatures of the social values which had dwindled and collapsed before and during our imprisonment. We dragged ourselves along in our sweat-soaked ill-fitting uniforms, with our bristly, emaciated faces, often trembling in the hope of an extra dixie-full of the foul food. . . .

The new masters struck him as ludicrous and contemptible.

> Which should have attracted us then, the wrecks of past glory or the set of thugs laboriously attempting to shine in their stead? The new type of success seemed as absurd as any of the former manifestations.

Paloczi-Horvath is another writer who has recorded his ordeal. He was supposed to provide evidence to incriminate others.

> On the 11th of December, 1951, we were taken to Security Police headquarters once more, and on the same day the trial took place. Only Security Police officers were present. I was the first witness. In the dock sat Janos Kadar and three others: Gyula Kallai, the former Foreign Secretary, Ferenc Donath, and Sandor Haraszti. The others had been tortured just as much as Kadar but their faces had gained somehow in dignity. Kadar's was frightening. He looked at me with a terrified stare. He knew that I had every reason to dislike him. He knew the methods of the Security Police and was prepared for the worst. The others looked at me with encouraging eyes. One smiled. Some people trust human beings. Some do not.

Kadar was sentenced to life imprisonment and Paloczi-Horvath, then still a believing Communist, was sent to the central gaol where as an important prisoner he found himself among

High Church dignitaries, former Horthy generals, and Spanish Civil War generals (on the Communist side, of course), the main war criminals, all the Rajkists, people like Prince Paul Esterhazy and Zsedenyi, a former President of the Republic, a galaxy of former Ministers and Under-Secretaries of State. On the first morning, when the convict-orderlies came on their rounds, we discovered that our floor was served by a former Cabinet Minister and a former Parachutist General. One of the gardeners was a Count, the plumber of our wing was an old-guard Communist who had served as Under-Secretary of State under Rajk. We met great names of the Hungarian, Roumanian, Czech, French, and Belgian Communist movements. In another wing Colonel Kalcsics was the orderly. He had fought through the Spanish Civil War and then the Belgian Resistance, and there is even a street named after him in one of the Belgian towns. In 1948 the Belgian Communist Party wanted him to stay. But Rakosi insisted. He pointed out that the great hero was of Hungarian origin and as such should help in rebuilding the Hungarian army. The great hero returned early in 1949 and was sentenced to life imprisonment as Rajk's accomplice.

In this prison in January 1953 an AVH lieutenant-general's uniform was observed hanging in the store-room. Gabor Peter, head of the AVH, had himself been arrested and he could be heard shouting down the corridor, 'Rakosi knew about everything.' The wheel had truly made a full circle.

An English Communist, Dora Scarlett, who was working for Radio Budapest, found that

Rakosi's real character was still a matter of debate among Hungarians, even in 1953, after six years of his personal leadership of the state. Some thought that he had never been a sincere Communist, others that he had begun sincerely, but was corrupted by

37   Matyas Rakosi talking during a Party function

45

the absolute power which he found within his grasp and took, and that he had in the process become completely cynical. Others maintained that he was most probably sincere, even when he killed Rajk and his companions knowing them to be innocent.

On every factory, on every public building, shone the red star. On their walls were painted slogans: 'Long Live Matyas Rakosi, Wise Leader Of The Working People.' 'For Better Work To Fulfil The Five Year Plan And Ensure The Happy Future Of Our Country.' The word *wise* was reserved by Party decree as an exclusive description of Rakosi. His portrait was everywhere. Slogans also pointed up the very latest Party commands. People who disagreed with them did not dare to say so, not to their friends, not to their family. On Rakosi's sixtieth birthday in March 1952 a whole volume was published in his honour containing the writings of the most prominent Hungarian authors. They believed in what they were doing, but had they not done so, they would have had to behave as if they did.

Two of the writers who contributed to that birthday book, Tibor Meray and Tamas Aczel, have described the way Rakosi dictated their state of mind.

And yet, the fear that filled the souls of even his most faithful disciples comprised only a part of their devotion. It comprised a strange, cold current under the waves of ecstasy. Its unbanishable presence served only to make happiness more poignant, delight more exciting, fulfillment richer in content. There was something overpowering in it, almost like intoxication or like standing on a peak near the blinding sun, from which it was so easy to tumble into the depths. This fear multiplied the importance of every little word, of every condescending gesture. One could 'live on it' for days, for weeks, for months, recalling it again and again and telling one's friends about it. 'Just imagine,' one could say, 'recently the telephone rang in my office. I picked it up. "Hallo, Rakosi here," he says. "Well, comrade, all I wanted to tell you is that, though that suggestion you submitted could have been worked out in greater detail, it was not bad, not bad at all. I shall personally recommend you for a decoration. How is your wife? . . ." I was so moved, I couldn't even reply. Anyway, he didn't wait for my answer. But that is not important. It is a great thing, old man, that he finds time to ring me up and even inquire about my wife, what with all the work he has to do, with the worries of an entire country on his shoulders. If you stop to think of it, he is doing everything in this blessed country.'

38 Imre Nagy addresses Parliament during the period of his 'New Course'. To his *right*, Rakosi. To his *left*, Gero

4 Rivalry among the Leaders

THE DEATH OF STALIN in March 1953 was accompanied like Julius Caesar's death at an earlier Ides of March, by threats and auguries. Plots thickened in Moscow. Jewish doctors were supposed to have conspired against the dying dictator. Stalin's daughter has since described in her memoirs this hot atmosphere of intrigue and danger. The tyrannical nature of Stalin's rule had long controlled high Party circles in Russia. Now a collective leadership was formed of those who might have stepped into Stalin's shoes, comprising Malenkov, Khrushchev, Bulganin, Molotov, and for a while in 1953, Beria, then head of the secret police. Collective leadership ensured that the struggle for supreme power did not become an ugly repetition of the pre-war purges and also guaranteed the primacy of the Communist Party as such over the claims of any one individual. Fossilised under Stalin, the Communist movement had lost its revolutionary impetus. The changes to their advantage in the world situation had given the Russians an interest in preserving the balance of power as it had become. But although the satellites had been reshaped entirely according to Russian wishes, each separate country could not help asserting its nationalistic character and claims in a way which cut across Communist theory and practice. The problem facing the collective leadership was to maintain overall direction of their empire without using the old rigid methods of control. Stalinism without the personal authority of Stalin was unworkable, and also inappropriate if Russia was to convince the world that she was a responsible power.

At first Stalin's death was lamented in public. Rakosi attended the funeral. In Budapest, Parliament convened to pay the customary tributes to his name. The vast Gothic-style building was filled with deputies in black who passed a unanimous resolution to revere Stalin's memory. Imre Nagy submitted the motion.

> My heart is heavy as I mount this speaker's platform in order to face our deeply mourning people. . . . To express their deep love for our greatest friend and liberator and teacher, the Hungarian people are rallying around the Party, the Government and our beloved Comrade Rakosi, and they are devoting all their energies towards carrying Stalin's great course to triumph in our country.

This speech of ritual praise gives no indication of the role in Hungary that Imre Nagy was to play for the next four years. As the usual sign of disgrace, Nagy had been obliged to make a confession of earlier political mistakes, and since then he had kept in the background, self-effacing. He did not seem a likely hero, nor a martyr. Of peasant stock, with a benign appearance, a thick but droopy moustache, and spectacles, Imre Nagy was as unpretentious as he looked and typically Hungarian. At first hand he knew the land-hunger and plight of the peasants. He had become a metal-worker in Budapest before the First World War, when like Rakosi he had been captured by the Russians. He had experienced the Bolshevik revolution and had at once joined the Soviet Communist Party, fighting in a special Red Brigade made up of Hungarian prisoners of war. He had worked in the underground Communist movement in Hungary, trying to start Party cells among the peasants. Escaping to Russia in 1930, he had lectured at the Institute of Agriculture, becoming director of a collective in Siberia in

47

1937, a year of terror for many politicians, including Bela Kun, the old Hungarian Communist leader in exile who was executed on Stalin's orders. In the years of eclipse after the Rajk trial, Nagy, expelled from the Politburo, became a professor of agriculture at Budapest University. In February 1951, he had once more been elected to the Politburo, having weathered the storm.

Elections were to be held in May, six weeks after Stalin's burial. At a mass meeting in the big square in front of Parliament in Budapest, Rakosi elaborately credited his government with the recent industrialisation and the new collective farming. After another such Five Year Plan, he said: 'Hungary would surpass most of the advanced capitalist countries in every field of activity.' The newspapers told readers that 'these great achievements are closely linked with the name of Comrade Rakosi'. On 17 May, the single list of deputies to the National Assembly was approved by 98.2 per cent of the voters.

A month later a revolt broke out in East Germany and Soviet tanks had to be used against the workers. In Czechoslovakia workers also demonstrated at Pilsen, a centre of heavy industry, and especially at the Skoda armaments factory, against a currency reform which reduced the value of money. Once the demonstration started, political demands were made and soon American flags were hanging out of the windows along with portraits of former Czech bourgeois statesmen. None too certain of the future anywhere, the new collective leadership in Moscow was anxious to forestall similar events in Hungary, which were all too predictable considering its economic deteriora-

39 On 19 June 1953 an uprising broke out in East Berlin, the first of such actions against Russian control

48

tion. Rakosi had a telephone line direct to the Kremlin and also a private aeroplane in which he made frequent trips there. Now he was ordered to bring with him his colleagues Gero and Farkas, and also Imre Nagy.

In Moscow, some time towards the end of June, Rakosi was obliged to listen to severe criticism. The forced industrialisation of Hungary was an adventure, collectivisation had not worked, the secret police had far exceeded their powers. Prices but not wages had risen. Khrushchev warned that the Hungarian government would be chased out with pitchforks. Beria is supposed to have mocked Rakosi:

> We know that there have been in Hungary, apart from its own rulers, Turkish sultans, Austrian emperors, Tartar khans, and Polish princes. But as far as we know, Hungary has never had a Jewish king. Apparently, that is what you have become. Well, you can be sure we won't allow it.

Collective leadership was to apply in Hungary as well as in Russia. The New Course was to be common to both countries, and Malenkov, its initiator in Russia, is believed to have worked for the promotion of Imre Nagy. At any rate Rakosi was permitted to remain First Secretary of the Party, but he had to hand the premiership to Nagy. At the end of the month, the Central Committee of the Hungarian Party passed a resolution which condemned 'the leftist adventurist policy of Matyas Rakosi, Erno Gero, Mihaly Farkas, and Jozsef Revai – a policy which has driven the country to the brink of a catastrophe'. The 'foursome', as they had come to be known, was dissolved, with Farkas and Revai dismissed from their ministerial posts. On 4 July, Nagy took office. Within a matter of weeks, the huge vote of the electorate had been shown to be meaningless.

On being appointed, Nagy announced the new policy to Parliament. Rakosi was sitting on a bench in the second row, listening to a rival unfolding plans opposed to his own, contradicting the fine speeches of May. Nagy talked openly of mistakes to the deputies. Heavy industry was to slow down its rate of expansion, collective farms could choose to disband, kulak lists were to be abolished; there was to be a return to the rule of law. Another chapter in the history of socialism was beginning, said Nagy. Not that he wished to undermine the centralised society, but only to change its direction. The deputies hardly knew what to make of this sensational speech, for they were sure that Rakosi would fight back. But in the country the New Course was at once popular. Peasants in some villages divided the collectivised land as if 'Communism was over' and fights broke out between them and the police. In the cities most of the self-employed traders or shopkeepers had been squeezed out. Now licences were granted to more than 10,000 of them, and once again there were private barbers, pastrymakers, opticians, art dealers, photographers, tailors.

Rakosi still had the Party machinery behind him. Intrigues began. Not all of the new measures were to be announced outside official circles. At Party meetings Rakosi reminded his audiences of his remaining powers. He gave orders to the AVH to prevent peasants from leaving the collectives. Unexpected help was given him when Beria was purged in Russia, having been found guilty of treason by his colleagues. There was no real proof of it, as Khrushchev has explained, but suspecting that Beria wanted absolute power for himself, 'we came to the unanimous decision that the only correct measure for the defence of the Revolution was to shoot him immediately. This decision was adopted by us and carried out on the spot.' Rakosi felt that his enemy in the Kremlin had been removed and that he could appeal to old loyalties there, gaining support in the power struggle against Nagy which was to last for the next year and a half. Bureaucrats in Hungary had to be sharp in order to spot whether their instructions were sponsored by Rakosi or Nagy. So long as Nagy was backed by the Kremlin, he had the final court of appeal.

Dramatically men began to reappear, men who had been dropped into oblivion as enemies of the people, spies, or traitors. Now some of these same men, whom it had been imprudent to remember, were sitting in cafés, telephoning, and looking for their wives, their clothes, and books. Sometimes their old friends shook their hands, and sometimes had to ask forgiveness for having denounced them. The AVH officer who released prisoners from the camps would make a little farewell speech. 'In the name of the Hungarian People's Republic, I ask your forgiveness for the injustice, the wrong and the indignity you were made to suffer.' One writer, Gyorgy Faludy, describes reaching the local village on his release, where an old man emerged,

> a long, skinny, barefoot peasant with greenish-yellow hair and moustache, almost like a Russian peasant straight out of Tolstoi. He shook hands with all of us. . . . 'We know everything,' he said, 'Everything.' Then he took nineteen large slices of bread from his knapsack, put a pinch of salt from his pocket on each and – according to the ancient custom of hospitality – offered us one each with a slight bow. He must have been watching us and seen us coming down the slopes.

Only a few hundred prisoners were released at this time, most of them former Communists, but some of those who had been illegally deported and interned were also allowed home. Their return to normal life had an impact out of all proportion to their number. People learnt at first hand what had happened. More important, many intellectuals and Communist sympathisers discovered that some of their heartfelt aspirations had been deceptions, that they had been exploited or misled by politicians. Plainly those who had defended the class war and who had justified the dictatorship of the proletariat as an end in itself, were responsible for the political climate in which such widespread crimes had been possible. Looking at their past work, many writers and propagandists were shocked and shamed by what they had done. 'It is my crime to have believed in yours' was a line in a much-quoted poem. Nor could these feelings be confined to intellectuals. Information filtered out, especially through the Communist Party. Janos Kadar was given a job as secretary of one of the Party branches in Budapest. Geza Losonczy, Sandor Haraszti, Ferenc Donath, all just released from prison, rose to prominence as a sort of group around Imre Nagy. A core of resistance to Stalinism in all its aspects had formed, and formed furthermore within the élite. That it did not spread further was due to Nagy's caution, even timidity. Any false move on his part would give Rakosi the chance to argue that Nagy was splitting the Party into opposing elements.

Always on the look-out for opportunities to regain lost ground, Rakosi had seized on the greater rivalry between Malenkov and Khrushchev. Malenkov wanted more of a consumer society for Russia, less investment in industry and armaments. Khrushchev could point to the speeches of President Eisenhower and his Secretary of State, John Foster Dulles, who harped on the tyrannies exercised by Russia over her satellites, and the need for their liberation. Khrushchev also had to defend his agricultural policies. Their fight reached a climax at a meeting of the Soviet Central Committee,

40   12,000 Russian troops and hundreds of tanks were
called in to subdue East Berlin

when Khrushchev had mobilised support from the military and the Party. Malenkov
had to resign as a 'rightist deviationist' a month later.

Once again the history of Hungary was made in Moscow. The handful of Hungarians who had been to Moscow to receive their orders to start the New Course in
June 1953 were summoned back in January 1955 to hear the switch. This time, Malenkov, under fire from his colleagues, attacked Nagy for liberalising too much and too fast.
Nagy had behaved much as Malenkov had. It was easy to pin on him, too, the label of
'rightist deviationist' and in only a matter of weeks Rakosi did so. There was a threat of
inflation in Hungary and the Stalinists had chosen the right moment to present themselves as a strong government. Nagy was criticised by the Central Committee and
dismissed from the premiership in April. Then he was expelled from all Party offices,
from his university chair, and from membership of the Academy of Science. Since the
beginning of the year, he had been ill after a heart attack, and was unable to defend
himself. A nonentity, Andras Hegedus, was appointed Prime Minister. He had been
picked by Rakosi. Nagy's first period in office had ended in failure. Whatever good
intentions he may have had did not materialise into an effective programme. He was
neither willing nor prepared to use Rakosi's political tactics. Yet many Hungarians
were ready to make allowances for him. They were also to remember the excitement of
the June speech, the first stirring of independence.

51

5 Two Steps Backward Three Steps Forward

LIKE THE BOURBON KINGS who returned to their throne after the French revolution, Rakosi had learnt nothing and forgotten nothing. Once again he tried to establish 'the cult of personality' around himself, restoring his former dictatorship. Some opponents were arrested, the prisons settled back to their usual routine. Throughout the year, *Szabad Nep* carried almost daily reports of the setting up of new collectives and co-operative villages, and everyone knew that the peasants were acting under compulsion. The standard of living was to be lowered in order to free capital for further investment in industry. But Rakosi was caught in an awkward fork. If he continued to be a Stalinist, the Hungarian people, aroused by the Nagy experiment, would reject him. If he destroyed the political structure of Stalinism, he would destroy himself.

Once he had ousted Malenkov, Khrushchev found himself somewhat similarly placed, anxious to maintain the Russian position, but also to assert leadership over the reformers in the Communist world. Among these, the most thornily persistent were the Yugoslavs, who had emerged very successfully from their quarrel with Stalin. Far from being toppled by Russian hostility, Yugoslavia was more independent and prosperous than at almost any other period of her history. Intellectuals and Party functionaries throughout Eastern Europe were looking with admiration at this example of a socialist country.

Khrushchev consolidated the Russian strategic domination of Eastern Europe by grouping all the satellites into the Warsaw Pact, a treaty of 'friendship, co-operation and mutual aid', which was signed in May 1955. This was a counterbalance to NATO, to which West Germany had just been admitted. The armed forces of all the Warsaw Pact countries were placed under Soviet command. At the same time Russia signed a peace treaty with Austria, and withdrew her troops from the Russian-occupied zone there. According to the 1947 Paris Treaty, she should have withdrawn her troops from Hungary, too, but now could argue that they were stationed in that country because of the needs of the Warsaw Pact. To reassure the West, Khrushchev made plain at a Geneva summit meeting in the summer that he believed in peaceful coexistence. Although he sometimes enjoyed telling capitalists that he would bury them, he was too shrewd to ignore the dangers of nuclear warfare. The Bolshevik view that war was inevitable had to be brought up to date.

Having smoothed out this legacy from Stalin, Khrushchev made his peace with Yugoslavia. In June 1955, at Belgrade airport, as if unable to wait before getting out an apology, he laid the blame for the past on the dead Beria. Tito held out for more, wanting an admission that each country was free to pursue its own road to socialism, and Khrushchev was ready to make the concessions, including the winding up of the Cominform, whose main task had been anti-Yugoslav agitation. This reconciliation threatened Rakosi. Not only were the Stalinists in Moscow being discredited, but Rakosi himself had been a leading opponent of Tito. That Tito had not forgotten was proved in a speech he made in July against the old guard:

41 Relations with Yugoslavia bedevilled Russian policy
after the war. Marshal Tito (*right*) meets the 1955 Russian
delegation come to make amends. From *left* to *right*:
A. Mikoyan, Marshal Bulganin and N. S. Khrushchev

These men have their hands soaked in blood, have staged trials, given false information, sentenced innocent men to death. They have had Yugoslavia mixed up in all these trials, as in the case of the Rajk trial, and they now find it difficult to admit before their own people their mistakes.

The reference to Rajk was very damaging. When the Belgrade speeches were published in the Budapest newspapers, it became obvious that if Tito was not the wicked imperialist agent of the West, then Rajk could not have been a traitor either. A journalist of *Szabad Nep*, Miklos Gimes, was expelled from the Party for asking at an editorial meeting that Rajk be rehabilitated. If Rajk were proved innocent, Rakosi could not survive the exposure. He was, in short, overtaken by Communist tactics, in that having once obeyed zealously the Moscow demands, he was left high and dry with the responsibility for them. That other tactics were called for to meet changing circumstances only proved that Rakosi belonged to the scrap-heap of history.

At home, Rakosi was confronted with this past. In July, Rajk's widow, Julia, was released from prison. Not allowed to resume her surname, she worked anonymously as a librarian in Budapest. A woman of fierce integrity and a Communist like her husband, she wanted his name cleared. Cardinal Mindszenty had his life sentence lifted, but was kept under house arrest. Imre Nagy, officially ostracised, was busy writing the book since published under the title *On Communism*. He was putting his thoughts in order, and his manuscript was circulating among his friends and admirers. These latter were increasingly daring in uttering their opinions, and many of them were writers or journalists. When the whole September issue of the *Literary Gazette* was confiscated, its

53

editor having already been dismissed, these writers had a focus for their revolt. The nine Communist members on the ruling committee of the Writers' Association resigned in a body. Early in November the protest spread. Fifty-nine of the most influential men in all fields of Hungarian cultural life signed a memorandum to the Central Committee attacking censorship and the stifling of opinion. In themselves the intellectuals carried no political weight, and could easily be coerced as they had no mass support. But they were the élite, and because the great majority of them favoured Imre Nagy, Rakosi could not ignore their opposition. A large Party meeting was held in the building of the Iron and Steel Workers' Union, where Rajk had been tried. In an atmosphere of a lynch trial, the intellectuals were condemned: some were expelled from the Party, others reprimanded. By inclination Rakosi would have liked to repress those he could not command. To do so would alienate even further a large section of the Party. Like many dictators faced with rebellion, Rakosi was uncertain whether force or compromise would be taken as an admission of weakness.

Events overtook Rakosi. The Twentieth Party Congress held in Moscow in February 1956 was one of the more dramatic moments of the Communist movement. Khrushchev's speech lasted several hours, well into the night, and was too revealing to be kept secret as intended. The Yugoslavs were the first to publish it to the Communist bloc. Khrushchev had reviewed much of the USSR's past. Partly he was out to prove his good intentions towards Yugoslavia, by condemning Stalin's policy. Partly he was out to show that if he could debunk the Stalin myth, he was the man to lead a new, revitalised Russia. Before more than a thousand delegates he laid the blame for all that had gone wrong in Russia on Stalin and 'the cult of personality' that went with him. Words were not minced. Some of the purges were described, and these doctrinaire killings were called abuses of power. This enterprise was risky, for Khrushchev and all the delegates in the audience knew themselves to be intimately involved in these deeds. Some of them may have expected that Khrushchev would go too far and so eliminate himself. In fact he succeeded in mobilising the pent-up desire for reform in Russia, and within months the old Stalinists like Molotov and Kaganovitch had lost their jobs in the government. Khrushchev's long term objective was to present a Soviet Russia returning to its early principles. If Stalin had been the criminal who had perverted these principles, then what about leaders like Rakosi who had been his creatures and had copied his every move?

Returning to Hungary after attending this Congress, Rakosi did his best to minimise Khrushchev's speech. An ex-Communist functionary has recorded that Rakosi told his friends not to worry: 'In a few months, Khrushchev will be the traitor and everything will be back to normal.' Which was not a bad guess, but wrong. To the Hungarian Central Committee Rakosi did his duty by attacking the cult of personality. He had hoped to be able to represent the imprisoned Gabor Peter, once head of the AVH, as the Hungarian Beria. But the pressure on him was too strong, and he was at last forced to make an admission, although he chose to do so in a small provincial town.

> After the unmasking of Beria, the imperialist agent, and in Hungary of Gabor Peter's gang, the Rajk case has, on the initiative of our Party, been reviewed. It has been established that the case was based on provocation. Therefore, in accordance with the Central Committee's June resolution, the Supreme Court has rehabilitated Comrade Laszlo Rajk and other comrades. Other cases have similarly been reviewed: the innocently condemned have been rehabilitated: others have obtained pardon. Succes-

54

sively cases of former Social Democrats have likewise been re-examined. Most of them have already been released; the last of them are being released these days. Those who were not guilty have been or will be rehabilitated.

In neighbouring countries Stalinists took defensive action by resigning. Rakosi was more stubborn. The campaign against him had revolutionary aspects because the drawn-out Rakosi-Nagy dispute had already brought into existence what amounted to an opposition. It must have been clear to Imre Nagy, as it was to many after the Twentieth Party Congress, that the pendulum had swung back in his favour. He was too old a Communist to do anything in a hurry. His house in Budapest was under constant watch by the police, but friends visited him openly, celebrating his sixtieth birthday with him in June. Tibor Meray and Tamas Aczel have described Nagy confidently biding his time.

> An elderly gentleman wearing a sports suit, a green hat, and yellow kid gloves appeared more and more frequently in the elegant streets of the Budapest shopping centre, looking into the shop windows and throwing covert glances from behind his pince-nez at the pretty women whispering excitedly behind his back. He was greeted by the male passers-by with a raising of hats, and whether he knew them personally or not, people stopped him to inquire about his health and ask what he thought of the political situation. The gentleman smiled delightedly, although it was obvious that he was a little ashamed of his contentment. Modestly, he replied to the inquiries about his health and brushed away the political questions. He behaved not at all like a fallen Communist prime minister who had been slandered and persecuted for years by the entire Party press. . . . He often had his grandchildren with him – a five-year-old boy and a four-year-old girl, whom he took to Budapest's best confectioner's, Gerbeaud's, for an ice cream, looking after them with grandfatherly tenderness. By then, his popularity was so great that bus drivers stopped between stations to pick him up, and young girls rose to give him their seats.

42 Mrs Julia Rajk with her eight-year-old son at the reburial of her husband, after the government acknowledged that he had been wrongfully killed. Next to her is the widow and child of another victim (*see page* 59)

TO18905

43   The Hungarian President (*left*) with a row of Ministers
and Politburo members in the cemetery where Rajk was
now placed among the 'Heroes of Communism' (*see page* 59)

The intellectuals were more impatient. Gyula Hay, an eminent playwright and a 'Muscovite', put their attitude bluntly in the *Literary Gazette*, now again published: 'The influence of the Twentieth Congress, the grandiose upsurge of humanity, the great triumph of human dignity, will not and cannot stop at our frontiers, they cannot by-pass our country.' At the end of 1955 some of the dissident intellectuals belonging to the Communist Youth League had formed a discussion club in Budapest, and they had called it the Petofi Circle, after Sandor Petofi, the young revolutionary poet who was killed in the Hungarian Revolutionary war of 1849. Its secretary, Gabor Tanczos, was a philosopher, and seventeen of its twenty organisers were Party members. A similar group of disillusioned Poles had recently become influential in Warsaw. After the Twentieth Congress, the Petofi Circle opened its doors to the public. A Communist Party organisation had freed itself from Party control, and it was offering open debate for the first time in Hungary since 1948.

The presiding chairmen were Party spokesmen, but as such they could count on no respect. It emerged from the talk of the country's leading nuclear physicist that valuable uranium deposits had been found near the Yugoslav frontier, but that Rakosi had signed away the concession to the Russians. Economic and educational policies came under attack. 'Contemporary Questions of Philosophy' was the title of an address given by Professor Gyorgy Lukacs, the most distinguished of contemporary Marxist scholars. Lukacs had been People's Commissar of Education during the Bela Kun regime in 1919, and had lived afterwards in Germany and Russia. A 'Muscovite' but a man of too subtle an intelligence to fit into any framework, Lukacs was always under suspicion for his unorthodoxy. Now he came out against Stalinist culture as a dreary desert of propaganda.

Mrs Rajk intervened during the debate on 'Socialist Legality'. Leslie Bain, an American journalist, opens his book about events in Hungary with his account of the

56

occasion. 'It was hard to believe that the gaunt woman who strode towards the lectern in an ill-fitting housedress had been but a few years ago one of the beauties of Budapest.' Taking the platform, Mrs Rajk issued a challenge recorded by Aczel and Meray in their book.

> Comrades, I stand before you deeply moved after five years of prison and humiliation. Let me tell you this: so far as prisons are concerned, in Horthy's prisons conditions were far better even for Communists than in Rakosi's prisons. Not only was my husband killed, but my little baby was torn from me; for years, I received no letters and no information about the fate of my little son. These criminals have not only murdered Laszlo Rajk. They have trampled underfoot all sentiment and honesty in this country. Murderers should not be criticised – they should be punished. I shall never rest until those who have ruined the country, corrupted the Party, destroyed thousands and driven millions to despair receive their just punishment.

The whole audience rose to applaud.

A final debate on the role of the press took place on 27 June. Held in the Officers' House of the People's Army, the meeting was attended by 6,000 people and lasted until dawn. The novelist Tibor Dery said that the root of the trouble was the absence of freedom. When Geza Losonczy said that Imre Nagy should be given a chance to defend himself, the public cheered and shouted for Nagy.

The next day a strike broke out at Poznan, one of the main industrial centres of Poland. The workers' demands had been persistently ignored. A general uprising developed there for two days until Russian tanks and troops surrounded the city. One hundred and thirteen people were killed. The Polish Prime Minister Cyrankiewicz warned that 'all hands raised against the Socialist authority in Poland would be cut off.' Bulganin in Moscow said: 'Every country should go its own way to Socialism, but we cannot permit this to be used to break up the solidarity of the peace camp . . . under the pretext of extending national peculiarities or democracies.' This uprising, and these official judgements, prefigure the Hungarian revolution.

Encouraged by the way the Poznan rebellion had been dealt with, Rakosi struck too, condemning the Petofi Circle, forbidding any future meetings, and drawing up a list of 400 people, including Imre Nagy, to be summarily arrested as members of an 'anti-Party plot'. Party agents were again sent to the factories to convince workers that the intellectuals had been preparing a return to capitalism. At a Politburo meeting in the Academy Street Party headquarters on 18 July, Rakosi presented his plans. He was interrupted by the arrival from Moscow, unannounced, of Anastas Mikoyan, Deputy Chairman of the Soviet Council of Ministers. Curtly Mikoyan told Rakosi to resign because his methods were unacceptable. Rakosi telephoned Khrushchev who confirmed Mikoyan's order. It had been Rakosi's habit to divide the Party by cabals. Recently, he had played to the Politburo the tape-recording taken on his instructions in 1949 of Kadar persuading Rajk to confess. Such manœuvres backfired. No section of the Party would now come to his help, and Rakosi could only make his self-criticism, resign, and leave for the Soviet Union. Had he stayed in Hungary, he might well have been arrested. Some weeks later, it seems, his wife returned to pack up their valuables.

If Mikoyan had insisted that the Central Committee choose Nagy to replace Rakosi, the Hungarian revolution might never have happened. Protest so far had been from a Communist standpoint against the Stalinism which was officially defunct. Moscow, and not the Hungarians, had removed Rakosi. Moscow also appointed Erno

57

Gero to succeed him, kept Hegedus as Prime Minister, and added to the Politburo Kadar and Marosan, victims of Rakosi's purges, but being groomed for the future.

Between July and October, Gero picked up the pieces of the former policies. Some particularly hated AVH officers, including Mihaly Farkas, were arrested. The rebellious writers were left alone, and the Petofi Circle was allowed to meet again in September. Compulsory teaching of Russian in school was reduced. The Iron Curtain, that stretch of mines, barbed-wire, and watch-towers along the frontier with Austria, was partially dismantled, and trips to Vienna were permitted. Once given a glimpse of the riches which accompanied the modern neutrality of Austria, the country which had formerly ruled them, Hungarians could not resist unfavourable comparisons. The summer, with

44   Sandor Petofi (1823–49), the Hungarian lyric poet who became an extreme democrat. He fought, with valour, under General Bem and was killed at the battle of Segesvar

45   (*opposite*) The Petofi Circle meets. The writer Tibor Tardos is speaking

the universities closed for the holiday season, gave Gero a short respite. He spent much of the time earning the goodwill of Moscow and of Tito, whom he met in the Crimea and by whom he was invited to Yugoslavia. After the revolution, Tito was to acknowledge that his friendliness to Gero had been a miscalculation.

> We wanted to establish relations with the Hungarian Workers' Party because we hoped that by not isolating the Hungarian Party we could more easily influence that country's proper internal development. . . . However, matters had already gone pretty far, a fact which we did not know, so that Gero's coming to Yugoslavia and our joint declaration [of friendship] could no longer help.

Diplomacy could not hide the public's dissatisfaction with Gero, the known henchman of Rakosi. An outlet for their feelings, almost an expression of their open victory, was provided by the reburial of Rajk, a scene which does justice to Mark Antony's judgement of Caesar, that 'the evil men do lives after them, the good is oft interred with their bones'. Mrs Rajk had insisted that her husband and those executed with him be given the honour of graves in the Kerepes Cemetery, where many of the great writers and statesmen of Hungary have memorials. The Party had agreed. The bodies of Rajk and the others were dug up from a forest clearing near Godollo, outside Budapest, where they had been hidden. Rajk's corpse was identified by his dentist. On 6 October, about 300,000 people filed into the cemetery to be present at the reburial. No policemen were to be seen, and none were needed because the crowd was impressively silent. Silent, too, when Politburo members made their formal speeches of apology. Gero and Kadar (once Rajk's protégé) were in Moscow. Near Mrs Rajk at the ceremony stood Imre Nagy, who afterwards walked up to her and embraced her. The *Szabad Nep* editorial said:

People were numbed not only by a deep sense of grief but also by burning hatred, by the memory that these comrades, these men were executed as enemies of the fatherland, of the people! We were led to believe – and we were willing to believe – the slanders about you. Forgive us for this, comrades!

Two days beforehand, Nagy had applied for readmittance to the Party. The Politburo took nine days to reply, and then cancelled the previous expulsion while making it clear that Nagy would have to confess to deviation. The intra-Party conflict was not going to be abandoned even at this late stage, after the reburial of Rajk, and with criticism, speculation, and revolutionary ideas appearing in many papers and journals. Hoping that Nagy's re-entry into politics was blocked, Gero on 14 October left at the head of the delegation to Belgrade, taking up Tito's invitation issued earlier in the Crimea.

While he was away, a crisis blew up in Poland, and this was the final event required to fire Hungary. Poland had been greatly shaken by Khrushchev's speech at the

Twentieth Party Congress. Stalin's treatment of the Poles had aroused the strongest national resentments. As in Hungary there had been a clash within the Communist Party between the Stalinists, their arguments strengthened after the Poznan riots, and the revisionists, those liberals who approved of Yugoslav ideas and hoped for a similar progress. At the Polish Central Committee meeting on 19 October, this split was resolved with high drama. Fearing a rebellion worse than Poznan, the old guard called on the Russians for military help. Russian tanks moved into Warsaw, and Khrushchev flew in with a large delegation including Mikoyan. Students and workers began to mobilise in the streets, the Polish army took up positions. If fighting had broken out, the liberals would have been forcibly suppressed. To head off the confrontation, Khrushchev decided to back down, presumably in the light of his recent attacks on Stalin's methods. Gomulka was accepted as the new First Secretary of the Party and on 21 October he announced that Poland was to go her own way to socialism. He spoke of the Stalinist past only to reject it fiercely. This was the 'October turning-point', as it has been called. The Russians were prepared to tolerate a form of communism which might not be identical with their own, and to which they might even have to adjust. Gomulka's career had many parallels to Imre Nagy's: he, too, had been disgraced and for the same reasons, although he had actually been imprisoned until December 1954. His return to power had been facilitated by the defection to the West of a senior police official whose revelations created a scandal similar to the Rajk affair. Intellectuals had openly backed Gomulka and the Warsaw crowds rallied to him because they hoped he might break the Stalinist grip. Hungarians learnt that it was possible to stand up to the Russians. In the Poles and their crisis they saw a reflection of themselves and their own aspirations, as they had done before at revolutionary moments in the past. The wires from Budapest to Warsaw were soon busy with messages of congratulations.

46 Cyrankiewicz and Gomulka, the Polish leaders who came to a temporary compromise with Russia during the 'Polish October' events which preceded the Hungarian revolution

6 Thirteen Days of Revolution

OVER THE WEEKEND OF 19–21 OCTOBER, students and intellectuals took advantage of the Polish crisis to publicise their demands. They would not have been able to do so without the past years of quarrel within the Party leadership, a quarrel bringing out the intimate link between Marxist politics and intellectual issues, but also lining people up behind Rakosi or Nagy. Like many revolutions in this century, the Hungarian October was given its immediate impetus by the actions of students. Youth groups which during the summer had left the official Communist youth organisations, took the lead. At the Technological University in Budapest, students outlined what was to be the official revolutionary policy a week later: that first of all the Russians should at once leave Hungary as laid down in the Peace Treaty, that Nagy be Prime Minister, that elections be held by secret ballot with participation of all parties, that political prisoners be freed and 'cadre-sheets' abolished. Rakosi, 'responsible for all the crimes of the recent past and for the ruin of the country', should be tried before a people's tribunal. Students gathered in many faculty buildings, in the College of Fine Arts on Academy Street not far from the AVH headquarters, in the law schools. Instead of discussing Poland, they turned to Hungarian affairs. In Szeged, capital of a large county in southern Hungary, Leslie Bain, the American journalist, had watched the stream of students moving in the sunny afternoon through the Ady Square towards the great hall of the university, and he had been impressed by 'their glowing faces, shining eyes, and excited voices'. He heard a Communist professor say, 'We do want a house-cleaning, and the students were right to take the lead.' From the start, students were not alone in showing their intentions. At Zahony on the frontier with Russia, military equipment was assembled and in Romania Soviet officers on leave and reserve officers speaking Hungarian were recalled.

In Gyor, another county capital, the writer Gyula Hay had chaired an open-air meeting at which he had asked for the withdrawal of Soviet troops from Hungary. On the next day, Monday, 22 October, this call was taken up at several further meetings, including one of young intellectuals at Buda. At the Lorand Eotvos University in Budapest, speakers emphasised that students should march shoulder to shoulder with peasant youth, and visit factories to inform workers of their ideas. Demands were everywhere different, with clusters of students moving across the city arguing and persuading and drawing up programmes which they wished to make public, and finally to broadcast on the radio. Towards evening a delegation went to Hegedus, the Prime Minister, with a petition of fourteen general points concerning their freedoms, a future election, and the departure of the Russians. They were assured that a Youth Parliament might meet in a fortnight. At the Student Council in Serb Street, a reunion of all the student bodies voted in favour of a demonstration of Polish-Hungarian solidarity, to take place at 1.30 p.m. on the following day. They would march to the statue of General Bem, a Polish general who had fought with the Hungarians in 1848. Petofi Circle leaders met and discussed until late at night, deciding to join the demonstrators. They also wrote a manifesto of ten points, more cautious than the students', its first proposition being that Imre Nagy should rejoin the Central Committee. Some 5,000 students and teachers spent the night debating in the main hall of the university,

61

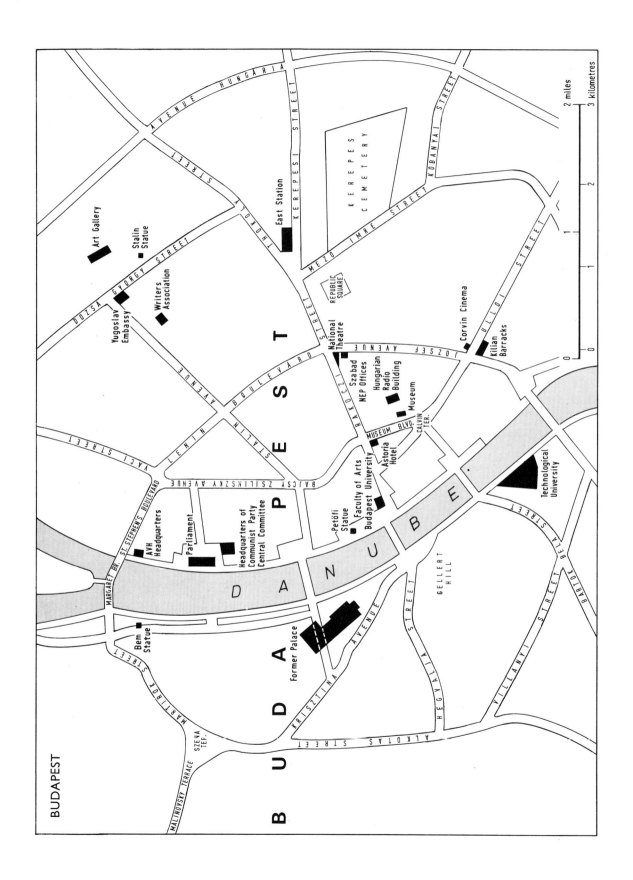

BUDAPEST

Art Gallery

Stalin
Statue

Yugoslav
Embassy

Writers
Association

AVENUE HUNGARIA

KEREPESI STREET

East Station

KEREPES CEMETERY

MEZO IMRE STREET

KOBANYAI STREET

REPUBLIC
SQUARE

Corvin Cinema

ULLOI STREET

Kilian
Barracks

National
Theatre

Szabad
NEP Offices

Hungarian
Radio
Building

Museum

JOZSEF AVENUE

CALVIN
TER.

MUSEUM BLVD.

Astoria
Hotel

Faculty of Arts
Budapest University

Petőfi
Statue

Technological
University

Headquarters of
Communist Party
Central Committee

Parliament

AVH
Headquarters

ST. STEPHEN'S BOULEVARD

MARGARET BR.

Bem
Statue

Former Palace

DANUBE

GELLERT
HILL

BELA STREET

BARTOK

VILLANYI STREET

HEGYALJA STREET

ALKOTAS STREET

KRISZTINA AVENUE

SZENA
TER.

MALINOVSKY TERRACE

MARTIROK STREET

DOZSA GYORGY STREET

THOKOLY STREET

NATIONAL STREET

RAKOCZI STREET

BAJCSY ZSILINSZKY AVENUE

STALIN BOULEVARD

LENIN AVENUE

VACI STREET

B U D A P E S T

0   1   1   2   2 miles

0   1   2   3 kilometres

resolving all the current arguments into an inclusive manifesto to be presented to the government.

Meanwhile at Badacsony, a village of the Hungarian Plain, north of Lake Balaton, a wine festival was taking place. Imre Nagy had a house there, and he was guest of honour at the festival. When friends telephoned him with the news from Budapest, he remained calm and continued to taste wines.

Tuesday, 23 October

The Hungarian leadership had no knowledge of these demands, nor of the discussions breaking out all over the country. Gero and Kadar and their attendant delegation were in a special Pullman returning from Belgrade. They could feel pleased to have obtained Tito's backing, having convinced him that as successors of Rakosi they were acceptable friends and allies. Tito seems to have been flattered by their attentions.

On arrival in mid-morning at Budapest station, Gero spoke confidently then and there of Hungarian-Yugoslav friendship. But his triumph was spoiled by the news of the students. He went to his office at Central Committee headquarters, where a delegation from *Szabad Nep* was waiting. Its editorial that day had said:

> Meeting follows upon meeting in our universities and our institutions of higher learning. Students of engineering, philosophy, law, and the creative arts are meeting in the universities of Budapest, Pecs, Szeged. These meetings of the youth are taking place in a passionate and stormy atmosphere, resembling a rampaging river overflowing its banks, rather than an artificially channelled stream.

The newspaper editors warned that the demands of the masses must be taken seriously. Backed by Kadar, Marosan, and Revai, Gero told them not to lose their heads. Revai was hysterical, shouting, 'We would fire! We would fire!' No concessions were to be made.

By one o'clock the radio had announced that the Minister of the Interior, Laszlo Piros, had forbidden the students to hold the demonstration decided upon the previous day. Tersely he had told the student leaders that the police were under orders to fire if the demonstration began. This ban was too late because hundreds of people were milling in the open, waiting expectantly. A large crowd had already assembled around the Petofi statue. Petofi had greatly admired the Poles for their anti-Russian fervour. This statue of the national poet stands in a small square on the Pest side of the Danube. People pressed in to hear a National Theatre actor, Imre Sinkovits, recite Petofi's poem *Arise Hungarians:* 'Now is the time, now or never. Should we be slaves or free? This is the question – choose!' The poem had sparked the 1848 revolution, which the Austrians had been unable to put down until calling upon Tsar Nicholas I for Russian help.

As planned, the march to the statue of General Bem started around two o'clock. Too late again, the radio proclaimed at twenty past two that the prohibition on demonstrating had been withdrawn, and also that Gero would later broadcast. At two o'clock, too, the Central Committee of the Hungarian Communist Youth League was opening a session to approve the events of the day and to send a telegram of appreciation to Polish youth for their revolution. In Warsaw, before the huge Palace of Culture, Gomulka was addressing 300,000 excited people. And early in the afternoon Imre Nagy returned from the country to his Budapest home.

63

The march to the statue of General Bem was an impressive tribute to the Polish October. The demonstrators, including well-known professors and a Polish poet who had flown in from Warsaw, crossed the fashionable centre of Budapest, over the Danube to Buda. They carried flags and banners. From the Technological University, the Agricultural University, the various high schools, other groups converged on this statue for speeches. Hundreds of people who had been to the Petofi statue also joined in. Peter Veres, the president of the Writers' Association, and a novelist of peasant life, read out to them all a resolution calling for an independent national policy, socialist but 'on the basis of the principle of equality', as far as the USSR was concerned, and he concluded that the people must elect their representatives by free, secret ballot. Soldiers in a nearby barracks were waving to show their approval.

By five in the afternoon these crowds had drifted back down St Stephen's Boulevard across the river. It was late autumn weather, the fullness of the year. Workers leaving factories to go home from the tram terminals at Marx Square, instead came to swell the numbers. This was the alliance of workers and intellectuals which Lenin had said was indispensable to a revolution. Yet there was nothing violent about the mass converging before the Parliament building whose vast dome is the nub of the capital, and visible from most vantage points. On the wide square in front of the building stand the statues of Kossuth, the leader of the 1848 revolution, and of Ferenc Rakoczi II, who had fought for national independence against the Austrians in the eighteenth century. As dusk gathered, the lights went on in some of the first-floor windows of Parliament. The silhouettes of one or two Ministers could be made out. Since midday the Politburo had been debating what should be done in the emergency, and the crowd knew it. When the lights in the square were abruptly switched off, the shout came, 'We have had enough of darkness!' Newspapers and pamphlets were rolled up and burnt like flaming torches.

47   A delegation from Budapest University (named after its
founder, Baron Eotvos Lorand) in the march from the
Petofi statue across the Danube to the Bem statue

At 8 p.m. Gero's speech was broadcast. It lasted twelve minutes. 'There are people', he said, 'who want to create a conflict between proletarian internationalism and Hunggarian nationalism.' Their socialist democracy was at stake, he warned. The tone of his voice, harsh and coldly arrogant, brought home to his listeners more than anything so far the nature of the power they wanted to reform. The American Leslie Bain was on Parliament Square while Gero was broadcasting. A dozen policemen crowded round him to listen to his car radio. Of Gero one of them said, 'He lies with every breath he takes.' Then it was announced that Imre Nagy would address the crowd. Only recently admitted back to the Party, Nagy was anxious not to push himself forward and had to be persuaded by his close supporters to make this address. Geza Losonczy had driven him that afternoon to Parliament. Calls of 'We want Imre Nagy!' had brought him out on a first-floor balcony. 'Dear comrades', began Nagy, but he was whistled at. 'We do not whistle at you but at your words', someone shouted. After a baffled pause, Nagy promised reforms, and asked the crowd to sing the national anthem. After only two minutes, he returned indoors, to speak to deputies. He had made a poor impression. That evening could be heard openly the slogan which was to stamp the revolution: '*Ruszkik Haza*' or 'Out with the Russians.'

After this dramatic appearance, Nagy went to Party headquarters and then his precise movements are unknown. For the next three days he was incommunicado and his telephone calls were checked. There is an eye-witness report of him sitting between two AVH policemen and nodding his refusal to give an interview. It was as if he were being held prisoner. It is not clear to what extent he participated in the discussions of the Central Committee that night. After all, he had been in disgrace until only a fortnight earlier, and he is said to have been afraid that he was being provoked by the Stalinists into making a false step which would once and for all end his career. Another eye-witness has reported that the scene at Party headquarters 'was one of confusion and

48   Peter Veres addressing the Writers' Association

calamity'. The leadership had to decide how to deal with the situation. It could take a soft line, and appoint Nagy Prime Minister in accordance with popular demand. The more liberal policies of 1953 and the New Course could then be resumed where they had been broken off. Or there was the hard-line alternative of calling in the Russians to maintain the government in office and bringing the crowds to heel by superior force.

In effect the Party leadership decided to adopt both lines at once, but to cover their tracks by involving Nagy in their appeal to the Russians. They must have been pushed to such deviousness by inclination as well as by the worsening of events in the evening while they were arguing. Having already achieved so much, the crowds were

49 The posters proclaim Polish-Hungarian Friendship and 'We will tolerate no provocateurs in our ranks'

50 Ropes and welding equipment had to be used to destroy the bronze statue of Stalin, set prominently in the capital, symbol of an era

not to be fobbed off with words when they had a manifesto prepared. But it was evident that any revolutionary action might fail for lack of publicity. No medium of communication was free from state control. The pavement orators demanded that their views be known to a wider audience, and in particular the sixteen points formulated the day before in the university. The radio station was an obvious objective, all the more because throughout the day it had been commenting on the demonstrations from the government's angle.

The Radio building was protected by an AVH unit which had been doubled at six o'clock. While Gero was making his speech, 200 more AVH men had taken up positions inside it. Truck-loads of soldiers were parked near Sandor Brody Street, and at first their attitude seemed uncertain. A student delegation went into the Radio building to negotiate the broadcasting of their manifesto. From time to time one of their number would come out to tell those outside how these talks were progressing. From Parliament Square more people kept arriving to find out what was happening. One worker has given this account of the confrontation with the AVH.

> We rushed up to the AVH men who were pointing their guns at us. They were obviously petrified that we might attack them. We were desperate and some of us began to plead with them: 'Aren't you ashamed of yourselves, pointing guns at your fellow Hungarians? Weren't you born of Hungarian fathers and mothers like ourselves?'

51 The head of Stalin, once knocked off the statue, was placed at a street inter-section and decorated with a No-Through-Road sign

52 All over Budapest, Communist emblems such as red stars or official statues were destroyed

> Many of the AVH men hesitated, some began to lower their guns to the ground. Some had tears in their eyes and told us: 'Only a bloody bastard would fight against you people, we will not use our guns against you.' At this moment an AVH machine-gunner, seeing that the police and the demonstrators were fraternising in the street, fired a round above the heads of the crowd.

How the shooting actually started is still not clear. The crowd wanted to be sure that the student delegation in the Radio building was unharmed. The report after-wards written by the United Nations Special Committee on Hungary described how an army major volunteered to present a paper containing the sixteen points to the head of broadcasting. At the main entrance to the building he was shot down by the police.

53 The Hungarian tricolour flag reappeared without a Communist badge on it

This was the opening signal for an armed insurrection, the United Nations Report concludes, the crucial turning-point when bloodshed became inevitable. 'Shortly after 9 p.m. tear gas bombs were thrown from the upper windows of the Radio Building and one or two minutes later, AVH men opened fire on the crowd, killing a number of people and wounding others.'

Between 10 and 11 p.m. army detachments were sent to support the AVH on instructions from the Central Committee. These lorries were stopped at the Astoria Hotel, not far from the Radio building, and the soldiers allowed the crowd to take their weapons. When a squadron of tanks arrived, the colonel in command assured everybody that he was a worker and had no intention of starting a massacre.

Dora Scarlett went to the Radio building where she worked.

> Along by the railing of the Museum garden and round the corner in Pushkin Street were a number of Hungarian army lorries full of troops. People were talking to them, sometimes arguing, but there was neither violence nor unfriendliness. The ground was a mess of mud; it was clear that hoses had been used and enough tear gas hung in the air to make the eyes smart and water freely. . . . The version of events which passed quickly round Budapest was that the AVH fired first into the air and the second time into the crowd. . . . It was half past midnight when I left the Radio. Had I stayed longer I should have been able to give a first hand account of the assault on the building but I did not know it was coming. My colleagues had walked unmolested out of the back entrance at 11 o'clock.

Once armed with army machine-guns and rifles, the crowd was able to bring heavy fire on the Radio building. Soon a siege was in progress. Four hundred special police from the Mosonyi Street barracks arrived, sized up the situation, and went away. Like the army, they had decided not to intervene on behalf of the AVH. By midnight

54 The Radio Building was the scene of the opening shots of the revolution. Broadcasting ensured that the whole nation partook in events

the city was swarming with revolutionary bands, and they were driving vans and trucks taken from factories.

Further away on Dozsa Gyorgy Street, another large crowd had gathered round the statue of Stalin to overthrow it. This immense block in a style all too broodingly realistic, fifty feet of bronze high above its vast pedestal of rosy marble, was a flagrant symbol of Russian supremacy, a monument to the bad times. Ropes were inadequate for the crowd's task, and it was not until about ten o'clock that metal-workers, using blow-lamps to melt the knees, managed to topple the metal effigy. Fragments of the bronze statue were to be a favourite souvenir for the next fortnight. The destruction of Stalinism had been unforgettably enacted.

Some revolutionaries realised at once that arms alone could fortify such gestures. At Soroksari Street, for instance, an ammunition depot was raided. Several ordinary police stations also opened their armouries. The United Lamp Factory, a cover name for an arms plant, provided at least a thousand rifles. Barracks were another source of supply. By the end of this first day, everybody with determination could have obtained a weapon if wanted. By then, too, scattered firing had broken out all over the city, aimed more at intimidation than at any opposition. Red stars and other Communist emblems were shot off buildings. Russian bookshops were raided and their stocks thrown out into the streets. The offices of *Szabad Nep* were also seized and there the AVH again opened fire, killing several, before they were themselves finally forced to withdraw.

The Politburo had been in session on the second floor of the Parliament building since Gero's speech, and the information reaching it made clear the revolutionary mood of Budapest. Major-General Hegyi, chief of the training section of the Ministry of Defence, had reported the insubordination of the armed forces; he had been personally threatened by the crowd. During these late hours the Politburo resolved its debate, and the larger Central Committee, urgently assembled during the day, had only to ratify what had been done in its name. It is not known whether any formal invitation to the Soviet army of occupation was given, although the Prime Minister Hegedus,

69

55 Young children who had grown up under communism fought the Russian intervention

shortly to be replaced, has been blamed for this, while Gyorgy Marosan, also of the Politburo, later boasted that he had called in the Russians.

Around midnight Nagy was informed that he was once more on the Central Committee and had also been appointed Prime Minister. He was then asked to sign a note to the Russians, which had to be antedated in order to hide the fact that the Russians had already taken their decision to intervene. This supposes liaison between the Hungarian Politburo and the Kremlin, or at least the Russian ambassador. But Nagy refused to sign. Soviet forces were on the move and needed no official document for what they were about to do. At about the time when the Radio building was finally seized, when the remaining AVH men were escaping from its back-doors, Russian armoured columns were closing on Budapest. Since the Russian soldiers were stationed outside the capital, some of them forty miles off, and would have needed time to organise their convoys, it may be assumed that orders to be prepared had been given them much earlier – perhaps even as soon as the ill-fated delegation had returned that morning from Yugoslavia. Hungarian military units had been put on the alert in the afternoon. Nevertheless, from the beginning Nagy had been skilfully enmeshed by the underhand method of his appointment. The twenty-four hours in which he might have taken control of events had passed. Confidence in his honesty had been undermined. The crowds thought that he had compromised with Gero, and the timidity of his public speech seemed to confirm their suspicions. The Russian action, however, meant that Gero would forfeit the advantage he might in turn have gained from nominating Nagy. It was to take time and effort to clear Nagy's reputation in the immediate future.

Wednesday, 24 October

Shortly after 2 a.m. Russian tanks entered Budapest. They came in time to reinforce the weakening AVH. Some AVH men had entrenched themselves behind quickly erected barricades. Others, notably those in some workmen's huts near the Radio building and those sent to defend the *Szabad Nep* offices, had surrendered. But the revolution was not a civil war. Its anti-Russian character was seen in the burning of the *Horizont* bookshops, where Soviet propaganda had been sold, and in the destruction of

70

56 Anti-Russian feeling was expressed by the burning of Soviet posters and propaganda

Soviet symbols. The entry of the Russian army gave the Hungarians a clearer purpose and a visible enemy. If their earlier demands had been too various to be politically effective, now they could focus on getting the Russians to withdraw. If the Russians were defeated to any extent, Gero's government would fall, and the Stalinist legacy with it.

The government made the revolutionary effort easier by its tactlessness and its refusal to deal fairly with the reasons for the insurrection. At 4.30 a.m. Budapest Radio wished its listeners a good-morning, and then gave its version of the news.

> Fascist and reactionary elements have launched an armed attack against our public buildings and against our forces of law and order. In the interests of re-establishing law and order, all assemblies, meetings and demonstrations are forbidden. Police units have been instructed to deal severely with troublemakers and to apply the law in all its force.

In spite of the previous night's shooting the Radio was neither occupied by freedom-fighters nor guarded by the AVH. The bodies of the AVH lay where they had fallen, along with some thirty dead demonstrators.

At seven o'clock the radio announced that Imre Nagy had been recommended during an all-night sitting of the Central Committee to be Prime Minister. It was stressed that Gero was continuing as First Secretary of the Party. The other changes in the Politburo showed how the Party had lost touch with events. Revai was dropped but other Stalinists remained, so that Nagy seemed a figurehead. Two more hours were to pass before the official announcement that the Soviet army had been called in by the government to put down the uprising, and that martial law had been declared. This gave the clear impression that Nagy was responsible for the unwelcome invitation as his first act in office. Two Soviet mechanised divisions had meanwhile crossed into Hungary from Romania.

The Russians may have intended no more than a show of force. If so, they had miscalculated. Small-arms had already been seized and distributed the day before, and now many more Hungarians broke into military and police arsenals. The insurgents ordered a general strike, and with all factories closed thousands of workers became freedom-fighters. The students had been replaced by the masses. Lacking central organisation and acting on impulse and emotion, the revolutionaries did not maintain contact with each other. Bands formed locally, and resistance to the Russians was spontaneous and confused. Tactically the Russians were at a loss. Their tanks could race up and down the streets, capture the bridges and commanding positions, but the revolutionaries had only to dodge or hide, and re-emerge unscathed once the tanks had passed. The Russians had sent no infantry for the hand-to-hand fighting which alone could carry the day in a large city. The tank crews were unwilling to climb out under sniper fire, and anyhow they did not show much enthusiasm for their task. Here and there in Budapest squadrons of tanks merely halted in a square or by the river. The streets soon emptied. But at four or five major cross-roads freedom-fighters early rallied as best they might. Using improvised hand-grenades and Molotov cocktails, they set about destroying the Russian armour engaging them.

Only the Hungarian army could provide proper armed opposition to the Russians.

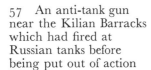

57   An anti-tank gun near the Kilian Barracks which had fired at Russian tanks before being put out of action

At several barracks and military academies the soldiers and cadets joined the freedom-fighters. The Kilian Barracks, strategically placed in the centre of Budapest, and with access only down narrow streets, saw severe fighting. Infantrymen and freedom-fighters also occupied the Corvin Passage and a cinema opposite the barracks, so commanding the approaches. There were some anti-tank weapons there, and soon the streets near by were blocked with burnt-out Russian tanks. A battle raged all day along the Jozsef Korut and at key points, the railway stations, and telephone exchanges. The Russian embassy and its military Commandatura were heavily protected by tanks.

Towards noon, Nagy delivered an appeal over the radio. 'Order, calm, discipline. This slogan is addressed to all. Blood should not be permitted to soil our sacred national programme.' After Nagy, the former President Tildy made a similar broadcast, as did a spokesman for the Petofi Circle. If these were Nagy's real opinions, he was not making clear who should take the blame for shedding blood. A week later, the chief of the Budapest police, Colonel Sandor Kopacsi, revealed in an article that Nagy had actually been a prisoner of the AVH when he made this broadcast.

When I heard of this, I immediately ordered a police shock detachment to stand by. I sent my personal representative to the Parliament Building – alone, to avoid attracting too much attention. He told the Prime Minister's captors that it was in the national interest that the Premier should have full freedom of movement and action. . . . The AVH gave way.

Kopacsi took another vital decision that morning, when he gave orders that the freedom-fighters be provided legally with weapons. The police, though not the separately administered AVH, had joined the revolution.

Radio Budapest repeated Nagy's proclamation of martial law, and his appeal for calm, and then went on, 'The Soviet soldiers are risking their lives to protect the peaceful citizens of Budapest and the tranquillity of the nation. . . . Workers of Budapest! Receive our friends and allies with affection!' Throughout the day false information was broad-

58   The Soviet tanks had been called in by the Gero government. They patrolled the streets while the people hid in doorways and waited until the tanks passed

cast that the freedom-fighters were obeying instructions and handing in their arms. More subtle approaches were also tried. In the evening for instance, the radio carried this message: 'The parents of Laszlo Tarjan, aged seventeen, have learnt that their son has taken part in the fighting. His mother has had a nervous crisis. He must go home immediately if he wishes to see her alive.'

Such calls were fruitless. Following the successful general strike, the workers were forming revolutionary committees at all levels of administration, from the factory floor to the county hall. The movement for self-government which so characterises this revolution was sweeping the country. Within the next few days, all the major towns had their revolutionary committees, Gyor, Debrecen, Sopron, Szeged, Szolnok. The Hungarians were plainly looking beyond the military uprising, and any possible anarchy, to a fresh reorganisation of their social institutions. Party control and its apparatus of police terror would be a thing of the past. The equitable form of socialism demanded by these revolutionary committees from the beginning disproves the charge of counter-revolution made over the radio.

In spite of the fierce combats all over Budapest, many delegations were sent by various bodies and committees to Party headquarters and to the Parliament building to learn what was going on. A history professor at the head of one such delegation of teachers and students was shot on the way by the AVH. But during the day the Writers' Association learnt from their committee that Nagy had not decreed the state of emergency with its martial law, and they were able to start influencing public opinion in his favour. The most important arrivals at Party headquarters, however, were Mikoyan and Suslov of the Soviet Presidium, who had flown from Moscow and were driven in by armoured car from the airport. They were to stay for three days, judging the situation from the Kremlin's point of view. They had every reason to be worried, and not only by the sight of smashed Russian tanks and the sound of gunfire as they talked. In Poland at a public appearance Gomulka had begged for law and order, but the Poles were not ready to listen. Crowds gathered and moved on Red army installations until dispersed with tear-gas. The Hungarian flag flew in Warsaw alongside the red and white flag of Poland. The world was hardly prepared for such news, and while the first foreign journalists were attempting to break into Hungary and reach Budapest, American spokesmen began to prepare statements that their country expected no military alliances or advantages from any change of government in Eastern Europe.

Thursday, 25 October

The Gero government had called in the Russians in order to have a kind of huge reserve police, to be used for political, not military, ends. Once Mikoyan and Suslov were in Budapest, these political ends could be manipulated on the spot. Mikoyan and Suslov had debated through the night with the new Hungarian Politburo, and it is to be assumed that the Kremlin would have endorsed their decisions. It is also likely that they were prepared to make concessions as they had done in Poland.

To the Hungarians on the streets, the battle of reaction and liberalisation was clearly also the battle of Hungary against Russia. Demands for national sovereignty did not mean the end of communism. They wanted what Yugoslavia had and what Poland had won. Reaction was embodied by Gero and the remaining friends of Rakosi, the Stalinists whom they wanted to throw out. Liberalisation meant Imre Nagy. Each

59 All over Budapest there was fierce street-fighting. The Russian intervention gave the freedom-fighters a clear goal – 'Russians Out', as the slogans said

74

country was to be free to find its own way to socialism, Communist leaders were loud in proclaiming, but slow in putting into practice. Had the Hungarians not risen, the Russian tanks would have succeeded in policing the disturbances; Gero would have stayed, and no doubt would have reverted to his old manner. The burning of Russian books, the destruction of red stars and hammers-and-sickles and official posters, marked the end of Soviet control, and all that went with it, including Gero. Everywhere the Hungarian tricolour flew, a hole in its centre where the Communist symbols had been cut out. Propaganda devices were no longer to be an encouragement to self-deception. Imre Nagy was the only statesman who could have given an unequivocal call for National Communism, a communism which would place Hungarian interests above any other. In the absence of such a call, the revolutionary committees would dictate the pace of events.

Radio Budapest opened its morning broadcast much as it had on the previous day. 'The Army, the State Security Forces and armed workers' guards have liquidated, with the help of Soviet troops, the attempt at a counter-revolutionary *coup d'état* on the night of 24/25 October.' There must have been very few people in Budapest who believed that. That morning, Istvan Bata, Minister of Defence, was still issuing orders to the armed forces to eliminate 'counter-revolutionaries.' From all government sources, the population was being warned not to go out of doors.

One of the army officers supposed to put down this 'counter-revolution' was Colonel Pal Maleter. In an interview on 1 November, Maleter said:

> Early in the morning of Wednesday, October 24, the Minister of Defence, in the course of his duties, gave me the order to lead a formation of five tanks against the insurgents in the Eighth and Ninth districts. Once I arrived there, it quickly became clear to me that those who were fighting for their freedom were not bandits, but loyal sons of Hungary. As a result I informed the Minister of Defence that I was going over to the insurgents.

60   The results of the street-fighting

75

61 Pal Maleter rose from the rank of colonel to be Minister of Defence. He epitomised the Hungarian will to resist Russian intervention

62 Here and there lay the dead, close to the barricades that had been erected. People were often buried close to where they had died

Far from putting down the resistance, Maleter's decision to disobey was the beginning of a spectacular, short, and tragic career, resuming in one person the whole fate of the militant revolution.

A freedom-fighter who was present has described the moment when Maleter made his first contact with the men in the Kilian Barracks.

> His eyes fell on a young man with an intelligent face. He asked him his name, his job, how he had acquired arms and the reasons which had driven him to take part in the armed uprising. The young man with the frank face answered straightforwardly, not in the least overawed. He spoke about the country's standard of living, about freedom which existed only on paper, and of patriotic feeling which during the recent years had been completely perverted and emptied of all meaning. He spoke equally of the sixteen points which the students had distributed on the street two days before, during the demonstrations, and as he could not properly recall one of those points, he put his hand in his pocket and took out his Communist Party card inside which – strange paradox – was the typewritten text of the students' sixteen points.

When Maleter was in turn questioned by the freedom-fighters, his views were the same as theirs: 'What I want, what we all want, I hope, is a free, independent and socialist Hungary. But for this, we need the support of everyone.' He then took charge of the defence of the Kilian Barracks.

Nor was Maleter the only person to find out for himself that the freedom-fighters were not fascists and counter-revolutionaries. Thousands of men and women had been assembling since early morning, and waving flags and shouting: 'This is a peaceful demonstration' and 'The Radio is telling lies'; they had been moving towards Parliament Square. It was a sunny morning and there was much fraternisation between these marchers and the Russian soldiers they encountered. Crossing the Buda bridge, some demonstrators even got a column of tanks to accompany them. Most people in the crowd realised that the Russians had not been bent on massacre the day before, and

76

63 The crowds demonstrating before moving into Parliament Square where the AVH were to open fire on them

that they were unhappy and baffled in their present performance. The demonstration and its escorting tanks filled the large square. More Russian tanks had been stationed in front of Parliament. Perhaps there was some confusion of identity, for the Hungarian army was equipped with Russian-made tanks. Perhaps the AVH men who had been posted on the surrounding roof-tops wished to cause a provocation which would allow them to shoot down the demonstrators. At any rate, machine-gun fire from the roof-tops opened up on the crowd in the square. Immediately the demonstration became a shambles. There was nowhere to hide. Bodies piled up, and were used as screens for the living. Estimates of the casualties vary, but the dead may have been as many as six hundred. The shooting at the Radio building had marked the opening phase of violence. Now the AVH went one step higher on the ladder of escalation by firing on unarmed civilians. Black flags of mourning were to be draped next to the tricolours.

Half an hour after the massacre, the Politburo, guided by Mikoyan and Suslov, decided that Gero must resign. On the next day he was escorted away from Party headquarters in a Soviet tank, and rumoured to have gone to the Devin Hotel in Bratislava, in Czechoslovakia. No pronouncement in his name on any aspect of the revolution has yet been made. Hegedus, the recent Prime Minister, took the chance to slip away from Party headquarters in his wake. Kadar was chosen by the Russians to replace Gero as First Secretary of the Party. Soon after midday the radio announced the changes, and Kadar came on the air to appeal for order. He promised that the rebels would not be punished and that Hungarian-Soviet relations would be reviewed. The uprising two days before, he said, had been peaceful and proper, but it had degenerated. Imre Nagy, a few hours later, was hardly more encouraging with a mention of 'a small group of counter-revolutionaries' who had provoked the disorders, but he did say that his government would negotiate for outright Soviet withdrawal. In spite of Colonel Kopacsi's efforts, Nagy may still have felt too intimidated to speak freely. Representatives from workers' committees had made their way to Nagy at Party headquarters and

77

reported up to fifteen AVH men on duty around him. Geza Losonczy and Ferenc Donath, his closest associates, had been urging him to take a firmer stand against the Stalinists, and not to be their tool. Another supporter, Gyula Obersovszky, had brought out an independent newspaper, *Truth*, the first free channel of news. It was to run for the next nine days, and Obersovszky, its editor, was to be imprisoned for it six months later.

Many of the new revolutionary committees were passing votes of confidence in Nagy. In Gyor there had been a mass demonstration. The local radio at Miskolc, in northern Hungary, said, 'Stop the slaughter of Hungarians in Budapest . . . let the Soviet troops leave Hungary. Make a truce!' Yet even if Nagy had been a free agent and a bolder man, there were still good reasons for him to hesitate. In Dunapentele, also an industrial town, the AVH had fired on an unarmed crowd as in Budapest, killing eight and wounding twenty-eight. Russian tanks continued to attack the Corvin cinema next to the Kilian Barracks, and several of them were knocked out. Robert Oakeshott, an Oxford undergraduate who had hurried out to Budapest, managed to obtain an interview with Maleter now installed inside the Barracks.

> I was very lucky, I got a pass card from the Central Revolutionary Students' Committee. . . . Maleter is absolutely adamant that the Tito solution is inadequate for Hungary. The Communist Party in his new Hungary, if he had anything to do with the new constitution, would be just one among any number of political parties.

In the afternoon a considerable group of demonstrators had presented to the British and American legations a petition that the case of Hungary be submitted to the United Nations. 'The heart of America goes out to the people of Hungary', President Eisenhower had said, and his words, broadcast to Hungary by Western radio stations, were taken as a sign of solidarity. The American government had in fact consulted with Great Britain and France on the possibility of debating the Hungarian question in the Security Council. Nagy must have known how political speculation was racing ahead of events, and like the other Party leaders he would have thought that nothing was to be gained by anarchy, or by any move which gave the Russians a pretext to use their full power. Military advisers had hoped that the firing would stop by nightfall. Instead, the morning's massacre was fuel to the revolution. Centres of resistance hardened on Rakoczi Avenue and Magdolna Street and in the Ferencvaros District. At 6 p.m. the

64 The Kilian Barracks after the fighting

78

Russians imposed a curfew until dawn, and the government appealed once more for a resumption of normal life. But once civilians had been shot in cold blood, appeals could not take the place of reforms.

Friday, 26 October

Kadar had jumped to prominence since his release from prison in 1953 when Nagy was Prime Minister for the first time. Only in July had he taken the place of Rakosi on the Central Committee, chosen by the Russians as a likely Hungarian to carry through their revisionist policy, in other words to govern according to the ideas of Khrushchev, not of Stalin. Since July Kadar had been on a round of introductions to leaders in the Communist bloc. He believed in the supremacy of the Soviet Union. Nagy believed that the friendship of the Soviet Union was indispensable, but should not exclude everything else. The Secretary of the Communist Party was at least as powerful as the Prime Minister, as Rakosi's career had shown. But Kadar was not a public figure like Nagy, and from the moment he was appointed he must have realised that without Russian help he would remain a mere Party official. He was to spend the next days keeping the shrinking and discredited Party together as best he could. Nagy was to spend the next days trying to rise above the tide of the revolution and so control it.

Since the arrival of Mikoyan and Suslov, Party headquarters had been the scene of almost continual consultations, broken only by broadcasts and the arrival of delegations to express their various opinions. The Central Committee, meeting there through most of the day, tried to put out statements of its resolutions. A new national government was promised, and following the Polish example, negotiations with Moscow were to begin on a basis of equality. The amnesty for the freedom-fighters, which had been ignored by them so far, was extended to 10 p.m. that night. The Party appeared to be giving way to the demands of the revolution, while not mentioning Russian withdrawal. But all the while Nagy was being thwarted in his efforts to build a government in which the people could have confidence. As in 1953 he was working with men heavily compromised by their Stalinist past.

While Nagy argued about the composition of his government, the fighting

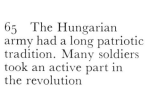

65   The Hungarian army had a long patriotic tradition. Many soldiers took an active part in the revolution

continued as fiercely as ever. The freedom-fighters remained in their groups, attacking at each opportunity. A single tank, or the last tank in a column, was a prime target for a freedom-fighter brave enough to climb on it and drop a grenade through its hatch. Or its tracks could be blown off with a home-made fire-bomb filled with petrol and ignited by a crude cotton-wool wick. At Szena Square, commanding a wide-open space in Buda, an elderly revolutionary led young boys and girls against Russian tanks, and as 'Uncle Szabo' he acquired a reputation as a local Scarlet Pimpernel. At the Corvin cinema another similar group was holding out. When Mikoyan and Suslov drove back to the airport that afternoon, to report to Moscow, they must have been able to hear firing, as when they had arrived.

The Polish paper *Po Prostu* published this account of its correspondent's entry into Budapest:

> We had left Warsaw convinced that Hungary had become peaceful, and here before reaching Budapest, we hear about the war, about 'front lines'. We hear shooting. . . .

66 At Magyarovar the AVH fired into an unarmed crowd – killing eighty-seven people. The massacre was witnessed by several Western journalists and photographers who had just crossed the Austrian border

> In front of us is the road to Budapest. At the Soviet post, heavy weapons, several nests of machine-guns. All the soldiers are in position, with their fingers on the triggers. An officer with a small machine-gun and several soldiers come forward with their guns pointing at us: 'From the Polish Embassy?' – He takes a rapid look at the passengers. We can proceed. Two kilometres further at a cross-road, we are stopped again. Another armed checkpoint: 'Lengyel (Pole)?' Friendly smiling faces. 'Poles are friends, Poles are brothers.' This happens again and again before our car enters the streets of a workers' suburb. Long walls of empty factories. Little houses in front of which a few people hover, ready to hide. Something uncanny in the air. An atmosphere which I cannot yet define. Is it horror, fear, hatred or despair? . . . Behind the iron gates of one of the industrial works, a group of armed people. They explain that they are workers, revolutionaries who are defending their factories. . . . At one of the insurgent posts, we are advised to take a longer road because on the Ulloi Street there is heavy fighting going on between Hungarian soldiers defending their barracks, and Soviet

tanks. . . . One thing emerges from all the chaotic information – the whole nation is on the side of the insurgents. The division is clear: the nation on one side, and on the other, the Stalinist faction of the Government and the AVH. There are thousands of Communists among the insurgents.

Noel Barber, *Daily Mail* reporter, had also just reached Budapest.

As I moved deeper into the city, every street was smashed. Hardly a stretch of tramcar rails was left intact. The jungle of hanging electric cables was denser even than in Buda. Hundreds of yards of paving stones had been torn up, the streets were littered with burnt-out cars. Even before I reached the Duna Hotel, I counted the carcasses of at least forty Soviet tanks. On the way in the Rakoczi Square, where the fighting had been particularly bitter, one street was barred by enormous tree-trunks, not chopped down, but uprooted. . . . At the corner of Stalin Avenue, where you branch right for the British Legation and then the Duna, two monster Russian T-54 tanks lumbered past, dragging bodies behind them, a warning to all Hungarians of what happened to

67   The chapel at Magyarovar where the dead were placed

the fighters. In another street, three bodies were strung up on a tree, the necks at ungainly angles but still not looking like bodies, more like effigies. A few corpses dotted the streets, though not so many as I expected. . . .

The men hanged on the trees belonged to the AVH, hunted down with ferocity after the massacre in Parliament Square. Sometimes these secret policemen were found to be carrying their pay, ten times that of a workman, and their bank-notes were left pinned to the bodies.

Budapest had given the lead but the provinces followed eagerly. The general strike applied throughout the country and many revolutionary committees decided to use it as a weapon enforcing the Russian withdrawal. A delegation from the town of Miskolc came to Nagy with such a proposal. In Szabolcs, Szeged, and Nyiregyhaza, all regional centres, demonstrators demanded that Nagy be at the head of an effective government, and they skirmished with the AVH. In Gyor the revolutionary committee had been established by Attila Szigeti, a friend of Nagy's, and who as a deputy in Parliament had moved a motion in his favour in the Rakosi days. One English writer who had driven the short distance to Gyor from the Austrian border at Nickelsdorf, heard the epic Beethoven Third Symphony relayed on an amplifier from its town hall. 'It had been a day of bright October sunshine and the hills and woods ahead, the undulating country of Transdanubia, lay under a blue haze.' On the way, he writes,

> we went into a small café where we drank *barack* and listened to the wireless. The girl said that the patriot station *Kossuth* was now operating, and that the government radio in Budapest could not be trusted. A babble of opinions were being voiced in the café, all obtained from the conflicting wireless reports, Hungarian and foreign. The Russians were leaving – they were not leaving – Nagy had left the government – Nagy had committed suicide – the students in Budapest were demanding a public trial for Gero – Tildy, the old president, had taken Nagy's place – Tildy had resigned – Cardinal Mindszenty was forming a Catholic Democrat party – six newspapers representing all the parties of the new democracy were coming out tomorrow. . . .

Not far away from Gyor, in the small town of Magyarovar, a demonstration no different from scores of others ended in tragedy, on an afternoon when the writer Gyula Hay was saying over the radio that 'A heroic life is worth more than an ill-timed unnecessary sacrifice.' As they had done the day before in Budapest and elsewhere, the AVH opened fire on the crowd, this time killing eighty-seven and wounding 160 people. Peter Fryer, then an English Communist and on the staff of the *Daily Worker*, arrived in Magyarovar shortly after a sharp battle for the AVH headquarters in which one police officer was killed, another lynched, and two more taken to hospital, from which one of them was carried to be hung by the ankles in the square.

> The townspeople [he writes] took us in slow, silent procession along an avenue of plane trees to the little chapel and mortuary in the town cemetery. Hundreds went with us; we passed many more coming away, having identified kinsfolk or sweethearts or friends or having stood in homage to dead workmates or fellow-students. Some faces were red and stern, others were contorted with weeping, and I wept myself when we reached the chapel and the mortuary. The mourners made way for us and gently pushed us to the front, so that we should see and know and tell what we had seen. The

68 Among the first victims was a small girl who had been standing at the front of the crowd

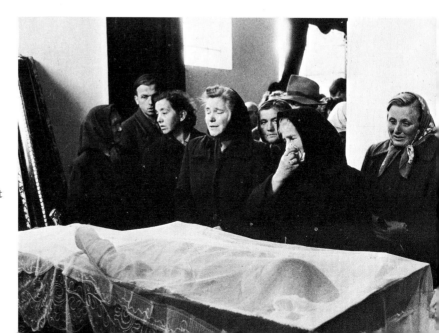

bodies lay in rows; the dried blood was still on the clothing. Some had little bunches of flowers on their breasts. There were boys who could not have been more than sixteen. There was a boy of six or so. Already in a coffin, lightly shrouded, lay the corpse of an eighteen-month-old baby. After eleven years of 'people's democracy' it had come to this: that the security police was so remote from the people, so alien to them, so vicious and so brutal that it turned its weapons on a defenceless crowd and murdered the people who were supposed to be the masters of their own country.

Saturday, 27 October

By midday Nagy was ready to announce his cabinet. Zoltan Tildy and Bela Kovacs, neither of them Communists, were to hold office. Bela Kovacs, broken after eight years' imprisonment once the Russians had kidnapped him, was still respected as the former secretary of the Smallholders Party. A well-known agricultural expert, also not a Communist, was appointed to the cabinet, and Professor Lukacs as Minister of Culture gave it further distinction. But the Stalinists remained in strength and the old-guard Communist character of the cabinet would not impress the insurgents to lay down their arms, as the radio was so frequently telling them to do. An Austrian journalist managed to get an interview with Colonel Maleter, resisting as stubbornly as before in the Kilian Barracks. Maleter spoke for many revolutionaries.

> For us, there is no choice. Either we win or we fall. There is no third possibility. We have confidence in Imre Nagy but we will not give up our arms except to Hungarian troops, and we will put ourselves immediately at the disposal of the new government if there is one truly worthy of the name.

Doubts must have arisen in his mind when hearing at 2 p.m. the new Minister of Defence, General Janza, ordering the armed forces to continue liquidating resistance.

The formation of the cabinet marked Nagy's personal liberation. Not only could he now move into the Parliament building, abandoning Party headquarters, but he had at last taken measures on his own, and openly. Several more notorious Stalinists followed the example of Gero and Hegedus and left the country to find refuge in Russia. The government changes, however, were not wide-sweeping enough to match the

69   The family of a student from an agricultural college killed by the AVH

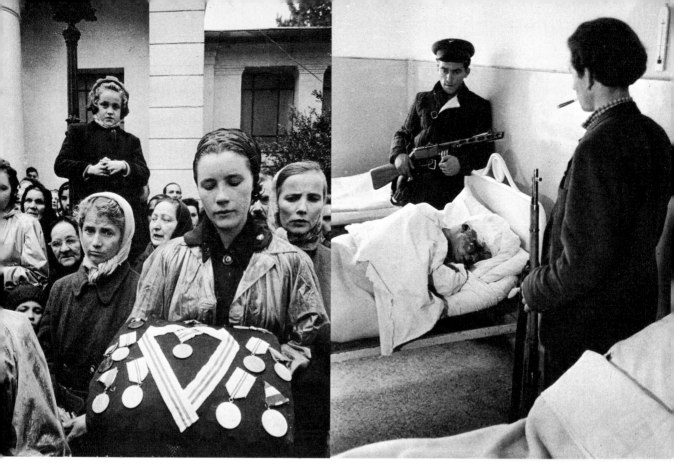

70 This woman's husband had been killed. For the funeral she carried the decorations he had won during the war

71 One of the AVH men who had fired on the crowd was taken to hospital after he had been beaten up. Others had been lynched

people's mood. Jozsef Kovago, mayor of Budapest before 1948 and since then a political prisoner, summed up these doubts and suspicions when he gave this account of a conversation with Tildy and his wife in the Parliament building.

> While we talked I wondered whether the two of them realized how unpopular they were with the people. Did they know that people were almost unanimous in disliking them, and that many regarded Tildy as one of the traitors of the nation? I wondered if there was any way of telling them of this and warning him that this time he should seize the helm of history with a firm hand, otherwise the nation would never forgive him.

Yet Tildy, former President of the Republic, was one of the men on whom Nagy was relying to gain public confidence. Bela Kovacs, meanwhile, was at his home in Pecs, and did not give his consent to his appointment.

The revolution at that point was a tussle between democratic socialism and the slower changes Imre Nagy had in mind. His cabinet reflected his indecision. No Social Democrats had been appointed; Tildy and Kovacs were figureheads. It must have been obvious to the revolutionaries that Nagy would only adopt their ideas if they maintained the pressure on his government, if they went on fighting. They were encouraged by the release from prison of more than 5,000 political prisoners whose cells were simply unlocked. Several provincial broadcasting stations which had freed themselves from central control, supported the freedom-fighters and now began to liaise between the various revolutionary committees and workers' councils throughout the country. The Central Council of Trade Unions proclaimed that 'the wish of the working class has been realised: enterprises will be managed by workers' councils'. Working in the same direction as the government, but not with it, the revolutionaries were gaining what they wanted. Food supplies were reaching Budapest again. Queues stood for two or three hours to buy bread or potatoes, but chickens and duck were available in the markets, packaged for export – food no Hungarian had seen in years. Unless the government and the freedom-fighters came to terms, a stalemate seemed assured, and the shooting would continue.

In Moscow these were presumably the days when Imre Nagy was under judgement. The revolution was open. For political purposes, it might be considered a fascist revival or a great manifestation of the working class, and if the latter, as the evidence suggested, then Moscow could approve providing the Communist Party steered it. That would depend on Nagy's relations with Kadar, the new Party Secretary whose colleagues were so well represented in the cabinet.

Sunday, 28 October

The Central Committee of the Communist Party, at a morning meeting, delegated its powers to a group of six members. Kadar presided over them, mostly his friends, and including Nagy. This small Presidium was a way of streamlining the Party. Radio Budapest commented on this: 'Everything has happened too late – only when the masses were ready to resort to coercion.' The Central Committee passed resolutions that the government must set itself the task of satisfying the legitimate demands of the people. A cease-fire was ordered immediately. As soon as there was calm, the AVH would be disbanded.

Such resolutions empowered Nagy to act with Party backing. By giving him this authority, Kadar was in effect telling Nagy that the Communist Party accepted the revolution and its achievements. A cease-fire was negotiated and slowly the fighting died down, although the insurgents were not all ready to hand over their arms. The Minister of the Interior, Ferenc Munnich, and General Janza, Minister of Defence, issued instructions to all soldiers and policemen to obey the new national government. All over Hungary, revolutionaries and the opposing Soviet troops patched up some temporary truce whereby neither side would be the first to fire. In the provinces, the Russians often drove out from towns and with relief made camp in the countryside. A clue to what had happened was that the word 'comrade' was abolished as the compulsory form of address in Hungary.

The free radio stations in all the provincial centres were jubilant, issuing political communiqués calling for Russian withdrawal and agreeing to support Nagy only if their demands were met. In the late afternoon Nagy answered them, on Radio Budapest. He conceded that the revolutionaries had carried the day, but the stilted phrasing of his speech indicates that he was not yet sure what to make of it.

> Last week, bloody events followed, one after another, with tragic rapidity. . . . The
> Government rejects the view that sees the present popular movement as a counter-

revolution . . . a great national and democratic movement embracing and unifying all our people unfolded itself with elementary force. This movement has the aim of guaranteeing our national independence and sovereignty, of advancing the democratization of our social, economic and political life. . . . The Government will support the new democratic autonomous bodies created on the initiative of the people and will endeavour to integrate them into the state administration. In the interest of avoiding further bloodshed and ensuring a peaceful clarification of the situation, the Government has ordered an immediate ceasefire. . . . The Hungarian Government is initiating negotiations to settle relations between the Hungarian People's Republic and the Soviet Union, including the question of the withdrawal of the Soviet troops stationed in Hungary. All this is in the spirit of Soviet-Hungarian friendship, equality among socialist countries and national independence.

For ten years the internal affairs of Hungary had been settled by the needs of Russian foreign policy. Nagy was saying in public that not only his government but also the Central Committee were endorsing 'the coercion of the masses'. Even the revolutionary committees were approved. The Central Committee, and therefore the Communist Party, was now more concerned about coming out on the right side of the revolution than about obeying any Russian demands. The Russians had to calculate whether this new national unity in Hungary undermined their foreign policy, or whether a generous acceptance of what they could not change diplomatically could earn them the even firmer allegiance of Hungary. The international implications began to loom large. Polish and Yugoslav messages of sympathy had been addressed to Nagy and Kadar. In the United Nations, where the Security Council was due that afternoon to consider 'the action of foreign military forces in Hungary in violently repressing the rights of the Hungarians', the Hungarian representative had voted against placing the question on the agenda. It turned out that this representative was actually a Soviet citizen and on the following day he was recalled by the Nagy government. The Soviet Union was certain to veto any condemnation of its actions, or any sanctions, and its representative called the Western appeals to morality 'crocodile tears'. Nevertheless Western public opinion was highly aroused, even emotional, at this rent in the Cold War.

Monday, 29 October

Soviet tanks and troops crunched out of this war-battered capital today carrying their dead with them. They left a wrecked city where the stench of death already rises from the smoking ruins to mingle with a chill fog from the Danube River. I arrived here from Warsaw by plane, car and foot, walking the last five miles. . . . No sooner were we on the road north to Budapest than we ran into a massive southbound Soviet convoy headed by two armoured cars. Ten T-54 tanks, their Red stars still visible through the grime of gunpowder, oil and blood, waddled behind leaving Budapest behind. Then came numerous motorcycles and trucks. On the back of one truck lay the corpse of a Soviet soldier, his eyes staring vacantly back at the Hungarian capital. Other bodies were in the trucks. The Russian tankmen in the black helmets looked tired and grim. . . . A Hungarian peasant spat at one tank as it passed him an arm's length away. The Russian crew did not notice. Hatred literally oozed from the Hungarians who silently lined the roadsides watching the Soviets evacuate Budapest.

So the United Press dispatch captured a memorable occasion.

The Russians were to be replaced, announced the Ministry of the Interior, by 'a unified democratic police force'. The AVH was in effect being abolished. Protection was offered to all AVH men who gave themselves up to the regular police or to freedom-fighters. Colonel Sandor Kopacsi has explained that

> Imre Nagy telephoned me from Parliament on October 29 and instructed me to organise the new special police, enlisting the insurgents in its ranks also, and to establish the top body of the National Guard, the Revolutionary Committee of the Special Police. He instructed me to look for an experienced well-trained man, possibly among the persons rehabilitated recently.

General Bela Kiraly was chosen for the job. When abandoned AVH buildings were taken over, preparations for a guerilla warfare were found, arms and ammunition, forged papers, civilian clothes.

72 In western Hungary there was support for Imre Nagy but also a movement to urge his government to stronger leadership, here being pressed by the Revolutionary Committee of Students in Sopron

73 Soviet tanks continued to occupy Budapest. It was not certain whether they intended to stay or go

It was urgent that Nagy tie together the many threads of the revolution, and start carrying out the promises he had made. He formed a secretariat of men he could rely on, Donath in charge of information and broadcasting, Gyorgy Heltai in charge of foreign affairs, his son-in-law Ferenc Janossi, and Gyorgy Fazekas, the brother-in-law of Colonel Kopacsi. The functionaries of Parliament, from Istvan Dobi the President downwards, took their orders. The press made full use of its new-found freedom of expression. Articles in *Truth* and the student papers explained how Nagy had been used by Gero, that as soon as he became a free agent he was 'the man of our revolution.'

74   Imre Nagy and friends outside Parliament

Pravda in Moscow had crudely criticised the revolution under a jargon heading, 'The Collapse of the Anti-Popular Adventure in Hungary.' *Szabad Nep* answered:

> This is an error. The events in Budapest were neither anti-popular nor an adventure; nor was there a collapse. . . . The revolutionary people of Buda and Pest want a people's freedom and a life without arbitrariness, without terror and without fear. They want more bread and national independence. Is this what *Pravda* calls an adventure against the people?

Once the facts became widely known, Nagy would be cleared of calling in the Russians, an acquittal all the more vital because some Western broadcasts and papers had gone on suggesting that he was to blame. Budapest Radio, however, made this confession on the air:

> Dear listeners! We are opening a new chapter in the history of the Hungarian Radio. For many years now the radio was nothing else but an instrument for disseminating propaganda and lies. Its main task was to carry out orders received from above and day and night it did nothing else but spread mendacities on all wavelengths. Even during the last days, in the hour of our nation's rebirth, this radio was compelled to continue spreading lies, although the struggle which in the streets was being fought to regain liberty and national independence, was also going on within the walls of this station. Here too it was triumphant: All those who have broadcast lies from this station in the past have been evicted.

That the past was truly the past was shown in another significant way, when Ferenc Nagy, Smallholder Prime Minister in 1947, and who had flown from America to Vienna, telephoned to friends in Budapest, but was advised to stay away from Hungary.

A delegation of writers who had supported Nagy through the difficult years, had on Sunday evening reached the Parliament building to present a declaration advocating free elections, workers' control, and a free system of agriculture. Nagy had returned to Party headquarters, and the intellectuals, one among many delegations, did not get to see him until Monday. As Tibor Meray describes it, Nagy was brusque. Leaving his chauffeur-driven car, he was making his way on foot to Parliament, over the debris and broken glass that littered the sidewalk. When recognised and questioned, he was advising people to return to work.

Nagy strolled gaily on towards the door of the Parliament Building nearest the bridge. Never before, perhaps, had he been so sure of what he was doing as he was on that morning of the twenty-ninth of October. He had read the demands of the Revolutionary Committee of Hungarian Intellectuals. He had found them excessive and had become angry. Instead of helping the government, these hot-heads were pressing it at the wrong moment. What was needed was a program whose points would stand the scrutiny of an objective and scientific analysis. It was his intention to proceed calmly and reasonably, and to get to the bottom of the problems. In the middle of a revolution, he still saw himself as a man of science.

Tuesday, 30 October

Were the Russians really leaving? Should the freedom-fighters lay down their arms? The *New York Times* correspondent, driving to the Kilian Barracks, through havoc which reminded him of the Second World War, saw fighting still in progress. Grey with exhaustion, the youthful insurgents, he reported, were indomitable. 'The air was electric, obviously anything might happen.' Near the university an AVH captain had tried to run from the crowd. He was hanged from a lamp-post.

In Rokk Szilard Street in the Eighth District a crowd of children, 12-to-14 years old, quietly surrounded a Soviet tank that was standing there. Suddenly several of them jumped on the tank, one of them produced a pistol and shot into it, while the rest stole the machine-gun of the Russian driver. Then they fled down the street under a hail of fire from other Russian tanks.

For the next three or four days Russian troop movements baffled observers. Some units withdrew, some advanced. Inevitably Russian sincerity was doubted. Yet on behalf of the Kremlin, Mikoyan and Suslov once again flew into Budapest bringing with them a declaration just published in Moscow, 'On Friendship and Co-operation between the Soviet Union and other Socialist States.' A liberal document, it acknowledged the justice of Hungarian claims to national sovereignty and was drafted cleverly but vaguely in the hopes of preventing further Hungarian defection.

Mikoyan and Suslov were in a position to see at first hand the breakdown of the one-party system. Shortly after one o'clock Nagy had broadcast that his government would be based on a coalition of all parties. Following Nagy, Tildy announced that free elections must be held. Kadar gave his support to the coalition. His hand had been forced. Probably like Imre Nagy, he was unhappy at this abdication of total power, but the claims of the Communist Party on the country had been exposed. Both men may have thought that only by such a move could the Communists dominate democratic socialism, as they had done in 1948. But Nagy may have wanted the remains of the democratic parties to join a sort of 'popular front' because some of the revolutionary committees in the provinces had almost separatist aims and were challenging the central authority of the government. Now the Smallholders and Peasant Parties began to wonder how to start organisations again. The Social Democrats were very slow to get going and indulged in fierce disputes among themselves.

A coalition would also protect Nagy from the dubious, if shadowy, people who might have taken advantage of the revolution. There is little or no evidence of political émigrés, whether former Horthyites or not, entering the country, but one strange buccaneer, Jozsef Dudas, had become the leader of a band in Budapest reputed to be about 3,000 strong. Born in Transylvania, Dudas had been in a Romanian prison from 1948 to 1954. Now he forced his way to an interview with Nagy at which he asked to be given the task of maintaining public order. Nagy dismissed him.

In order to prevent any such appearance of anarchy or possible fascism, the National Guard was formed. The Communist Party told its members that it was their duty to present themselves without delay at the recruiting centres of the National Guard. This National Guard was in fact the freedom-fighters under another name, and its formation was a way of securing them to the government, giving them a recognised function. It was also a way of stopping lawless children attacking Russian tanks while delicate negotiations were beginning, and of checking men like Dudas. The National Guard came under control of a Revolutionary Committee of Armed Forces. General Kiraly and Colonel Maleter had command of it, and their work of consolidation enabled the revolutionaries to resist again when the Russians counter-attacked at the end of the week. That evening a car from Parliament fetched Maleter from the Kilian Barracks and drove him to Parliament where for the first time he met Nagy, placing himself and the Revolutionary Committee of the Armed Forces completely at the government's disposal.

There were still people taking the law into their own hands. On Republic Square stood the headquarters of the Greater Budapest Communist Party. A detachment of AVH men, most of them new recruits, had been posted there at the beginning of the revolution but given no further orders. While the AVH was being disbanded, they had remained in position. In the morning, a truck with food rations drew up. A queue of housewives had lined up at food shops nearby, and they now saw provisions given to the AVH. An angry crowd went into the big Party building but was pushed out. The leader of these attackers was taken before Imre Mezo, secretary of the Budapest Party organisation, who was in the middle of discussing with two army colonels how the new National

75 Freedom-fighters from western Hungary on their way to Budapest to make their demands known to Nagy

76 Freedom-fighters moving up to attack the Greater Budapest Communist Party headquarters where some AVH men were in position

Guard could best defend factories. Aroused, the crowd tried to free their leader, and soon besieged the Party building. Firing broke out, and after three hours Imre Mezo gave the order for a surrender. The crowd was merciless. The AVH men were mown down as they stepped out of the building. The two colonels were hung by their feet and beaten to death. Imre Mezo died of his wounds in hospital. Foreign journalists had been present, and a French photographer was accidentally killed during the shooting. The incident showed how deeply loathed the police state had been, but it may have had a more serious repercussion than anyone could imagine. Imre Mezo had been a close friend of Kadar's, who may have thought that this futile death proved the need to control the revolution. So he may have prepared his betrayal.

At about the time when Imre Nagy was somewhat anxiously telling the country about the intended Soviet withdrawal, the British Prime Minister, Anthony Eden, was giving the news in the House of Commons of the British and French ultimatum to Egypt. This crisis had been simmering lengthily, but at some remoteness from Hungary. The Middle East was an area of instability which the Russians had been hoping to penetrate to their advantage following the evacuation of British military bases there. Their break-through had come with an arms sale to Egypt in 1955. The Cold War now extended to another part of the globe. The Americans had long been uncertain of the political direction Egypt would take under Nasser's rule. Having offered to finance the construction of a huge irrigation project, the Aswan Dam on the Nile, they decided in July 1956 not to go ahead with it. In retaliation Nasser nationalised the Suez Canal at the end of the month. The British were concerned to protect oil supplies and shipping, and military plans were at once prepared in Whitehall. Yet the summer was to slip by while the French and the Israelis were brought into these plans. Not until 29 October, at the high point of the Hungarian revolution, did the Israelis mobilise and sweep down to the Suez Canal in a matter of hours. The ultimatum then issued by the British and French governments called on the Egyptians and the Israelis to pull back ten miles on either side of the Canal, and this was justified as 'separating the combatants'. Egypt naturally refused the ultimatum and the British and the French were committed to using

77 An AVH policeman caught by the crowd. 'I am your brother, as you are mine,' he said to them. But he had turned a machine-gun on them and the crowd sentenced him to death

78 Sniping on the streets of Budapest

force. Not so well prepared as the Israelis, the British spent the next week mounting their invasion. The bombs falling on Egyptian airfields were more than a background to the Hungarian revolution; they raised alarmingly the prospect of a wide East-West confrontation, with its danger of nuclear warfare. Power politics were nakedly revealed. Whatever compromise solution the Russians might have been devising for Hungary took on a new aspect. If the Cold War were about to enter a more open phase, it would only be prudent on the Russian part to ignore the clamour for freedom in the satellites, and in particular in Hungary, a small country of 10 million people conveniently locked away behind the Iron Curtain and in no position to play a part more powerful than that of the pawn it was.

Wednesday, 31 October

At a cabinet meeting to discuss relations with Russia, writes Gyorgy Heltai, then Deputy Minister of Foreign Affairs, a cable was brought in.

> Nagy read it aloud: 'British and French forces are bombing Egypt.' The silence was deafening.
> 'God damn them!' Losonczy exploded.
> Nagy forced a tired smile and looked at his watch. 'Mikoyan expects us,' he said, 'Let's go.'
> 'Aren't we going to put out feelers to the Western Powers *even now?*' someone asked.
> 'Certainly not *now*.' Nagy replied.

At the talks which dragged out Kadar was present. Mikoyan and Suslov were reputedly in good spirits, shaking hands with everyone in sight when they left Party headquarters to return that afternoon to Moscow. As they left, rumours spread of Russian troops on the move. The atmosphere in Budapest became feverish. The strike

79　The bitterness of the people at the
years of tyranny had found its outlet.
Western photographers were present

80　When the Party Headquarters was
stormed after three hours' shooting, the
freedom-fighters exacted a terrible revenge

was still on and little groups discussed politics at every corner, or read the endless
leaflets and manifestos.

One freedom-fighter has described the activity at the offices of the Smallholders
Party.

> There was already a long row of cars outside. . . . Everything went well until ten
> o'clock, but after that there was such a rush that one could not avoid the impression
> that the whole city wanted to get into the house. . . . People were flocking in from every
> direction: worthy peasants from the country, foreign journalists carrying photographic
> equipment, delegates from industrial revolutionary committees and so on.

The Smallholders were at last on a firm footing. The Social Democrats also had an
official publication, and had elected Anna Kethly president. Born in 1889, she had been
one of the first woman deputies in Hungary. Nagy himself saw that she obtained a visa
to a socialist conference taking place in Vienna.

> The Smallholders Party has full liberty to reassemble but the question is whether,
> in its constitution, the party will proclaim its old ideas again. No one should dream of
> going back to the world of aristocrats, bankers and capitalists. That world is definitely
> gone! A true member of the Smallholders Party cannot think along the lines of 1939 or
> 1945. The last ten years were bitter but they also provided a useful lesson.

So ran part of Bela Kovacs's first political speech in years, made at Pecs. He had been
astonished, he said, to find the names of former Communist leaders in the Nagy government, but had not resigned because he wished to help build a neutral Hungary.
Nevertheless he was pessimistic about the outcome and did not arrive in Budapest
until the next day. In a conversation with Jozsef Kovago, he confided his fears that the
Soviet Union would always fight the establishment of a Western-style democracy on
her borders, and his doubts that the West was ready to risk a world war.

The Communists were the losers in the political free-for-all started by the return

93

to coalition government. A Yugoslav journalist found that his Communist contacts were frightened of possible assassination. But Professor Lukacs, now Minister of Culture, gave a more objective view in a talk to a Polish journalist. He thought that a new Marxist party would have to be formed.

> The new Party will not be able to expect rapid success – Communism in Hungary has been totally disgraced. . . . In free elections the Communists will obtain five per cent of the vote, ten per cent at the most. It is possible that they won't be in the government, that they will go into opposition. But the party will continue to exist; it will save the idea; it will be an intellectual centre, and after some years or some decades from now, who knows. . . .

The release of Cardinal Mindszenty gave the Catholic parties a leader. From prison he had been transferred to a manor-house, once church property, at the village of Felsopeteny. The AVH had guarded him, until an army major with a detachment of tanks drove up on instructions from Tildy to release him and to escort him back to the episcopal palace in Budapest. This major, of an aristocratic family but with Arrow Cross and Communist affiliations, was to be executed for his part in freeing Mindszenty. The Cardinal gave his blessing to those who gathered at the palace to watch and then made a radio statement. 'We must find a solution later. For the moment I shall inform myself. Two days from now, I shall address an appeal to the nation in the hope of leading it toward that solution.' He had lived in isolation for six years. Nagy signed a proclamation that the proceedings against Mindszenty lacked all legal basis and the accusations levelled against him by the Rakosi regime were unjustified. Mindszenty was the second Cardinal to be let out of confinement that week, for in Poland Cardinal Wyszynski had also been allowed to take up his duties.

Shakily, with confusion, democratic politics emerged somewhat on the pattern of 1945. It was as if the parties had been put to sleep by a spell, and now, awakened with the roughest of kisses, were none too sure what to make of it.

81 Scenes such as this aroused fears of counter-revolution and probably led to Kadar's betrayal of the Nagy government to the Russians

Thursday, 1 November

For a week Nagy had been tugged along by the revolution. It must have been a heavy strain on a 'man of science', a 'Muscovite', a lifelong Communist, to make concessions, one after another, to a country insatiable for its freedom. Nagy may have liked the masses, he disliked a mob. Maybe he felt that he alone could present Hungary favourably to the Russians, that his brand of communism was the only way of preventing a catastrophe. The endless delegations petitioning him, the free radio stations with their advice, the violence on the streets, may have convinced him that he could no longer be content to respect the revolution, but would have to embrace it.

The Russian troop movements had been contradictory until now, and reasons for their delayed withdrawal could be found. When Nagy reached his office during the morning, he could no longer avoid the conclusion that the Russians were not retreating, but reinforcing their units. Train-loads of soldiers estimated at more than 75,000 men and 2,500 tanks were moving across the frontiers from Russia, from Romania and Czechoslovakia. When the whole of Hungary had given such proof of its determination to be free from Soviet domination, it was impossible for Nagy to give way before a show of strength. Having seen the revolution through to victory, having been carried along with it to the point where he could form a coalition government, Nagy could hardly do anything except take a more intensive lead. He was neither feeble nor a cynic. Urgently he summoned the Russian ambassador, Andropov, to protest against the troop movements and to warn him that if these soldiers did not return to their bases at once, the government would break with the Warsaw Pact and proclaim Hungarian neutrality. This step was dictated by the logic of the situation, but in Russian eyes it was an act of aggression, and coming after the formation of a coalition cabinet, must have confirmed their fears that soon Hungary would be rejecting everything to do with Soviet Communism. Nagy had been placed in a predicament where he had to risk the future for the sake of what had been achieved.

82   Impromptu debates took place on street corners. The freedom-fighters were organised into the National Guard and were allowed to carry weapons

Throughout the day the telephones in the Parliament building kept ringing with more information about the Russian troops pouring into the country. Questioned by Hungarians, these soldiers would explain that they had been ordered to put down the fascists. Nagy sent a telegram to the Soviet Presidium asking that a time and place be fixed for talks on the departure of these Russian forces as agreed in the Declaration of 30 October. Simultaneously a teleprinter on the twentieth floor of the United Nations building in New York began clocking out a cable. Nagy had told Hammarskjold, Secretary-General of the UN, to place the question of Hungarian neutrality on the agenda for discussion at the next session of the General Assembly. The connection with New York stayed open.

At 2 p.m. Nagy telephoned Andropov to say that since troops were still advancing, Hungary was withdrawing from the Warsaw Pact. The cabinet met, and at 5 p.m. summoned the Russian ambassador to hear the official proclamation. In front of Andropov, Kadar exclaimed that as a Hungarian he would fight with his bare hands if necessary against Russian tanks. His emotion seemed genuine to those present. Andropov regretted the Hungarian measures and urged Nagy not to declare neutrality. The heads of other diplomatic missions were then called in to be informed of the cabinet decisions, and of the cable sent to the UN. At 6.15 p.m. Nagy broadcast that the government,

> giving expression to the undivided will of the Hungarian millions declares the neutrality of the Hungarian People's Republic. The Hungarian people, on the basis of independence and equality and in accordance with the spirit of the UN Charter, wishes to live in true friendship with its neighbours, the Soviet Union and all the peoples of the world. The Hungarian people desire the consolidation and further development of the achievements of its national revolution without joining any power-blocs. The century-old dream of the Hungarian people is being fulfilled. . . .

Six minutes later the teleprinter in New York sprang to life with this message which was circulated to UN delegates, but, says one reporter, 'it bore no marks of urgency'.

An English journalist that afternoon crossed Parliament Square, which was deserted,

> save for a few weeping women who crossed themselves before the candles under the walls of Parliament. A Hungarian officer approached smiling. I told him I wanted to

83 Members of the AVH are known to be hiding in the building opposite this improvised post

96

84   A news bulletin
broadcast from the Town
Hall; broadcasting was
to become Hungary's last
link with the outside
world

speak to Nagy or Kadar. . . . Two soldiers, carrying tommy-guns and grinning hope-
fully, led me through a maze of rich Byzantine corridors. The incredible thing about
Hungary's ten days of liberty was the fact that journalists from all over the world,
rushing up and down the Vienna–Budapest road, were the unofficial ambassadors of
the Hungarian government to the outside world. The two dirty soldiers in their Russian
uniforms, walking down these golden passages, gave an impression of Russia 1917.
After the atmosphere of the streets the warm waiting room was soothing for the nerves,
apart from the fact that armed patrols kept passing incongruously across the rich
carpets. One of Nagy's assistants spoke fluent English. . . . In the next room Nagy was
arguing with Soviet Ambassador Andropov. The assistant told me that in half an hour's
time Nagy intended to declare Hungary a neutral country and ask the UN for protection. 'Russian troops are pouring in from the Ukraine. They are digging in around
Budapest. I am very pessimistic. I hope I am safe in telling you this. But you could
not communicate it anyway.' There was a swift passing of messages for relatives in the
West, a handshake and he advised me to leave Budapest at once.

It was in somewhat the same spirit of doom that Bela Kovacs at last met Imre
Nagy in Parliament and after a ninety-minute talk was sworn in formally as a member
of the cabinet. He had satisfied himself that the new democracy was acceptable, but
such integrity had delayed any influence he might have had. In the evening Kadar
broadcast. The Communist Party, he said, would defend democracy and socialism 'not
by slavishly imitating foreign examples, but by taking a road suitable to the economic
and historic characteristics of our country'. To achieve this, the old Communist Party
would be dissolved and a new one formed. The committee members to organise the
Party's future were besides himself to be Nagy, Donath and Losonczy, Lukacs, Kopacsi,
and Zoltan Szanto. This was a nucleus of present leaders, but all six nominated by
Kadar were shortly to be arrested, imprisoned, or executed when he came to power.

Kadar went on to praise the revolution but also to say that it had come to a
crossroad.

97

A grave and alarming danger exists that foreign armed intervention may reduce our country to the tragic fate of Korea. Our anxiety for the future of our country leads us to do our utmost to avert this grave danger. We must eliminate the nests of counter-revolution and reaction.

With hindsight it is possible to see in this warning a clue to Kadar's own behaviour. For soon after this broadcast, he vanished out of the Parliament building. Ferenc Munnich, a firm Stalinist, had taken him in a chauffeur-driven car to the Russian embassy. The chauffeur was to report that another car had been waiting for them both, and he had the impression of a pre-arranged plan. For a while Kadar remained missing without trace. He had in fact gone to Uzhgorod, a town in the Carpatho-Ukraine, where he could act like a latter-day 'Muscovite' and offer himself to head the government which would be installed once the Russians had militarily regained control of Hungary. At ten o'clock the following morning Nagy wanted to discuss the new Party programme with Kadar, and he then learnt of Kadar's unexplained movements. Gyorgy Heltai, foreign affairs adviser, writes, 'It was decided not to publicise Kadar's disappearance.'

Friday, 2 November

The UN General Assembly opened with a debate on Suez. Not until several hours had passed did the Indian delegate refer to 'some difficulties' in Hungary, by which time Nagy had addressed a second telegram to Hammarskjold, appealing for recognition of Hungarian neutrality by the Great Powers. In the small hours the American resolution against Britain, France, and Israel obtained sixty-four votes to five against. In the Security Council, meeting in a special session, the Russian delegate flatly denied that Soviet troops had crossed into Hungary. By the time that he could be confronted with the truth, it was too late to do anything. While he was actually speaking, Hungarian railwaymen were counting the armoured trains entering. Late that night, 'a night filled with uncertainty and mysteriously silent', two student journalists made their way through Budapest suburbs to an airfield. There they encountered Russians from Temesvar, in Romania. It turned out that Budapest International Airport was also surrounded. Three times during the day Nagy protested to Andropov against such seizure of railway lines and stations and airfields. Andropov answered that the troops had to ensure the safe evacuation of Russian civilians.

Because it was All Souls Day, the Day of the Dead, candles had been lit throughout the city, and commemorative lights flickered beside the many graves where freedom-fighters had been buried as they fell. Tibor Dery had ended an article in the *Literary Gazette* published that day:

> When the first rifle bullet was heard, my blood drained from my head. Safeguard our revolution! Until now it had such nobility which only justice and humanity could lend to a cause. Let us concentrate on one thing: this is not the hour of revenge but of justice. . . . Respect the dead!

Dery, like others, was concerned with the purity of the revolution, with making sure that no White Terror erupted, because any anti-Communist spirit of vengeance could only play into the hands of the Russians. As it was, the Moscow newspapers and commentators were already accusing the Hungarians of hounding Communists. When they came to publish a justification of their acts two years later, a justification which was also an indictment of Imre Nagy, they claimed that under the Nagy government 239 Communists had been killed. Considering the mood of Budapest after the Russian intervention, this figure is strikingly low. A few of the victims will have been men like Imre Mezo, but most were AVH officers and policemen. Witnesses of all nationalities have testified that there was no looting in Budapest during these ten days, in spite of the temptations offered by smashed shop-windows. On the streets, too, were open boxes to collect money for the families of the fallen revolutionaries, and it was not necessary for guards to stand over these collections. Hungarian Jewry in a statement 'identified with the free and independent homeland', which it was able to do because there was none of the anti-Semitism hitherto found in Hungarian nationalism. Nor were any of the old claims on Transylvania raised.

The Russians would have to delve hard to find evidence of the counter-revolution which they alleged. Twenty-five newspapers were published in Budapest instead of the five usual Communist ones, and none of them had a reactionary viewpoint. Here and there, on walls, in slogans, were comments that the revolution had not yet gone far enough. In a paper controlled by his band of followers, Dudas called for a congress of revolutionary forces. In a bizarre incident, a group of Dudas's supporters entered the Foreign Ministry and took possession of it. They were persuaded to leave and Dudas was removed into protective custody. It seems that he believed the political rivalry of the democratic parties was all a Communist trick. A Pole who interviewed Dudas found that the man's ambitions were not modest, that he thought he should be in the cabinet. Dudas, he said, had a large, expressive but repulsive face, a Tyrolean hat, a coat thrown around his shoulders like a cape, a gun at the belt, black trousers. Was this really a fascist, he asked. The Russians were to cast the theatrical Dudas in the role of a counter-revolutionary villain. It was harder for them to do the same with the Americans. The American minister had left for a new posting in July and the legation had no head throughout the crisis. The new minister arrived from Brazil on 2 November, the day his staff was evacuated to Vienna, and he himself never managed to present his credentials.

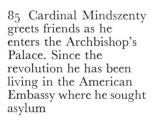

85 Cardinal Mindszenty greets friends as he enters the Archbishop's Palace. Since the revolution he has been living in the American Embassy where he sought asylum

Saturday, 3 November

In the morning, tens of thousands of people hastened towards their places of work. Not all of them had to go by foot because the streetcars had started to run along those lines where the rails had not been torn up and where the wires were intact. To many, it was a pleasure to be able to climb once again the steps of one of those yellow cars, and they paid their fares almost cheerfully. Many factories had sent out trucks to fetch their workers. The strike was almost over. . . . Queues of shoppers lengthened along the streets, waiting to buy bread and potatoes, and the housewives could be sure that they would not have to return empty-handed. There was no threat of famine in the capital. In the *espresso* shops, there was already black coffee to be had and some were even able to serve *patisserie*.

Tibor Meray was not alone in assuming that Monday would bring normality with it. Because no Russian attack had taken place the day before, it was possible to feel that the danger was past. A Catholic paper enjoyed one issue, in its editorial renouncing the nationalised possessions of the Church. Young Communists stood on the streets, handing out the first leaflets issued under the auspices of the New Party, with passages from Kadar's speech of the previous day. They were unaware that Kadar was completing plans with the Russian general staff.

Kadar's name was included in the new government which Nagy announced in mid-morning. Several Communists who had been junior Ministers were dismissed, some of them on the request of their civil servants. The parties of the coalition were represented as they had been in 1945, in the period of the Allied Control Commission. Anna Kethly entered the government, but could not actually join because a Russian road-block obliged her to return to Vienna. Maleter was appointed Minister of Defence. He was interviewed by an English journalist.

He still wore his little partisan star of 1944 (and another Red Star awarded for successful coal-digging by his regiment at Tatabanya) at a time when the whole officers' corps was dragging off its Soviet-style epaulettes. 'If we get rid of the Russians,' he said to me, 'don't think we're going back to the old days. And if there's people who do want to go back, well we'll see.' And he touched his revolver holster.

86 Anna Kethly was the leader of the Social Democrats. She had been imprisoned in 1948. Imre Nagy gave her permission to attend a socialist conference in Vienna. There she was greeted by the Austrian Minister of the Interior (*right*)

At midday a Russian military delegation presented itself at Parliament to begin negotiations, as the Kremlin and Ambassador Andropov had been promising. They were given full honours. The delegation was headed by General Malinin who wore a green uniform on which were rows of medals. Maleter, promoted to the rank of general, headed the Hungarian negotiation committee. General Kiraly, Commander of the National Guard and of the defences of Budapest, caught Maleter coming out of the committee room and asked how things were going.

> I came back at 6 that evening [Kiraly wrote later], and cornered another member of the committee, General Istvan Kovacs, the army chief of staff. I asked the same question. 'It is practically agreed,' he said. 'First, Russia will evacuate all her armed forces from Hungary. Second, to avoid disrupting transportation the Russians want to leave by degrees. A committee of experts will be set up to arrange a time-table. Third, the Hungarian garrisons must cease denying the Russians food and fuel. Fourth, the Russians are not prepared for a winter movement and the Hungarians must be patient; the troops will not be able to leave until January 15. Lastly, they say the Russian army did not want to attack the Hungarians but only did what the Hungarian government asked. Therefore the evacuation must be not only peaceful but friendly. The troops must leave in a festive air and the Hungarians must cheer them as they leave.' In effect, said General Kovacs, the committee had agreed to all the Russian demands, even the friendly farewell, but insisted that departure date be stepped up by a month. The meeting was to be continued that night at 9 p.m. at the Russian military headquarters at Tokol, on Csepel Island. . . .

In the Parliament building a large press conference for foreign journalists was given by Tildy and Losonczy. When asked about a possible clash with the Russians, Tildy replied, 'I consider that a clash as tragic as that could not take place.' Losonczy emphasised that the government would make no concessions as far as the achievements of the last twelve years were concerned. Capitalism was not to be restored.

Shortly after this tense press conference, Cardinal Mindszenty made a broadcast to the nation. Pal Ignotus, elected after his release from prison to the committee of the Writers' Association, was present at the temporary centre of the Free Kossuth Radio in the Parliament building where the broadcast was made. The muddle and enthusiasm were touching, he says, here was a revolutionary headquarters at its best.

> My speech was recorded for broadcasting late at night. At the peak hour, Cardinal Mindszenty was to speak. I stayed to see him. It was a fantastic sight; the diehard Primate Cardinal arriving with an armed guard of honour amidst the Communist revolutionaries. He was received by a cabinet minister, once President of the Republic, originally a Protestant parson, Zoltan Tildy; later a political prisoner, released in April 1954. The Cardinal walked in with swaying steps and glaring eyes, the strange expression of which may or may not have been the result of his ordeal in AVH imprisonment. I listened to his speech. Its text can be read and checked in several volumes of documentary literature. The spokesmen of Soviet policy on Hungary have since made a habit of referring to it as a counter-revolutionary incitement to restore the old estates. This is nonsense. The Cardinal's speech was moderate and cautious. But it was not appropriate to the extraordinary moment when it was made. One could not help feeling that a ghost was speaking from the past.

The Cardinal acknowledged that good relations between Hungary and Russia had to be maintained, even strengthened.

Our entire situation depends on what the Soviet empire, that vast empire of 200 million inhabitants, will do with its troops within our borders. The radio has announced that the number of Soviet troops in Hungary has increased. We are neutral. We give the Russian empire no cause for bloodshed. Do not the leaders of the Russian empire realise that we will respect the Russian people even more if they do not oppress us?

Few Hungarians would have disputed those words. As for internal affairs, the Cardinal demanded free elections. 'We want to live in a constitutional state and in a classless society and to increase democratic progress. We are in favour of private property within just and equitable limits of our society's best interests.'

Whatever the Cardinal said, or might have said, in these final few hours of Hungarian independence, was doomed to be ineffective. The Austrian minister had called on Nagy earlier in the day to inform him that the Austrian frontier remained closed to prevent unauthorised crossings. The neighbouring Communist countries, except Yugoslavia, had begun all-out propaganda attacks against the Hungarian uprising. Rumours that a UN fact-finding team had arrived from Prague were false. Had such a team existed, it could have landed only at a Russian-occupied airport. In New York the American resolution deploring the use of force to suppress the Hungarians was vetoed by Russia, and the Hungarian question was postponed until after the week-end. The Russians were not only poised round Budapest and provincial towns, but had also sprung the trap round Hungary.

Hope died hard. Jozsef Kovago, once again mayor of Budapest as he had been nine years previously, accompanied Bela Kovacs to Parliament where Nagy and Tildy wished to speak to them.

> We found a highly optimistic Tildy. He was convinced that the Russians would not attack. General Maleter and his associates had already held one conference with Russian military authorities and were about to start another. . . . He also mentioned the mysterious disappearance of Janos Kadar and of some of his associates. His interpretation was that they might have started direct negotiations with the Soviets, which in the long run, might come out well for us.

At 8 o'clock General Maleter drove to Tokol in a Russian car to renew the negotiations at the Russian military headquarters. It had been suggested to him that he was walking into a trap, but he answered that even if so, his duty had to be done. He was accompanied by General Kovacs, Colonel Szucs, and a politician, Erdei of the National Peasant Party. Telephone lines were open from Tokol to Parliament and to Moscow. The talks began at 10 o'clock. Sandor Horvath, a soldier of Maleter's bodyguard, has written:

> Everything appeared to go off perfectly in the office where the talks were taking place. At least that was our impression in the ante-chamber, from the noise of conversation we could hear. . . . Towards midnight, about twenty military policemen in green caps burst into the room. . . . They shouted a password and covered our delegation with their sten-guns. . . . Through the broken door I was watching our boss . . . the others were pale . . . only his face didn't change. 'So that was it, was it?' he said to the Russians, standing up calmly. I seized my own sten-gun, thinking that before dying I would still shoot a few rounds at the men in green caps, but it was too late. Two military policemen were already holding me. I tried to get free of them. There was a struggle; I was the stronger. I had again seized the barrel of my sten-gun when the boss called out: 'Stop

it! It's useless to resist.' What could I do? His words were my orders and I let my sten-gun be taken away.

The United Nations Report provides this account:

> Towards midnight, telephone contact with the Hungarian delegation at Tokol was broken off. Reconnaissance parties sent towards Tokol by General Kiraly also failed to return. The Committee has been informed that the discussions between the Soviet military delegation and the Hungarian military delegation at Tokol were in fact interrupted by the entry of a personage 'who bore no insignia of rank' – General Serov, Chief of the Soviet Security police. Accompanied by Soviet officers, he announced that he was arresting the Hungarian delegation. The head of the Soviet delegation, General Malinin, astonished by the interruption, made a gesture of indignation. General Serov thereupon whispered to him; as a result General Malinin shrugged his shoulders and ordered the Soviet delegation to leave the room. The Hungarian delegation was then arrested. In vain therefore, did Mr. Nagy, at 5:56 a.m. broadcast an appeal to Generals Maleter and Istvan Kovacs and other members of the mission to return to their posts at once to take charge of their offices.

The delegation, the whole government, had been duped. The Russians had used the negotiations to cover their military preparations and to capture Maleter, the soldier who could rally resistance. The revolution was over.

87   High-school students on a revolutionary committee read the new posters and proclamations (*contrast with page* 123)

103

7 The Return of the Russians

Attention! Attention!
Attention! Attention!

Now Imre Nagy, President of the Council of Ministers of the Hungarian People's Republic, is going to address you!

This is Imre Nagy speaking, the President of the Council of Ministers of the Hungarian People's Republic. Today at daybreak Soviet forces started an attack against our capital, obviously with the intention to overthrow the legal Hungarian democratic government.

Our troops are fighting.
The Government is in its place.
I notify the people of our country and the entire world of this fact.

SO FREE RADIO KOSSUTH OPENED at 5 a.m. on 4 November. Nagy was speaking from the Parliament building where he had spent the night. A few cabinet Ministers and friends were with him: the remainder were telephoned to come at once. At about the same time, on a frequency normally used by a transmitter in west Hungary, Ferenc Munnich, who had gone over to the Russians with Kadar, announced a breakaway government. Kadar himself, speaking from Uzhgorod, declared:

> The Hungarian Revolutionary Workers and Peasant Government, acting in the interests of our people, our working class, and our country, requested the Soviet Army Command to help our nation in smashing the dark reactionary forces and restoring order and calm in the country.

With Kadar's act, the circle begun on 23 October had come full round – the Russians had again arranged for a Communist Party Secretary to screen aggression with a rigged appeal. And for Janos Kadar 'the glorious uprising of the people' which he had been speaking about, had become, within seventy-two hours, a counter-revolution.

In Vienna the Associated Press office received a dawn call from *Szabad Nep*.

> Since the early morning hours Russian troops have been attacking Budapest and our population. Please tell the world of the treacherous attack against our struggle for liberty. Our troops are already engaged in fighting. Radio Petofi is still in our hands. Help – Help – Help.

Listeners to the radio then heard that the Security Council in New York had acknowledged Nagy's early statement. This was followed by the music of Schubert's *Ave Maria*.

After Nagy had made his 5 a.m. appeal, Gyula Hay, the playwright and a friend of Nagy's, arrived in the Parliament building and scribbled down a further cry for help.

> This is the Hungarian Writers' Association speaking to all writers, scientists, writers' associations, academies and scientific organisations of the world. We appeal for help to all intellectuals in all countries. Our time is limited. You all know the facts. There is no need to review them. Help Hungary! Help the writers, scientists, workers, peasants, and all Hungarian intellectuals. Help! Help! Help!

Hay's wife was reading over the air her German translation of this message when the Russian advance columns reached the Parliament building.

88 (*opposite*) Men, women and children took part in the resistance to the second Russian intervention

In order not to be captured then and there, Imre Nagy left the building, and sought refuge in the Yugoslav embassy. Many of the political leaders of the revolution and his closest advisers during the last ten days accompanied him, Losonczy and Donath, his son-in-law Janossi, Professor Lukacs, Gabor Tanczos of the Petofi Circle, Mrs Rajk, the president of the Journalists' Association, Sandor Haraszti, and fifteen women and seventeen children of their families. Just before the Russians stormed the Parliament building, Cardinal Mindszenty had turned up there, as if attracted back to the scene of his broadcast in the twilight of the revolution. With his private secretary, a monsignor, the Cardinal managed to escape through a side door, and in a small car almost alone on the streets, dodged the oncoming tanks to seek asylum in the American legation. There he has remained, trapped and unyielding over the years, the subject of occasional but unsuccessful correspondence between the Hungarian government and the Vatican, his fate as lonely as it is symbolic.

> Then, suddenly, there was the rattle and rumble of trucked vehicles. A Hungarian artillery formation, with medium guns and anti-tank guns, was moving past to take up defensive positions on the outskirts of the city. It was 3:30. Not much longer to wait. Soon the skies were flickering with the flash of gunfire, and the roar of guns shook the air. The Battle of Budapest had begun.

So the inhabitants of the city had been awakened, and Nagy's call on the radio had only confirmed the noise of the past hour. The Hungarian army command, however, could not be relied on, even though the soldiers appeared ready to fight for the revolution. Several senior officers had been sent back from staff courses in Moscow in these last three days of the Nagy regime. General Kiraly was at the headquarters of the National Guard which he commanded when the Russians attacked. He has described how he telephoned to the Ministry of Defence to issue orders. His call was taken by General Janza, the dismissed Stalinist Minister of Defence who was not even authorised

89 Watching from a window inside the Parliament
building the arrival of the Russians

90 The Russian armoured columns enter Parliament Square. In the background stands what was once the Supreme Court

to be there. Janza asked Kiraly to prevent the activities of fascists. Apart from its will and its politics, the Hungarian army was not equipped to withstand the Russians.

In the circumstances the freedom-fighters would have to bear the brunt of the onslaught as they had done ten days before when the Russians had first intervened. The National Guard leadership had a command post pre-arranged in the Manresa, a former Jesuit monastery on the Szabadsaghegy, a hill overlooking Budapest, and there they received information about the various resistance groups. General Kiraly took charge of those who were 'in principle reluctant formally to renounce the goals of the revolution' by putting themselves at the mercy of the Russians. But central organisation could not be maintained by the National Guard unsupported by the government, and in the face of so heavy an attack. The Russians had thrust at once into the centre of Budapest, had occupied the crucial Danube bridges, and had begun to bomb several strategic points from the air. As best they could, freedom-fighters resumed their earlier tactics. They destroyed isolated Russian tanks, those posted at crossroads or on patrol. They threw 'Molotov cocktails' and laid booby-traps, they sniped from windows or roof-tops at any Russian who showed himself. This time the Russians were ruthless. If a shot came from any house, their tanks would reply with cannon-fire. Among the many hundreds of buildings smashed out in this way was the office of the Soviet-Hungarian Friendship Association. In the provinces, too, the Russians had ringed the towns and then closed in. One by one the main centres fell, and during the morning the revolutionary broadcasts and appeals became fewer, finally to cease.

In Budapest the teletype line of the Hungarian News Agency sent out dispatches until nearly 11 o'clock.

> People are jumping up at the tanks, throwing hand-grenades inside and then slamming the driver's windows. The Hungarian people are not afraid of death. It is only a pity that we can't stand for long. . . . Our building has already been fired on, but so far there are no casualties. The roar of the tanks is so loud that we can't hear each other's voices.

107

Now I have to run over to the next room to fire some shots from the window. . . . The tanks are now firing towards the Danube. Our boys are on the barricades and calling for more arms and ammunition. There is most bitter fighting in the inner city.

The despair of resistance could be heard in the remaining radio appeals, which were to leave an indelible mark on listeners and readers:

Civilised peoples of the world! We implore you in the name of justice, freedom, and the binding moral principle of active solidarity to help us. Our ship is sinking. Light is failing. The shadows grow darker every hour over the soil of Hungary. Listen to our cry, civilised peoples of the world, and act. Extend us your fraternal aid.

'Just before midnight we heard the rumbling of heavy Soviet tanks, some of them passing our building in the direction of Andrassy Street', writes one correspondent.

There they were concentrating and making a laager for the night. The whole street was floodlit to keep snipers at bay. It was a fantastic sight. But the precautions were in vain. The temptation was too great. Thousands of freedom fighters moved into an extemporised attack before dawn. This attack on the tanks led to one of the heaviest battles. I watched it from my window. More than thirty tanks were destroyed. And after that the Soviet tanks never stayed in the centre of the city at night. Every night, before midnight, they moved out, to come back at dawn. . . .

Peter Fryer was another eye-witness.

On the Sunday and the Monday while the din of the artillery bombardment and the ceaseless tank-fire mingled with the groans of the wounded, the battle spared neither civilians nor those bringing aid to the wounded. Bread queues were fired on by Soviet tanks and as late as Thursday I myself saw a man of about seventy lying dead outside a bread shop, the loaf of bread he had just bought still in his hand. Someone had half-covered the body with the red, white, and green flag. Soviet troops looted the Astoria Hotel as far as the first storey, even taking the clothes from the porters' rest room. . . . Some of the rank-and-file Soviet troops have been telling people in the last two days that they had no idea they had come to Hungary. They thought at first they were in Berlin fighting German fascists.

Groups continued to resist, particularly the workers of Csepel. Lack of communications and arms made their efforts suicidal. The Kilian Barracks held out for three stubborn days until the last forty men to leave it, under amnesty, were all mown down. The Russians prepared for an all-out assault on the National Guard headquarters on the Szabadsaghegy. The headquarters withdrew from Budapest. General Kiraly led them:

We bivouacked on various ridges of the Pilis, Vertes, and Bakony Mountains while Soviet helicopters hovered overhead, tracking our line of retreat. Anxiously we listened to foreign broadcasts, waiting and hoping for an eventual change that somehow at some point would force the Soviet Union to negotiate with Imre Nagy after all. We hoped that then we could offer him again the services of the only surviving central organ, the Headquarters of the National Guard and the Revolutionary Council of National Defence to help him rebuild.

91 (*opposite*) The Russians had no hesitation now. They had decided to repress the revolution

92   Russian tanks occupied strategic bridges and inter-
sections in the centre of Budapest

When the last urban pockets laid down their arms on 14 November all resistance
ceased.

On 7 November Kadar returned to Budapest. For three days of fighting there had
been no government at all, and it took Kadar some weeks to regain minimum control.
At first his declared programme was a dim echo of Nagy's reforms without their central
features of free elections, a multi-party system, and neutrality. Kadar was therefore a
continuation of Gero, and he justified the second Soviet intervention in much the same
language as Gero had justified the first. The working class which had fought so tenaci-
ously could not be expected to give in tamely to the instruments of their Russian
attackers. Nor were they likely to be reassured by the methods of the new regime. The
AVH were out in their uniforms again, escorting Russian soldiers, and picking out
former insurgents for arrest. Lorries full of young men were driven to Russian-occupied
barracks. Deportations began, as indiscriminate as in 1945, trains full of people packed
off at random to Russia. Along the railway lines fluttered the notes they threw out of the
carriages.

The general strike remained the chief weapon against Kadar's government. As
fighting came to a halt, the Workers' Councils of the Budapest factories created a
Central Workers' Council. It would have been impossible for them to stay away from
work indefinitely, but the Central Workers' Council was dissolved only after the arrest of
all its leaders in December. The movement for workers' control was stopped. It was
resented widely and bitterly that the government which claimed to be acting on
behalf of the people should in fact be stifling the people's first democratic experiences.
Kadar was not believed when he argued that with the Russians he had suppressed a

counter-revolution. Slogans on the walls of Budapest mocked this line: 'Former aristocrats, cardinals, generals, and other supporters of the old regime, disguised as factory workers and peasants, are making propaganda against the patriotic government and against our Russian friends.' Or, 'The forty thousand aristocrats and fascists of the Csepel works strike on!' The Writers' Association called the Soviet intervention 'a historic mistake' and members called Kadar a scoundrel with whom one either had to break relations or compromise. Refusing to change its attitude, the Writers' Association was dissolved in 1957 for having 'assaulted the Socialist system'.

Kadar spoke on Radio Budapest on 11 November. 'I, who have myself been a member of Nagy's Government, hereby state that according to the best of my knowledge, neither Imre Nagy, nor his political group, has willingly supported the counter-revolution.' He followed this up when speaking to an official delegation of workers. 'Imre Nagy is not under arrest and neither the Government nor the Soviet troops wish to restrict his freedom of movement. It depends entirely on him whether or not he participates in politics.'

The presence of Nagy in the Yugoslav embassy was an uncomfortable challenge. Not only was Nagy more popular than ever, he was also the legitimate head of government. Kadar had talks with the Yugoslav Foreign Ministry and finally it was confirmed in writing that the Hungarian government 'did not desire sanctions against Imre Nagy and the members of his group for their past activities'.

'The next day, 22 November at 6:30 p.m. a bus arrived at the Yugoslav Embassy to take the party to their houses', continues the United Nations Report.

> Soviet military personnel arrived and insisted on entering the bus, whereupon the Yugoslav Ambassador asked that two Embassy officials should accompany the bus, to make certain that Mr Nagy and his party reached their houses as agreed. The bus was driven to the Headquarters of the Soviet Military Command where a Russian Lieutenant-Colonel ordered the two Yugoslav officials to leave. The bus then drove

93   A Russian lorry and gun which had been blown up

away to an unknown destination escorted by Soviet armoured cars. In a *note verbale*, the Yugoslav Government condemned the Hungarian action as 'a flagrant breach of the agreement reached'.

Perhaps Kadar's government felt that the Yugoslavs would swallow this behaviour because Tito in a big speech on 11 November had condemned the first Russian intervention, but managed to accept the second. This stance lost him much credit in Eastern Europe. But nobody could varnish over the fact that Nagy and all those seeking asylum with him had been hijacked. They were imprisoned outside the country, at Sinaia in Romania.

94 A view of the Ulloi Street, with the Kilian Barracks

The border with Austria remained open for some weeks after the revolution, however, although there were police incidents: 200,000 people took this chance of escaping, and became refugees. Housed in camps and shelters in Austria, they moved on to whichever countries in the West would accept them. Only 10 per cent of them were to return to Hungary. Many of these refugees were talented and ambitious and Hungary could ill afford to lose them. Perhaps the government thought that if such people were discontented, it would be safer to let them go and not risk another internal explosion. It was not long before the minefields and barbed-wire were reinstalled and the Iron Curtain was back as it had been. 'For years to come, the Army will only act in a police capacity and will not be trained for battle manœuvres.' So spoke the general placed in charge of the Hungarian army's political division. In contrast an agreement was rapidly reached which permitted the Russians to station troops permanently in Hungary. Communist leaders and military experts from Eastern Europe came to give Kadar's government aid and advice.

By the end of the year the Communists had returned to methods of terror to gain their ends. The non-Communist parties had submitted their conditions for co-operating with Kadar. It was pointless, for the very day they did so, the Communist Party resolved not to surrender any of its authority to other parties. Bela Kovacs publicly declared that he was retiring from politics. Nagy supporters, now possible leaders of the opposition, were arrested, many of them removed from their homes, or picked up from the street by the AVH. Not only were the workers' councils and committees which had come into being with the revolution outlawed, but martial law was introduced with summary punishment for those found with weapons. A decree was passed whereby the

95 The number of those killed during the revolution has been estimated as high as 25,000. Many houses in Budapest still show damage ten years afterwards

96 Soviet officers were not pleased to see photographers recording them

Public Prosecutor, on police recommendation, could order detention without trial. Secret sentences were soon being hurriedly carried through and the concentration camps were once more filled. It was again the day of the AVH. The bodies of AVH men killed in the revolution were dug up and reburied with military honours.

Throughout that January and February, while Kadar spoke of the 'major tasks' facing his regime, Budapest Radio carried news of the execution of counter-revolutionaries, including that of Jozsef Dudas. Two thousand people are estimated to have died in this repression and 20,000 to have been imprisoned. Apart from the intellectuals who were especially exposed to persecution for their part in the revolution, they were mostly workers, students, soldiers, ordinary men and women. Those involved actively with Nagy were eliminated from public affairs. Sandor Kopacsi was sentenced to life imprisonment. Ferenc Donath received twelve years. Tildy, sentenced to six years, was released after four, and died in 1961. Attila Szigeti, head of the Revolutionary Committee of Gyor, died in prison. Professor Lukacs was fortunate to be released in 1957 and has since been allowed to retire to complete the Marxist philosophical studies of a lifetime.

The Communist Party had shrunk to a membership of 90,000, a mere 10 per cent of its pre-revolutionary number. But opportunists rallied to it, as they had done in 1948. Membership had doubled by the middle of 1958, and by 1961 had reached half a million. At the first elections to be held after the revolution, in November 1958, the usual single list of candidates was presented for approval. All were Communists, and they received a vote of 99.8 per cent, more than Rakosi had ever managed. After these elections, and again in 1960, Kadar felt able to declare amnesties, and to free prisoners.

With the elections over, collectivisation was enforced and soon the collectives and state farms comprised 90 per cent of all arable land, again far more than Rakosi had achieved. The peasants had not taken much part in the revolution, and they were readier to put up with what they could not alter, an attitude which over the centuries they had been obliged to adopt. They now form an agricultural proletariat with little prospects for betterment, and their children leave to find industrial jobs in the cities. Industry again had to pay for this collectivisation. Wages were frozen and norms raised as a result, although the regime had to be cautious in its treatment of labour because of its support of the revolution.

97 Refugees at a station in Austria. In all, 200,000 people left Hungary and were resettled outside the country

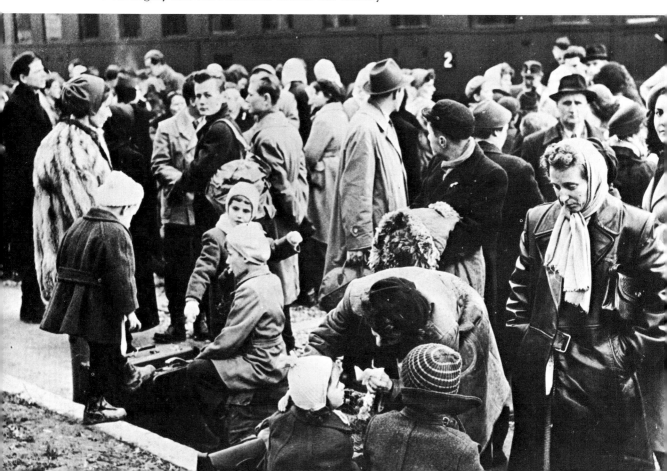

Nagy and those kidnapped with him were kept alive in Romania until June 1958. During that time, official speeches became more and more hostile to Nagy and the counter-revolution which he was now accused of fomenting. Finally the Kadar government left no doubt that they would execute those whom they had supplanted. The trial which eventually took place was secret. It was said that Nagy refused to plead guilty or to make any kind of confession. His sentence of death was announced on 17 June and it was added that no appeal was to be permitted. Such an appeal would anyhow have been impossible, for Nagy had in fact been executed a few days before the announcement of his sentence. General Pal Maleter, the journalist Miklos Gimes, and Nagy's secretary Jozsef Szilagyi, were also shot. Geza Losonczy, also one of the accused at the trial, had already died in prison in unexplained circumstances.

Ten years after Nagy's execution, Gyula Hay wrote in a Hungarian journal published in Paris an account of Nagy's secret trial which he had witnessed. This article, quoted in the London newspaper *The Observer* in July 1968, gave Nagy's final words to his judges after the death sentence had been passed:

I have twice tried to save the honour and image of Communism in the Danubian valley, once in 1953 and again in 1956. Rakosi and the Russians prevented me from doing so. If my life is needed to prove that not all Communists are enemies of the people, I gladly make the sacrifice. I know that there will one day be another Nagy trial, which will rehabilitate me. I also know I will have a reburial. I only fear that the funeral oration will be delivered by those who betrayed me.

98   For many it was a desperate flight with such belongings
as they could carry

8 Aftermath

AT DAWN ON 5 NOVEMBER, while the Russians were retaking Budapest, British and French paratroopers were dropped at Port Said, shortly to be followed by the main force. They were still seventy-five miles from Suez, their objective, when a cease-fire was called by the United Nations, hardly more than twenty-four hours later. Severe pressure had been exerted by America against this ill-timed expedition. The American government resented the collusion of two of its major allies, and saw in their use of force a return to colonial methods which also prejudiced American aims. Although the US Sixth Fleet was standing off Alexandria, ready to strike if need be, Washington was in fact caught unprepared for these events. Not only was the Secretary of State, John Foster Dulles, ill in hospital, but a presidential election was about to take place, on 6 November. Because it was more concerned with the aberrations of its allies than of its enemies, the American government helped to divert the attention of the world from Hungary to Suez. It took the Russians a long time to accept that the Americans had not inspired, but opposed, the Anglo-French operation. By then the impotence of the United Nations to act had been demonstrated and the Hungarian revolution had been ended with far less public scandal than the Russians might have expected. The Americans took the initiative in the General Assembly later in November and a resolution was passed calling for the immediate cessation of Soviet intervention in Hungary and providing for UN representatives to observe conditions in that country and to submit a report. No UN representatives were in the event allowed into Hungary, not even Hammarskjold, and such condemnations as the UN could offer were easily digested by the Russians.

Moscow and Washington could both reason that any change in the balance of power not initiated by them was likely to be too dangerous to be tolerated. Emmet

99 By the end of the year, the Iron Curtain was again impregnable. The Russians dynamited this bridge over the Einsler Canal

John Hughes, a speech-writer on President Eisenhower's staff, has described the muddle and hesitancy which gripped the White House. On 31 October, President Eisenhower was lamenting, 'I just don't know what got into these people. It's the damnedest business I ever saw supposedly intelligent governments get themselves into.'

In an interview on television, a few years after, President Eisenhower was to sum up.

> There was no European country, and indeed, I don't believe ours, ready to say that we should have gone into this thing at once and tried to liberate Hungary from the Communist influence. I don't believe, at this time, that we had the support of the United Nations to go in and make this a full-out war. The thing started in such a way, you know, that everybody was a little bit fooled, I think, and when suddenly the Soviets came in in strength with their tank divisions, and it was a *fait accompli*, it was a great tragedy and disaster.

Public opinion in America and Western Europe was greatly aroused by the Russian interventions in Hungary, and there were people who would have approved anti-Russian measures, however extreme. In general, the Hungarian revolution was seen as a brave and tragic cause, an appeal of the just few against the tyrannical many. Russian embassies in capitals around the world were angrily besieged. Crowds demonstrated, petitions were signed, and a handful of students or volunteer workers with medical supplies did reach Budapest where their presence was at least a sign of goodwill. Many more volunteers and relief agencies were to look after the refugees in Austria. Some official American institutions, from the State Department to Radio Free Europe, had been making anti-Communist statements throughout the Cold War. These statements were too loosely considered to cover a real political emergency although they seem to have been taken seriously by some Hungarians. During the first ten days of November, the extensive rumours in Hungary of active Western intervention, or of UN missions, were widely believed. To that extent, American Cold War propaganda had

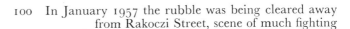

100   In January 1957 the rubble was being cleared away
from Rakoczi Street, scene of much fighting

101   Janos Kadar addresses his first Parliament in
May 1957. Immediately to his right is President Istvan Dobi,
and beyond him sits Ferenc Munnich, who engineered
Kadar's betrayal of the revolution

been harmful, inspiring hopes which could only be disappointed, and at a most anguish-
ing moment.

Yet there was little that the Americans could have done, so rigid had the Cold War
become. Hungary was surrounded, with one exception, by Communist states, and
American or United Nations forces, had any been available, would have had to violate
their territory or air-space in order to have access to Hungary. The Communist states
would certainly have appealed to Russia for protection. The exception – Austria – took
a firm stand from the beginning of the revolution, and would permit no movement of
foreign troops on her soil and watched her frontiers very closely for unwelcome émigrés
or agents. This was prudent, because had fighting broken out Austria would have
provided the unwilling battle-ground.

Had America persisted, she would have had to face the consequences of a war with
Russia, and even those most militantly opposed to the Russian interventions would not
have cared to risk the destruction of their own society by nuclear bombs for the sake of
Hungary. All considerations of morality apart, therefore, the Russians could always
have crushed Hungary with impunity as they did, and in the face of world opinion.
They were asking to be judged by world opinion, however, especially as Marxist theory
lays down the inevitability of the victory of the Communist system. The methods used
to achieve such victory spoke for themselves. The Suez episode diverted much of the
odium which would have fallen on Russia, and its timing must have seemed a stroke of
fortune to the Kremlin. Robert Murphy, Secretary for Political Affairs in the State
Department, expressed in his memoirs the frustration felt in Washington: 'Perhaps
history will demonstrate that the free world could have intervened to give the Hungarians the liberty they sought, but none of us in the State Department had the skill or
the imagination to devise a way.' The Americans had discovered that the anti-Russian
incitement of the Cold War years led nowhere, certainly not to the military liberation of

118

102   With Kadar in front of Moscow station sits M. Suslov.
An agreement was signed permitting further Soviet
troops to be stationed in Hungary

Eastern Europe. They, too, learnt the lesson of the Hungarian revolution, and after-wards worked for a policy of change by evolution. In fact the decision not to intervene in October 1956 had already been taken in 1944. The West was paying the price for the Russian alliance which had been so necessary to defeat Hitler.

As for Khrushchev, he visited Hungary in January 1957, April and June 1958, and December 1959. During his April 1958 journey, he mentioned how awkward the Hungarian revolution had been for the Kremlin.

> We had strength and right on our side, but it was difficult to make a decision because part of the workers were on the side of the counter-revolution. . . . Bullets do not choose between striking class enemies or misguided workers. Believe me, my friends, we spent painful days and nights before coming to a decision.

The Kremlin may well have been split between those who wanted to make some political bargain as in Poland, and those who favoured a military solution.

Having staked so much on de-Stalinisation and finding one unwelcome consequence in Hungary, Khrushchev may have felt particularly responsible for the success of the Kadar government. No amount of Marxist theory about the dangers of deviation and revisionism could still the violent emotional surge that the Hungarians had experienced, nor the bitter aftermath. Khrushchev continued to be harassed by the difficulty of keeping united the international Communist movement. The Chinese Party came to resent his demolition of the 'personality cult' of Stalin, and its leaders thought of Khrushchev himself as a revisionist, a man who would degrade their interpretation of Marxism, and especially the inevitability of a total clash between communism and capitalism. It is known that they were anxious for the Russians to intervene in Hungary in order to serve a warning on revisionists – and Imre Nagy was certainly one. The arch-revisionists were the Yugoslavs with ideas like Nagy's, and who had chosen to remain outside the

119

Communist treaties and organisations, and even to accept American aid. Khrushchev's relations with the Yugoslavs took a turn for the worse in 1957, and it is possible that Imre Nagy was sacrificed, much as Rajk had been before him, to prove how greatly the Russians disapproved of any kind of national communism. Nagy's death served no other purpose, and was seen in Hungary and abroad as another mean abuse of power.

To Communists everywhere the most unacceptable fact about the Hungarian revolution was that it had been prepared by intellectuals, sparked off by students, and maintained by the industrial masses, all elements in society which should have owed most to communism. The uprising had appealed through all classes to the whole nation. The concept of class warfare which the Communists had argued to be an essential part of bourgeois societies proved to be of no significance when national independence was at stake. The attempts by the Kadar government and the Russians to blame the Church and Cardinal Mindszenty and the old aristocracy and the capitalists were threadbare. The White Books which were published in defence of the Russian intervention only show that there were very few members of the former upper classes left in Hungary, that they were old, and had ceased to have any political pull. It was not surprising that a long wave of pessimism engulfed most Hungarians. As one young writer was to express it,

> We were enthusiastic twice (in 1945 and 1956) and disappointed twice, on both occasions so cruelly that we could hardly survive even with our elastic spirit. It is not easy for us to be enthusiastic; instead of ideas, we try to find strength within ourselves on which we can depend.

Nevertheless Hungary could not regress in isolation: the country was not cut off from developments within the Communist world. Russian leadership of the Communist movement was threatened by the Chinese who were insistent in accusing Khrushchev of failing to stand up to the West in orthodox Marxist-Leninist fashion. Kadar was a faithful adherent of Moscow on this important but divisive issue, and as an ally he came to be increasingly trusted by the Kremlin. As this ideological struggle with the Chinese Party grew until it appeared that it might overshadow world politics in the coming years, co-existence between Russia and America became firmer and more convincing. The climate of gradual thaw in the Cold War permitted reforms in the satellite countries. With the 1960s a more tolerant society emerged in Eastern Europe, including Hungary. 'Those who are not against us are with us', became Kadar's working slogan. The Party could follow the example of the freedom-fighters and cease to brood on the revolution. In order to hold a top job, it was no longer necessary to join the Party. Kulaks were allowed to become members of collective farms, and were not treated as social outcasts. Children of middle-class origins could receive higher education where once they had been discriminated against. Books and films and the theatre – 'that series of mutual alibis' in the words of one critic – were less crudely directed and censored.

Since it was impossible to infuse intellectuals again with Marxism, their importance has declined. No longer expressing the purposes of the nation, the intellectuals have no great public role, and the less they are heard, the more they can be tolerated. Condemnations of the Rakosi years are a useful safety valve, in politics and the arts, for Rakosi has been wholly identified with the disgraced Stalin, and all past abuses may be put down to them. On 4 August 1963, *The Times* carried an obituary:

It is understood that Mr Rakosi died last week in the Soviet Union where he has been living since 1956. So far no official confirmation is available. Reuters report from Vienna that travellers returning from Hungary yesterday said news of his death was received at the Communist Party headquarters in the Hungarian capital last Sunday – Mr Rakosi fled to the Soviet Union shortly before the 1956 uprising and was last reported to be living at Krasnodar in southern Russia with his Mongolian wife. Last year he was formally deprived of his party membership by Mr Kadar's administration, which has recently introduced a more moderate course regarding the country's internal affairs.

Many of the old Stalinists have been obliged to adjust. Gabor Peter was reported to be working in a tailor's shop in Budapest. Mihaly Farkas was also amnestied and has not served his long prison sentence. Former Prime Minister Hegedus has become a sociologist. Jozsef Revai fled to Czechoslovakia during the revolution, but returned to side with Kadar and violently to attack Imre Nagy, demanding revenge. In 1959 he died. In that year Mrs Rajk was released from prison; her husband is rarely mentioned. Another widow, Mrs Bela Kun, was also allowed to return to Hungary, her husband rehabilitated. The past has been reshaped to accord with the Kadar present.

Seen against the slow changes in the nature of communism, the Hungarian revolution may appear a painful failure – estimates of the dead in the fighting alone rise as high as 25,000. Until the invasion of Czechoslovakia in 1968 it could be argued that the revolution was not only a failure but also an obsolete protest. The Russian empire, that is to say, was in 1956 no more what it had been in 1948. The pace of its decolonisation has been unsteady, but the Twentieth Party Congress did begin the slow retreat from central despotism. The Yugoslav defiance succeeded. Poland has enjoyed some liberal reforms. Romania has struck out on a foreign policy of her own, making political alignments and trading contracts without consideration of Russian aims. In

103   3 August 1968. East European leaders at a wreath-laying ceremony at the memorial for Czechoslovak and Russian soldiers near Bratislava. *Front row*, from *right* to *left:* Dubcek, Ulbricht (E. Germany), Gomulka, Brezhnev, Svoboda, Zhivkov (Bulgaria), Kosygin, Podgorny, Kadar

order to appease her powerful neighbour, Romania has maintained strict Communist control in internal affairs.

In Czechoslovakia the Stalinists clung to power with determination and their delaying tactics created the suspense in which the liberal leadership came to office. Antonin Novotny had been First Secretary of the Party for nearly fifteen years, and for most of that time also head of the state. In January 1968 he was finally voted out by the Party and replaced by Alexander Dubcek. General Ludvik Svoboda became the President of the Republic, a veteran statesman with the distinction of having earned decorations from Czarist Russia and Soviet Russia alike. At once a rapid process of liberalisation began. Censorship was virtually abolished; there was a freedom of speech in the press and on television which had been quite unknown in Eastern Europe. Czech economists began to suggest that loans for investment might be raised in the West. Once closer ties with West Germany, the arch-enemy of the past, had been mentioned, the Czechs could also examine their own recent history. In April a professor published an article suggesting that Jan Masaryk, the Foreign Minister who was found dead in unexplained circumstances after the Communist take-over in 1948, had been murdered. Thousands of people marched to lay wreaths on his tomb, and on that of his father, T. G. Masaryk, founder of the Czech republic in 1918, whose achievements had been banned from discussion by the Communists. The rehabilitation of the 50,000 Czech victims of Stalinism started, but was handicapped by the mysterious suicides of four of the senior officials concerned with this politically explosive task. The country took pride in the swift progress of the 'socialist democratic revolution', as it was called, and gave unqualified support to the new leadership.

At first the Russians appeared to accept the Dubcek regime. Delegations flew between Moscow and Prague. But in May the Russians showed their suspicions by mounting military manœuvres in southern Poland along the Czech border, and a month later sent 25,000 troops into the country under cover of Warsaw Pact exercises. By July, Communist governments were expressing their 'deep anxiety' over internal Czech developments. The example of the Hungarian revolution and the fate of Nagy must have been forcefully present in the minds of the Czech government. At the end of July, at the Slovak frontier village of Cierna, the Czech Presidium met the entire Soviet Politburo for talks which after four days seemed to offer hopes of a compromise. The Czechs gave assurances of socialist solidarity and the Russians agreed to allow them their own road to socialism – an echo of the former Hungarian predicament. President Tito and President Ceausescu of Romania flew to Prague to show their public support, as Communists, of the Czechs. But during the night of 20 August the Russians launched an airborne invasion and within hours had seized all the main cities of Czechoslovakia. They had forced their Warsaw Pact allies to send contingents, so that troops from Poland, East Germany, Bulgaria, and Hungary crossed the frontiers, numbering altogether upwards of half a million men. 'And you, did you not have enough?' was one of the slogans chalked by Czechs on Hungarian tanks.

The events of 1956 were repeated, but there were differences. The Czechs offered only passive resistance, realising that heroism on the Budapest model brought deadly retaliation. This time the Russians had not been able to prepare an equivalent of the Kadar government for Czechoslovakia, and they were seriously embarrassed by the unshakable national loyalty of the Czechs to their leaders. On 24 August talks began in the Kremlin between Dubcek and his colleagues and the Russians. Tension grew in

Prague as thousands of young people defied Soviet curfew orders and sat for twenty-four hours a day in the city's main square. At the end of the talks the Czech leaders returned. Exhausted by the rough handling and the physical and moral humiliation he had received on his journey, Dubcek was moved to tears when he broadcast to the nation. His emotion was also aroused by the inevitable capitulation of his government to Russian demands. In September Vasily Kuznetsov, Russian Deputy Foreign Minister, came to Prague where he acted as a watchdog, supervising that the Czechs were indeed falling back into line. The population reluctantly bowed to force. Some thousands of Czechs, including a few in prominent positions, either left the country, or chose not to return from their visits abroad.

The Russians had minimum co-operation when removing politicians and intellectuals, reimposing the old controls including censorship. Such intervention proved once again that the Russians insist on dictating the politics of each satellite. It may be that in the Kremlin, too, the memory of 1956 was painfully fresh. In 1968 the Russians based their arguments for the use of force not so much on counter-revolution as on simple power politics. As many Czechs pointed out, it is a reflection on the nature of the Russian empire that the individual liberties sought by the Czechs as citizens as well as socialists should provoke a massive military invasion. It may also be a sign of weakness, in that the satellites can only be kept from changes by such displays of armed might. Whether rightly or wrongly, the Russians believed that their interests demanded the crushing of Czechoslovakia, as of Hungary. Russian forces remain garrisoned throughout Eastern Europe, excepting Romania. Since 1948, revolution and even change in Eastern Europe have been directed against Russia and therefore have been at the mercy of greater power. Compelled to bow to this power, Hungarians and Czechs could still respond to their ideals of their national identity. The Hungarian revolution broke out against political logic and because it was against political logic, it created the conditions of change which in turn enabled the Czechs to reach out for personal and national freedoms. Hopes are no less intense because they are frustrated and both the Czechs and Hungarians have shored up a self-respect which is a strong defence against foreign domination. The Russians may well draw the conclusion that their policy of absolute control must be short-lived because it does not accept the aspirations of the countries under their rule, but serves instead to prolong for all to see the stubborn uncertainty of Eastern Europe.

104   28 August 1968. Young Czechs demonstrate in Wenceslas Square, Prague, after Dubcek's speech telling the country of the Russian conditions for withdrawal of Soviet troops

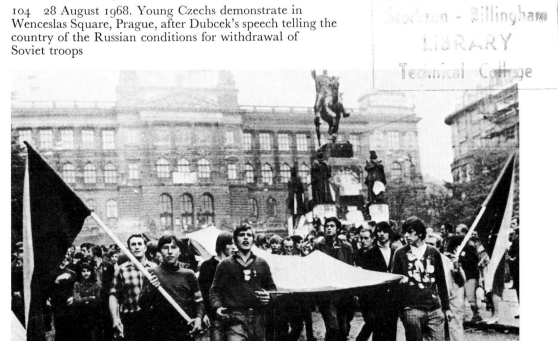

ACKNOWLEDGEMENTS

THE AUTHOR's thanks are due to Mr Pal Ignotus who was kind enough to read the manuscript.

THE AUTHOR AND PUBLISHERS wish to record their grateful thanks to copyright owners for the use of the illustrations listed below:

The Associated Press Ltd for: 3, 33, 41, 43

Barnaby's Picture Library for: 28, 36

Bibliothek für Zeitgeschichte, Stuttgart for: 4

Camera Press Ltd for: 6, 18, 30, 31, 34, 35, 57, 97, 98

Rolf Gillhausen and *Stern*, Hamburg for: 56, 60, 62, 63, 66, 67, 68, 69, 70, 71, 77, 78, 80, 81, 82, 88, 91, 95

Keystone Press Agency Ltd for: 5, 10, 11, 12, 13, 15, 24, 25, 38, 46, 51, 52, 61, 75, 86, 92, 100, 101, 102

Erich Lessing and the John Hillelson Agency Ltd for: title page, 37, 45, 48, 85

Pictorial Press Ltd for: 7, 16, 17, 19, 20

Paul Popper Ltd for: 2, 23, 26, 39, 40, 47, 49, 53, 55, 58, 59, 64, 73, 93, 99

Pressbyrå, Kungl Utrikesdepartementet, and Reportagebild, Stockholm for: 14

Radio Times Hulton Picture Library for: 1, 54, 65, 72, 76, 79, 83, 84, 87, 89, 90, 94, 96

Süddeutscher Verlag, Bild-Archiv, Munich for: 74

Syndication International (*Daily Mirror*) for: 21, 22, 32

Ullstein Bilderdienst, Berlin for: 44

United Press International (UK) Ltd for: 27, 29, 42, 50, 103, 104

Yad Vashem Archives, Jerusalem for: 8, 9

and for Quotations:

Cassell and Co. Ltd and Houghton Mifflin Company for the extracts from *The Second World War*, Volume VI: *Triumph and Tragedy* by Sir Winston Churchill

Dennis Dobson (Publishers) for the extracts from *Hungarian Tragedy* by Peter Fryer

Routledge and Kegan Paul Ltd and Crowell Collier and Macmillan Inc. for the extracts from *Political Prisoner* by Pal Ignotus

Martin Secker and Warburg Ltd and George Paloczi-Horvath for the extracts from *The Undefeated*

Thames and Hudson Ltd and Frederick A. Praeger Inc. for the extracts from *13 Days that Shook the Kremlin* by Tibor Meray and *The Revolt of the Mind* by Tibor Meray and Tamas Aczel

Index

Printed in Great Britain
by Jarrold & Sons Limited,
Norwich

FOR OVER A THOUSAND GENERATIONS THE JEDI KNIGHTS WERE THE GUARDIANS OF PEACE AND JUSTICE IN THE OLD REPUBLIC...

...BEFORE THE

DARK TIMES...

STAR WARS™

MYSTERIES OF THE JEDI

WRITTEN BY
ELIZABETH DOWSETT
AND **SHARI LAST**

CONTENTS

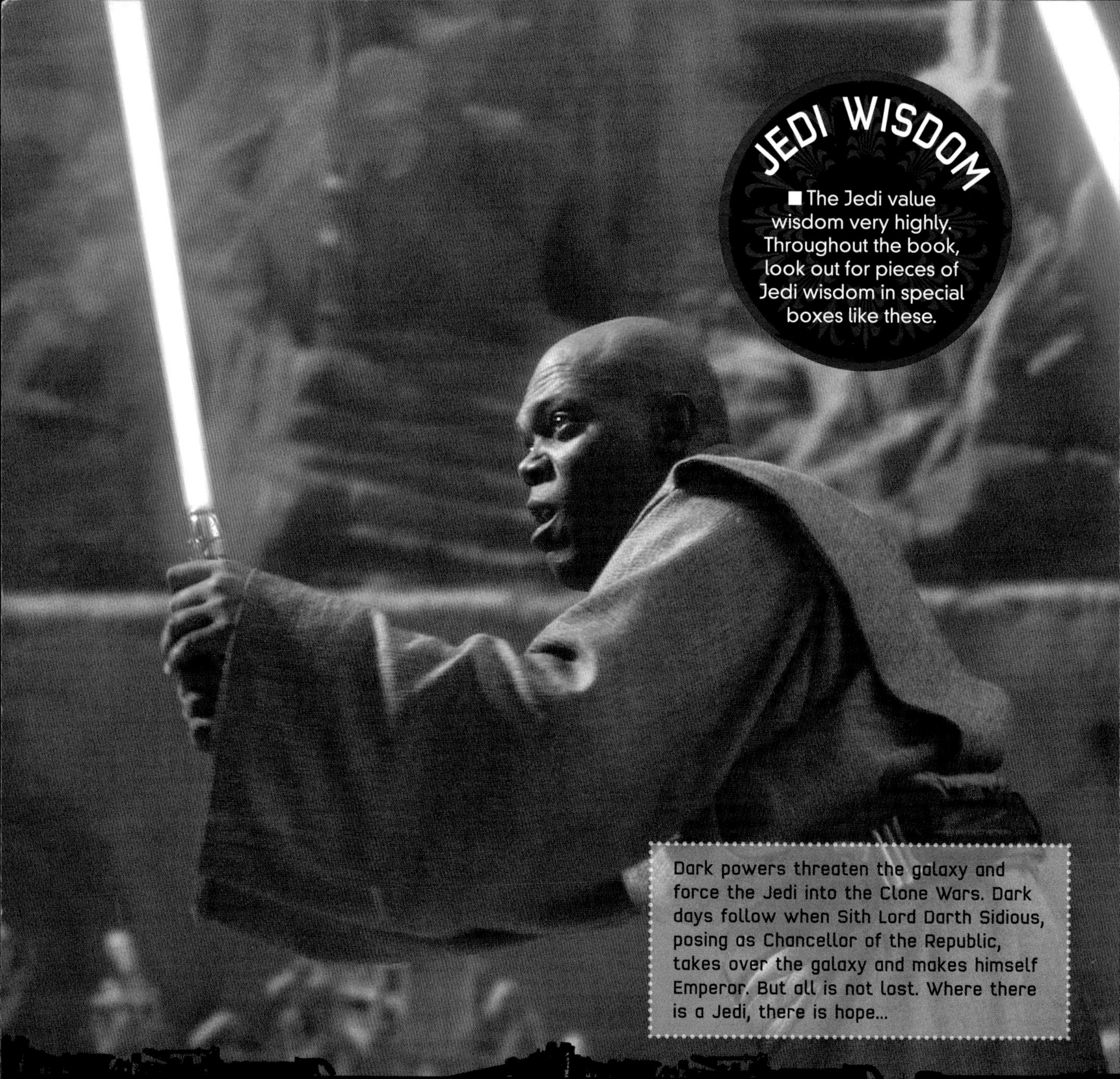

JEDI WISDOM

■ The Jedi value wisdom very highly. Throughout the book, look out for pieces of Jedi wisdom in special boxes like these.

Dark powers threaten the galaxy and force the Jedi into the Clone Wars. Dark days follow when Sith Lord Darth Sidious, posing as Chancellor of the Republic, takes over the galaxy and makes himself Emperor. But all is not lost. Where there is a Jedi, there is hope...

41 BBY: Birth of Anakin

32 BBY: Battle of Naboo

22 BBY: Battle of Geonosis

19 BBY: Birth of Luke and Leia

19 BBY: Jedi Purge

50 BBY

40 BBY

30 BBY

20 BBY

REPUBLIC ERA

THE CLONE WARS

THE JEDI

The word Jedi is known throughout the galaxy. It carries respect and wonder. Mention of the Jedi conjures up images of noble defenders of peace and justice, selfless heroes who put the Republic before themselves.

Despite the popularity of the Jedi, however, little is actually known about the inner workings of this ancient Order. Who exactly are these powerful knights? How do they use a kind of mystical energy known as the Force? How do you become a Jedi and what is it like to dedicate your life to a higher purpose? Welcome to the mysteries of the Jedi...

NOTE ON DATES: Dates are fixed around the Battle of Yavin in year 0. All events prior to this are measured in terms of years Before the Battle of Yavin (BBY). Events after it are measured in terms of years After the Battle of Yavin (ABY).

0 Battle of Yavin

2 BBY: Rebel Alliance is founded

3 ABY: Battle of Hoth

4 ABY: Battle of Endor

10 BBY   **0**   **10 ABY**   **20 ABY**

THE FORCE HAS TWO SIDES

THE FORCE IS AN invisible energy that flows through all living things. Studying the Force will grant you knowledge and power. You must use this power wisely, or face the consequences.

THE LIGHT SIDE

The Jedi study the light side of the Force and use their wisdom to uphold justice and protect the innocent. Using the Force allows Jedi to live in harmony with the galaxy, feel things before they see them, react quickly to danger and use a lightsaber with incredible skill.

- **BRAVERY**
- **WISDOM**
- **LOYALTY**
- **INNER STRENGTH**
- **JUSTICE**

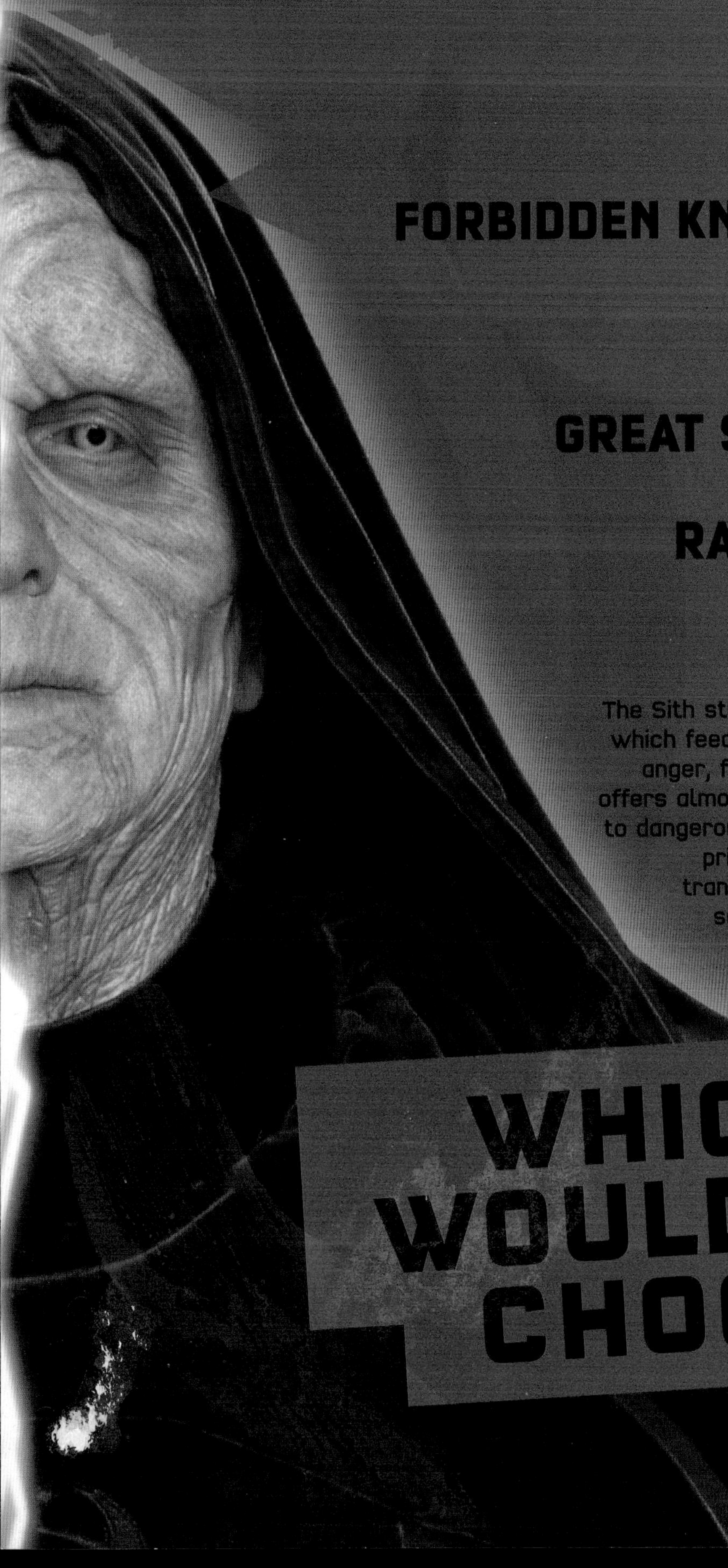

PASSION ■

FORBIDDEN KNOWLEDGE ■

FREEDOM ■

GREAT STRENGTH ■

RAW POWER ■

THE DARK SIDE

The Sith study the dark side of the Force, which feeds on negative feelings such as anger, fear and jealousy. The dark side offers almost unlimited power and access to dangerous knowledge, but at a terrible price. Submitting to the dark side transforms the Sith into something so evil, they cease to be human.

WHICH WOULD YOU CHOOSE?

FORCE JUMP
CHANNEL THROUGH: Full body
BEST FOR: Leaping out of harm's
way; quick movement during a
duel; surprising enemies
from a great height.
LEARN FROM: Yoda, who evades
his enemies during a duel with
multiple Force jumps.
DANGER LEVEL: Moderate

USING THE FORCE
The Force might
be invisible, but it can
be channelled through a
Jedi's body for a range
of different results.

FORCE DEFLECTION
CHANNEL THROUGH: Hands
BEST FOR: Shielding yourself from incoming attacks.
LEARN FROM: Yoda, who repulses deadly Sith lightning
fired at him by Chancellor Palpatine.
DANGER LEVEL: High

FORCE PILOTING
CHANNEL THROUGH:
Hands and eyes
BEST FOR: Steering
through busy airways.
LEARN FROM: Anakin, who
flies safely at super
speed above Coruscant.
DANGER LEVEL: High

FEEL THE FORCE

THE FORCE IS AN ENERGY FIELD that flows through
every living thing and is accessible to those with the
right mindset and training. Jedi spend many years
studying how to apply its many uses without causing
harm to themselves or others. Do you seek advice?
Are you being attacked? The Force can help.

TELEKINESIS

CHANNEL THROUGH: Hands
BEST FOR: Moving objects without touching them; summoning your lightsaber.
LEARN FROM: Yoda, who uses the Force to stop heavy objects from crushing himself and others during his battle with Count Dooku.
DANGER LEVEL: Moderate

BEAST CONTROL

CHANNEL THROUGH: Hands and mind
BEST FOR: Taming wild beasts that threaten your safety.
LEARN FROM: Anakin, who takes control of a particularly vicious reek in the execution arena on Geonosis.
DANGER LEVEL: High

FORCE GHOST

CHANNEL THROUGH: Spirit
BEST FOR: Living on after death to advise and guide others.
LEARN FROM: Obi-Wan, who becomes one with the Force after sacrificing himself on the Death Star.
DANGER LEVEL: Low, but only possible for a few rare Jedi.

FORCE DISTURBANCE

CHANNEL THROUGH: Heart and mind
BEST FOR: Sensing disturbances in the Force; letting you know what is happening elsewhere in the galaxy.
LEARN FROM: Yoda, who senses the start of the Jedi Purge.
DANGER LEVEL: Low

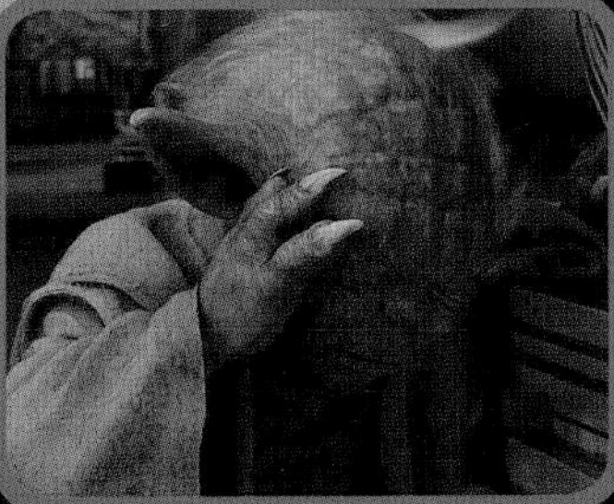

SITH COMBAT

The Sith use the dark side of the Force to fight viciously. Force choking weakens or kills through strangulation. Count Dooku uses it to attack Obi-Wan Kenobi. Force lightning is deadly blue crackling energy. These cruel uses of the Force are forbidden for Jedi.

JEDI MIND TRICK

CHANNEL THROUGH: Hands and mind
BEST FOR: Persuading others to leave you alone or to do what you want.
LEARN FROM: Obi-Wan, who convinces a stormtrooper patrol to let him pass through a checkpoint at Mos Eisley.
DANGER LEVEL: Low, but mind tricks work only on the weak-minded. A Jedi must be very careful not to abuse this power.

SMALL BUT STRONG
Never underestimate Yoda! Being small doesn't mean he can't be deadly. Yoda's strength comes from the Force. He achieves any height he needs in battle thanks to acrobatic Force jumps. When Count Dooku realises that Yoda is more than a match for him, he flees in his Solar Sailer.

Yoda is an immensely powerful Jedi who can control blue crackling Force lightning. It is a cruel weapon of the Sith so he never normally sees it. But he knows that sometimes you must destroy your enemy with their own weapons.

YODA

Yoda is Grand Master of the Jedi Council. He shoulders the great responsibility of leading the Jedi Order. Famous for his unmatched wisdom, Yoda has a strong connection with the Force and often turns to it for answers.

JEDI STATS
SPECIES: UNKNOWN
HOMEWORLD: CORUSCANT
BIRTHDATE: 896 BBY
HEIGHT: 66 CM (2 FT 2 IN)
RANK: JEDI GRAND MASTER
TRAINED BY: UNKNOWN
WEAPON: GREEN-BLADED LIGHTSABER
PREFERRED COMBAT STYLE: FORM IV (ATARU)
TRADEMARK: WISDOM

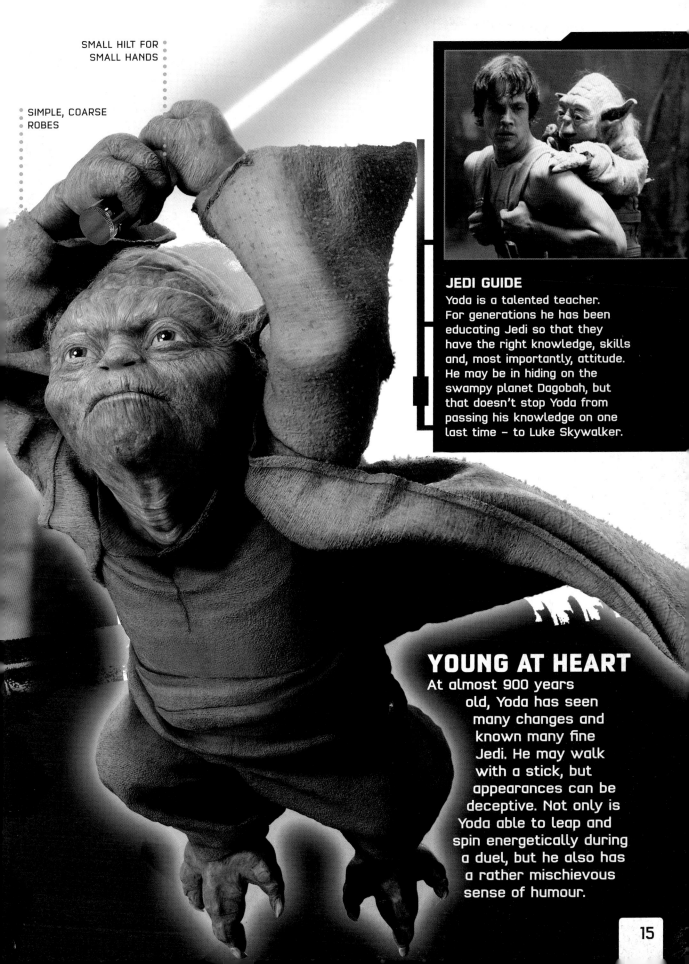

SMALL HILT FOR
SMALL HANDS

SIMPLE, COARSE
ROBES

JEDI GUIDE

Yoda is a talented teacher. For generations he has been educating Jedi so that they have the right knowledge, skills and, most importantly, attitude. He may be in hiding on the swampy planet Dagobah, but that doesn't stop Yoda from passing his knowledge on one last time – to Luke Skywalker.

YOUNG AT HEART

At almost 900 years old, Yoda has seen many changes and known many fine Jedi. He may walk with a stick, but appearances can be deceptive. Not only is Yoda able to leap and spin energetically during a duel, but he also has a rather mischievous sense of humour.

HOW DOES YODA FIGHT SOMEONE SO MUCH BIGGER THAN HIM?

YODA KNOWS THAT size matters not. The aged Jedi Grand Master is a skilled lightsaber warrior who can leap high and fight hard. When he takes on Darth Sidious in the Senate building on Coruscant, Yoda proves that his strength and power have nothing to do with his size.

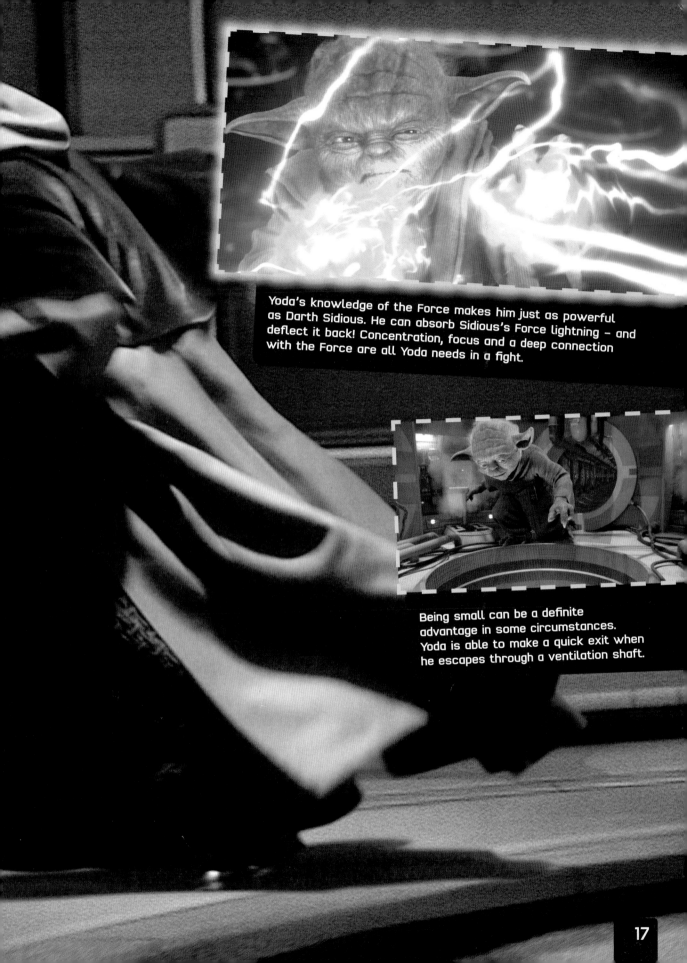

Yoda's knowledge of the Force makes him just as powerful as Darth Sidious. He can absorb Sidious's Force lightning – and deflect it back! Concentration, focus and a deep connection with the Force are all Yoda needs in a fight.

Being small can be a definite advantage in some circumstances. Yoda is able to make a quick exit when he escapes through a ventilation shaft.

THE JEDI CODE

Welcome to the Jedi Order. As a Jedi you will learn to harness great power – but you must never use it for personal gain. To live the life of a Jedi, you will need to follow the Jedi Code. It explains the path you must take to become powerful yet remain selfless. The Jedi way of life rests on three basic principles: self-discipline, knowledge and the Force.

SELF-DISCIPLINE

Your role as a Jedi must come before your own desires. That means having no possessions and not becoming emotionally attached. If a Jedi cares more for something or someone than he does about his mission, he might make a poor decision and jeopardise the safety of the galaxy.

THE FORCE

A Jedi must study the Force and live in tune with it. You must be able to control the Force, communicate with it and know its will. When you interact with the Force, you will possess great power. But you must use it wisely.

KNOWLEDGE

As a Jedi, you will value knowledge and wisdom in yourself and others. You must learn how to distinguish truth from lies, and how to seek out information so you can solve problems and resolve conflict.

**"THERE IS NO EMOTION, THERE IS PEACE.
THERE IS NO IGNORANCE, THERE IS KNOWLEDGE.
THERE IS NO PASSION, THERE IS SERENITY.
THERE IS NO CHAOS, THERE IS HARMONY.
THERE IS NO DEATH, THERE IS THE FORCE."**

The quick-thinking Jedi blast their way out of the trap and turn the situation to their advantage. Checking out the ship, they find a huge army and learn that Naboo is about to be invaded. They escape aboard Trade Federation transits to send warning of the attack.

JEDI WISDOM

■ The Trade Federation is an organisation that supports business across the galaxy. It is not normally violent, but it has come under the control of the Sith Lord Darth Sidious.

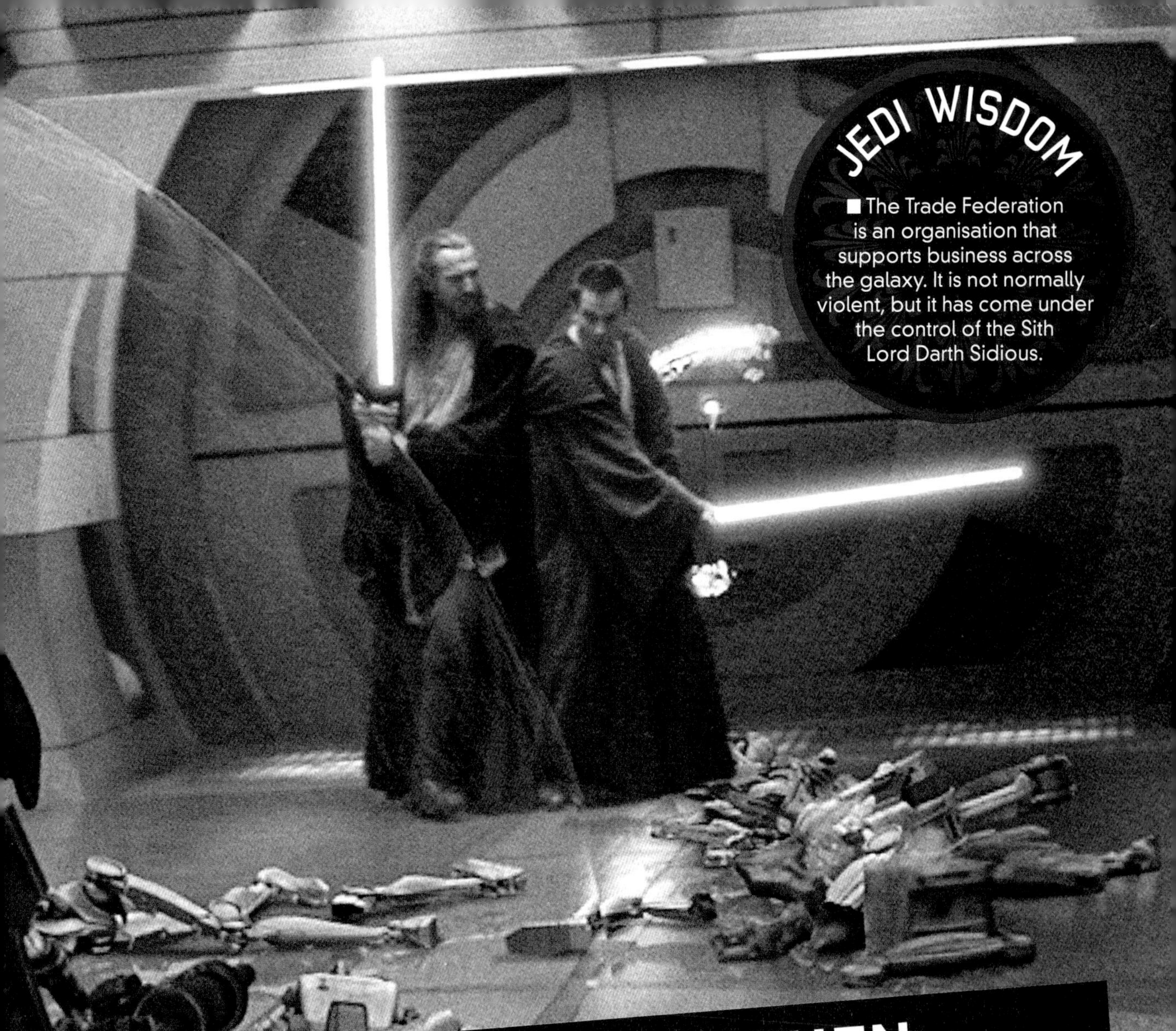

WHAT HAPPENS WHEN NEGOTIATIONS FAIL?

JEDI SEEK TO KEEP PEACE THROUGH discussion and reason, but sometimes actions speak louder than words. Qui-Gon Jinn and Obi-Wan Kenobi arrive on a Trade Federation transport on a diplomatic mission to negotiate a solution to the Naboo blockade crisis. However, it is a trap. Before they are even able to enter talks, the two Jedi are attacked. Having sensed all was not well with the Force, they are quick to respond, defending themselves against battle droids and droidekas.

HOW CAN YOU BECOME A JEDI?

Not everyone can become a Jedi – it requires dedication, hard work and a sensitivity to the Force. It can take more than 20 years of training and there are several stages to go through. If you show promise and are selected, your Jedi career starts here. Good luck!

JEDI COUNCIL

The Jedi Council is made up of 12 Jedi, who are in charge of running the Jedi Order. They resolve disputes, make decisions and uphold the Jedi Code.

YOUNGLING

Great news! You have been selected to train as a Jedi. You will start as a Youngling and will live in the Jedi Temple, where you will study the basics of the Force. Most Jedi begin their training when they are babies, but some successful Jedi have started later. Get ready to work hard!

GRAND MASTER
YODA

GRAND MASTER

You'll have to be right at the top of your game to reach this rank. As Grand Master, Yoda is the head of not just the Jedi High Council, but the whole Order. Along with other Council members, he selects who will become Younglings.

PADAWAN ANAKIN SKYWALKER

JEDI TRIALS

When your Master thinks you have finished your training as a Padawan, you will sit the Jedi Trials. These gruelling tasks will push you to your limits to prove you are ready for Jedi Knighthood.

PADAWAN

Well done! You have excelled as a Youngling and have been selected by a Jedi to be their Padawan. From now on, you will travel with your Master and get one-to-one training from them. Going on missions is dangerous but it's the best way to learn.

JEDI KNIGHT AAYLA SECURA

JEDI MASTER LUMINARA UNDULI

JEDI KNIGHT

Congratulations! You must have shown great courage and strength in the Jedi Trials because you passed and are a qualified Jedi Knight. Now you can go on your own missions and even train your own Padawan.

JEDI MASTER

Once you have trained your own Padawan, you may be promoted to Jedi Master. As a Master, you will continue the duties of a Jedi and can choose another Padawan. If you show exceptional devotion and skill, you may be invited to sit on the Jedi High Council – a great honour.

WHY SHOULD A PADAWAN LISTEN TO HIS MASTER?

Anakin's impulsive attack gives Count Dooku the chance to overpower him and Obi-Wan easily. Anakin's haste also costs him his arm when Dooku's lightsaber slices it off.

Yoda arrives just in time to save Obi-Wan and Anakin, but Dooku escapes, taking with him plans for a superweapon called the Death Star. The Jedi miss the chance to learn more about their mysterious Sith enemy, to end the Clone Wars before they have really begun and to prevent the building of the Death Star, partially because Anakin failed to heed Obi-Wan.

JEDI IN TRAINING do not study only in safe classrooms. They face real cases of life and death, with only the experience and wisdom of their Masters to guide them. When Obi-Wan and Anakin face Count Dooku, Obi-Wan knows they should fight him together. But the Padawan's anger makes him rush to attack the Sith.

WHO TAUGHT WHO?

LEARNING THE JEDI ARTS isn't easy! Every young Padawan is teamed up with a Jedi Master who shares his or her wisdom and experience with them. For centuries, skills have been passed from generation to generation as Padawans become Masters and then take on their own Padawans.

THE JEDI ▶

Ki-Adi-Mundi

Ki-Adi-Mundi began Jedi training at the age of four, which was considered late. However, thanks to his skill, dedication and guidance from Yoda, he caught up with his peers and became a good Jedi.

YODA

Yoda has been training Jedi for centuries. This natural teacher is dedicated to helping those who want to learn, but he expects complete commitment from them in return. He is quick to point out a student's shortcomings, but also offers guidance on how to overcome them.

Count Dooku

Count Dooku often expressed controversial ideas about the Jedi Order. After his training with Master Yoda, Dooku passed on his unconventional views to his own Padawan, the young Qui-Gon Jinn.

THE SITH ▶

DARTH SIDIOUS

DARTH PLAGUEIS

Sith also follow a Master/pupil system, but the Rule of Two states there may be only two Sith at a time. When Darth Sidious murdered his Master, the mysterious Darth Plagueis, he then searched for his own Apprentice.

Darth Maul

From a young age, Darth Maul was trained as Sidious's Apprentice in secret. He revealed his existence to the Jedi, which eventually led to his death.

Not all teachings begin with Yoda. There are many strands of Masters and Padawans. They represent ancient lines of Jedi wisdom that are still being passed on today. Here are just a few.

 YADDLE Oppo Rancisis

 MACE WINDU Depa Billaba

LUMINARA UNDULI Barriss Offee

CLOSE BONDS

It is an honour to pass on your skills to young Jedi. However, it's not always easy. Masters don't just teach Padawans facts, they must mould their characters with Jedi values, develop their skills and take care of them in dangerous situations. In these intense relationships, Jedi often form strong bonds that last beyond training.

Qui-Gon Jinn

Qui-Gon was rebellious and outspoken, but he was loyal to the Jedi Order – unlike his former Master, Count Dooku. Qui-Gon's Padawan, Obi-Wan Kenobi, often disagreed with Qui-Gon's opinions, but he also respected Qui-Gon's wisdom and skill.

Obi-Wan Kenobi

At first Obi-Wan struggled to find a Master due to his rash temperament. However, thanks to Qui-Gon's patience and guidance, Obi-Wan became a model Jedi. As Qui-Gon was dying, he made Obi-Wan promise to train Anakin Skywalker.

Anakin Skywalker

Anakin and Obi-Wan developed a very close bond, even though Anakin didn't always agree with his Master. Anakin was often difficult and stubborn, so when he was assigned a Padawan he was given someone equally as stubborn. Anakin learned a lot about teaching when he trained Ahsoka Tano.

Ahsoka Tano

Ahsoka was proud to be Anakin's Padawan. Although their strong personalities clashed at first, they went on to develop a great relationship.

Luke Skywalker

Under the Empire, after the Jedi Purge, the Jedi arts were at risk of being lost. Through Luke, they were preserved and went on to flourish.

Darth Tyranus

For his next Apprentice, Darth Sidious chose the Jedi Count Dooku. He tempted him over to the dark side with promises of great power. Dooku took the Sith name Darth Tyranus, but was ultimately betrayed by Sidious to make way for his next Apprentice, Darth Vader.

Darth Vader

Darth Sidious set his sights on another Jedi for his next Apprentice – Anakin Skywalker. Anakin eventually turned to the dark side and took the name Darth Vader.

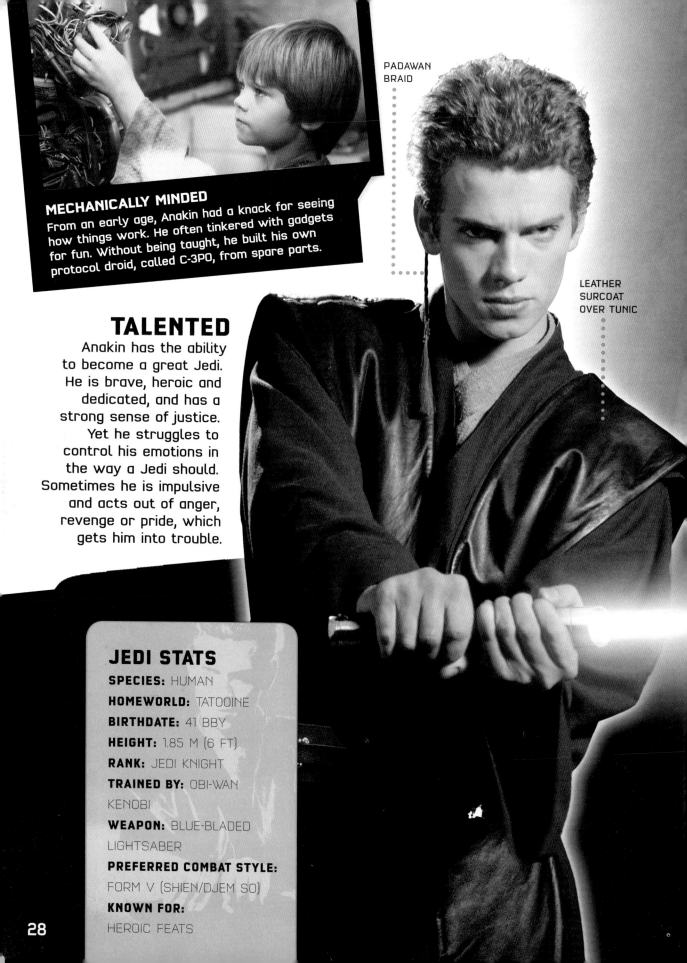

MECHANICALLY MINDED
From an early age, Anakin had a knack for seeing how things work. He often tinkered with gadgets for fun. Without being taught, he built his own protocol droid, called C-3PO, from spare parts.

PADAWAN BRAID

LEATHER SURCOAT OVER TUNIC

TALENTED
Anakin has the ability to become a great Jedi. He is brave, heroic and dedicated, and has a strong sense of justice. Yet he struggles to control his emotions in the way a Jedi should. Sometimes he is impulsive and acts out of anger, revenge or pride, which gets him into trouble.

JEDI STATS

SPECIES: HUMAN

HOMEWORLD: TATOOINE

BIRTHDATE: 41 BBY

HEIGHT: 1.85 M (6 FT)

RANK: JEDI KNIGHT

TRAINED BY: OBI-WAN KENOBI

WEAPON: BLUE-BLADED LIGHTSABER

PREFERRED COMBAT STYLE: FORM V (SHIEN/DJEM SO)

KNOWN FOR: HEROIC FEATS

Anakin's fighting style uses strong, powerful attacks. As a Padawan, however, he underestimates Count Dooku – which costs him his arm.

Anakin
SKYWALKER

As a young boy, Anakin discovers that he is the Chosen One who will bring balance to the Force. But prophecies do not always play out as expected. Anakin has the potential to be the most skilled Jedi ever known, but only he can determine his future.

SHOW-OFF
Anakin is good at being a Jedi – and he knows it. He likes proving that he is better than his Master Obi-Wan, whether he's finding a better way to catch an assassin or flying super fast.

HOW CAN A HUMAN SURVIVE A PODRACE?

JEDI WISDOM

■ Some aliens are good Podracers because they have super-fast reflexes, but it doesn't mean they have the other skills needed to be a Jedi.

Anakin has a talent for understanding how things work. He even built his own Podracer. When it gets damaged, he can fix it himself in mid-air, without having to leave the race.

Podracers don't always play fair – they sometimes try to win by smashing each other's vehicles to pieces. Anakin uses the Force to stay calm and focus on the race so he is unfazed by the attacks from his fiercest competitor, Sebulba.

PODRACING ON TATOOINE is so dangerous that even the best racers are lucky to survive. It's too fast for humans, but Anakin Skywalker is no ordinary human – he has Jedi reflexes. His ability with the Force means he can navigate every swerve and tight corner of the Boonta Eve Classic Podrace, all at super-high speeds. Not only does he survive; he wins!

Practice for the Trial of Skill begins at a young age in classes at the Jedi Temple.

TRIAL OF SKILL

The JEDI

The Jedi Trials are an occasion to prove that you are ready to become a Jedi Knight after years of gruelling study.

• FOCUS • KNOWLEDGE • INTELLIGENCE

TRIAL OF SKILL

Simply repeating what you have learned in class will not get you through the Trial of Skill. You must be able to demonstrate that you can apply your complex knowledge, values and skills under pressure and in different situations.

TRIAL OF FLESH

Brace yourself. As a Jedi, you will have to endure physical and emotional pain and suffer extremes of hunger, heat and cold. In the Trial of Flesh, you must prove you can rise above these hardships and focus your thoughts elsewhere.

• DETACHMENT • ENDURANCE • STRENGTH

TRIAL OF FLESH

Anakin experiences his Trial of Flesh when he loses part of his arm, including his hand, in combat with Count Dooku. From then on, he has a mechanical hand.

32

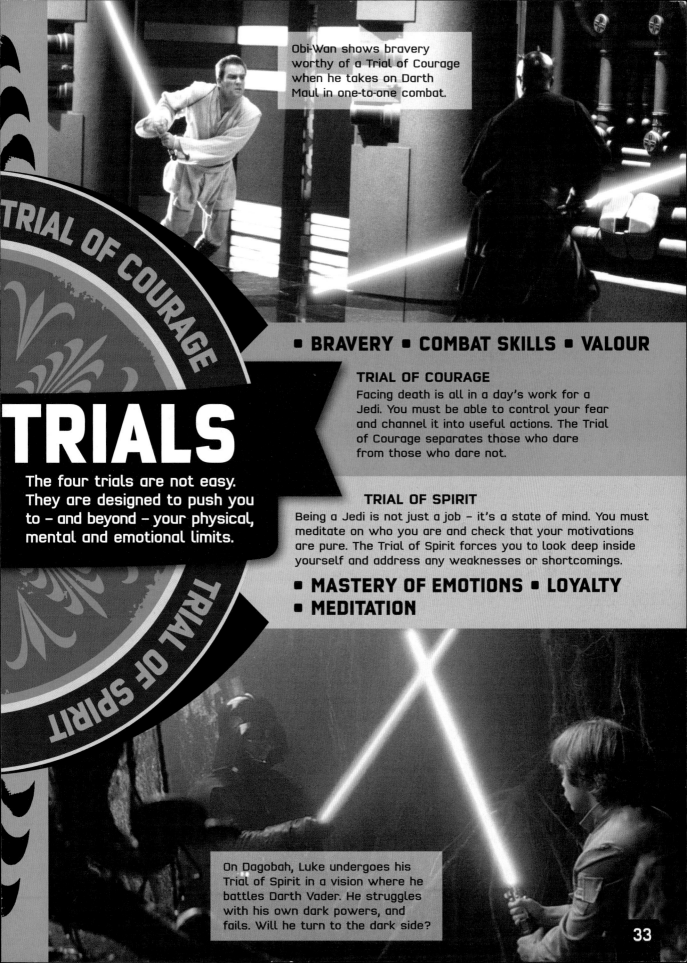

Obi-Wan shows bravery worthy of a Trial of Courage when he takes on Darth Maul in one-to-one combat.

TRIAL OF COURAGE

TRIALS

The four trials are not easy. They are designed to push you to – and beyond – your physical, mental and emotional limits.

• BRAVERY • COMBAT SKILLS • VALOUR

TRIAL OF COURAGE
Facing death is all in a day's work for a Jedi. You must be able to control your fear and channel it into useful actions. The Trial of Courage separates those who dare from those who dare not.

TRIAL OF SPIRIT
Being a Jedi is not just a job – it's a state of mind. You must meditate on who you are and check that your motivations are pure. The Trial of Spirit forces you to look deep inside yourself and address any weaknesses or shortcomings.

• MASTERY OF EMOTIONS • LOYALTY • MEDITATION

TRIAL OF SPIRIT

On Dagobah, Luke undergoes his Trial of Spirit in a vision where he battles Darth Vader. He struggles with his own dark powers, and fails. Will he turn to the dark side?

A Jedi needs to be very skilled with a lightsaber, but also lucky. Qui-Gon's luck runs out against the Sith Lord Darth Maul, but he meets his death valiantly.

MAVERICK

Qui-Gon is quick to speak his mind. He believes in the Jedi way, but his interpretation of it sometimes brings him into conflict with the Jedi Council. This rebellious streak has cost him a seat on the Council. However, Qui-Gon is not interested in politics; he prefers to be true to himself.

TWO-HANDED GRIP FOR PRECISION

Qui-Gon
JINN

Qui-Gon is a wise and powerful Jedi Master. He follows the values of the Jedi Code, but is not afraid to think for himself. He is very conscious of the living Force and is mindful of its will. Qui-Gon likes to live in the moment and focus on the present.

JEDI STATS

SPECIES: HUMAN
HOMEWORLD: UNKNOWN
BIRTHDATE: 92 BBY
HEIGHT: 1.93 M (6 FT 4 IN)
RANK: JEDI MASTER
TRAINED BY: COUNT DOOKU
WEAPON: GREEN-BLADED LIGHTSABER
PREFERRED COMBAT STYLE: FORM IV (ATARU)
TRADEMARK: MAVERICK

ALL HEART

Qui-Gon has a compassionate nature that often spurs him to go beyond the call of duty to help others. On Naboo, he speaks up to save Jar Jar Binks from certain death. In return, the grateful Gungan gives Qui-Gon his loyalty and service, which prove invaluable for the Jedi during the Battle of Naboo.

WELL-WORN
JEDI ROBE

LONG HAIR IS A SIGN OF
HIS REBELLIOUS NATURE

DETERMINED

Qui-Gon is very self-assured in his opinions. When he finds Anakin on Tatooine, he is convinced that the slave boy is the Chosen One. Qui-Gon is so sure that he risks his own ship in a bet with Anakin's greedy owner, Watto, to win the boy's freedom. He also insists that Anakin be trained as a Jedi, even though it goes against the Jedi Council.

WHAT DOES IT TAKE TO DEFEAT A SITH?

Such is Darth Maul's skill with his double-bladed lightsaber, that Qui-Gon and Obi-Wan must both dig deep to duel him. While Obi-Wan is trapped behind a laser door, Qui-Gon falters in the heat of battle and pays the ultimate price.

With his Master slain, Obi-Wan now fights Darth Maul. The Jedi appears to be at the Sith's mercy: hanging over an abyss, his weapon lost. Using his quick thinking, strength and the element of surprise, Obi-Wan uses the Force to jump high and grab Qui-Gon's lightsaber. He defeats an unsuspecting Maul with one swift blow.

THE SITH ARE FIERCE warriors who wield great power. They have been in hiding for centuries, honing their skills and biding their time. Finally, they reveal themselves to the Jedi. Darth Maul briefly appeared on Tatooine. Now he is on Naboo and it takes two great Jedi to battle him.

YOU CAN TELL A LOT BY A JEDI'S
BODY LANGUAGE

JEDI MISSIONS ARE OFTEN highly dangerous and shrouded in secrecy. However, by paying attention to a Jedi's body language and clothing, you may pick up some clues about what they are up to.

HANDS CLASPED

Clasped hands under a cloak cannot reach easily for a weapon. Jedi stand like this on diplomatic missions as a sign of peace, service and respect.

BLENDING IN

If you spot a Jedi wearing non-Jedi clothes, don't approach him. He is probably on an undercover mission and wants to keep his Jedi identity secret.

HOOD ON

If you see a Jedi with his hood on, don't disturb him – it means he's on a secret mission. A Jedi will wear his hood to help deflect attention when it's not safe for him to be out in the open.

CLOAK OFF

When you see a Jedi discard his or her cloak, get ready for action! Their long cloaks are not practical when fighting; a Jedi needs to be able to move freely.

TOUGH TASKMASTER

Luminara expects the same high standards of her Padawan and her troops as she does of herself. She is demanding and strict, but is respected so she gets the best out of people.

JEDI STATS

SPECIES: MIRIALAN
HOMEWORLD: MIRIAL
BIRTHDATE: 58 BBY
HEIGHT: 1.70 M (5 FT 7 IN)
RANK: JEDI MASTER
TRAINED BY: UNKNOWN
PREFERRED COMBAT STYLE: FORM III (SORESU)
TRADEMARK: ADHERENCE TO RULES

HUMBLE ADVISOR

Luminara is a trusted contributor to the Jedi Council, but is mindful of her position. She stands back respectfully and offers her opinion only when asked for it.

Luminara UNDULI

FLOWING MIRIALAN ROBES

Jedi Master Luminara Unduli is a stickler for the rules. As far as she's concerned, there's little room in the Jedi Code for self-expression. For her, the cornerstones of the Jedi Order are discipline, discipline, discipline.

JEDI STATS

SPECIES: MIRIALAN

HOMEWORLD: MIRIAL

BIRTHDATE: 40 BBY

HEIGHT: 1.66 M (5 FT 5 IN)

RANK: JEDI KNIGHT

TRAINED BY: LUMINARA UNDULI

PREFERRED COMBAT STYLE: FORM III (SORESU)

TRADEMARK: RESPONSIBILITY

A HEALING FORCE

Barriss has a strong connection to the Force. This helps her wield her lightsaber like a pro. But even more valuable in the middle of war, Barriss is an expert at using the Force to heal sick or injured people.

MIRIALAN TATTOOS

Barriss OFFEE

Barriss Offee is a model Padawan. She is loyal, obedient and respectful to her strict Master, Luminara Unduli. After earning her knighthood during the Clone Wars, she continues to serve alongside Luminara.

STEPPING UP

Barriss is only a Padawan when she is flung into the Clone Wars. Her lightsaber skills and cool head help her rise to meet the challenge.

41

HOW TO BUILD A LIGHTSABER

THE LIGHTSABER is an ancient sword known for its elegance as well as its power in battle. It is the weapon of choice for both the Jedi and their enemies, the Sith. Lightsabers consist of a handle, or "hilt", that emits a coloured blade of plasma energy. As part of their training, every Jedi learns how to build their own lightsaber. All lightsabers contain these eight basic parts, but you can vary the design to suit your own taste and needs.

JEDI WISDOM

■ During the Knighting Ceremony when a Padawan becomes a Knight, a lightsaber is used to cut off the Padawan's braid.

MAIN HILT ■

The plasma for the blade is created here in the blade energy channel from a special type of gas.

■ BLADE EMITTER

This is where the plasma blade beams out. The metal ring houses the base of the blade and makes sure it keeps its cylindrical shape.

FOCUSING LENS ■

The focusing lens channels the plasma for the blade and makes sure it has a fixed end point. Most blades are one meter (3¼ feet) long, but they can vary.

BLADE ENERGY CHANNEL

CRYSTAL

A crystal sits at the heart of every lightsaber and gives the blade its bright colour. Most Jedi lightsabers glow blue or green because they use crystals mined on the planet Ilum. The Sith prefer to make their own artificial crystals so their blades glow a more fearsome red colour.

The crystal also determines the length of the blade. Having more than one crystal means you can vary the length of your blade. Many Jedi believe that three is best number of crystals to have.

POWER CELL ■

Energy from special diatium batteries stored in the power cell heats up gas to create plasma for the blade.

POMMEL CAP ■

The pommel seals the end of the lightsaber. It often contains a back-up battery. If you want, you can add a ring that clips to your belt.

■ CONTROLS

Buttons activate the blade, but Jedi who are very skilled in the Force can control these things using the Force instead.

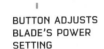

BUTTON ADJUSTS BLADE'S POWER SETTING

ENERGY GATE

BUTTON ADJUSTS BLADE'S LENGTH

■ HANDGRIP

This outer part of the hilt is covered in ridges so that the lightsaber doesn't fly out of your hand while you are swinging it around.

DOS AND DON'TS

■ Don't plunge your blade into water – it will sizzle out unless it has been specially adapted to work underwater.

■ Take care of your lightsaber – if you lose it, it can take a month to build a new one.

■ Make sure your power cell is covered with an inert power insulator, otherwise you could get electrocuted!

■ Keep fit: the forces acting on the weightless blade mean that a lightsaber requires strong arms to control it.

■ Study the Force: anyone can wield a lightsaber, but only those with Force powers can unlock its true potential.

■ Be careful: the blade can slice through almost anything. (Any injuries you get won't bleed because the blade is so hot it seals the skin, but that doesn't mean they won't hurt!)

■ Keep your lightsaber in good condition and it could last forever and never run out of power.

WHAT HAPPENS WHEN A CYBORG STUDIES JEDI SKILLS?

General Grievous is a fearsome fighter, and his lightsabers make him all the more deadly. But he doesn't understand the Force. Obi-Wan shows him that four lightsabers are no match for one lightsaber wielded by a true Jedi.

Grievous thinks he is better than the Jedi. However, no Jedi thinks himself above anyone. Grievous's arrogance is his downfall. Obi-Wan struggles in their duel, but in the end, his emotional detachment brings him victory.

COUNT DOOKU HAS trained General Grievous in the Jedi arts. These lightsaber skills have made the part-machine, part-organic warrior even more dangerous. However, just being able to wield a lightsaber doesn't make him a Jedi. Not that he wants to be a Jedi: Grievous likes nothing better than killing Jedi and adding their lightsabers to his creepy collection.

JEDI WISDOM

■ General Grievous was a reptilian Kaleesh warrior who was injured in battle. Now all that remains of his body are his brain and the organs encased in his metal chest.

45

HOW DO YOU FIGHT WITH A LIGHTSABER?

Wielding a lightsaber may look easy, but it is a difficult skill that requires much training. There are seven main forms of lightsaber combat. Every Jedi has a favourite, but the most skilled can switch between all the styles depending on the situation.

TRAINING HELMET

SHII-CHO BASIC STANCE

Luke begins with Shii-Cho as a way of learning to channel the Force and master his lightsaber. This exercise involves deflecting blasts from a training remote.

FORM I: SHII-CHO

When trainee Jedi get their lightsabers, the first thing they learn is Form I. It introduces them to all the basic parts of lightsaber combat: how to attack and how to defend or "parry". To master it properly, Younglings practise all the steps again and again in drills known as "velocities".

ALSO KNOWN AS: Way of the Sarlacc or Determination Form

FORM II: MAKASHI

Makashi is a development of Shii-Cho that is designed for lightsaber-to-lightsaber duels. Precision and discipline are key to Makashi, rather than strength or power. The style requires very accurate bladework and elegant, well-balanced footwork.

ALSO KNOWN AS: Way of the Ysalamir or Contention Form

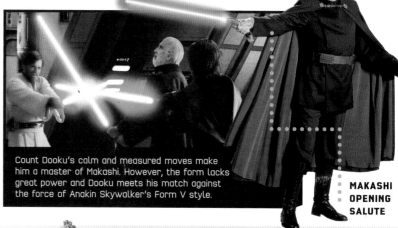

Count Dooku's calm and measured moves make him a master of Makashi. However, the form lacks great power and Dooku meets his match against the force of Anakin Skywalker's Form V style.

MAKASHI OPENING SALUTE

BLADE PROTECTS BODY

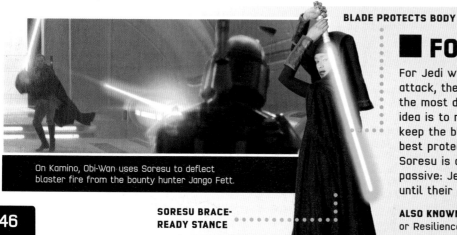

On Kamino, Obi-Wan uses Soresu to deflect blaster fire from the bounty hunter Jango Fett.

SORESU BRACE-READY STANCE

FORM III: SORESU

For Jedi who find themselves under blaster attack, then Soresu is a good choice. It is the most defensive of the seven forms. The idea is to make only small movements and keep the blade close to the body to give the best protection from blaster fire. Although Soresu is defensive, it does not have to be passive: Jedi sometimes defend themselves until their opponent tires – then they attack.

ALSO KNOWN AS: Way of the Mynock or Resilience Form

FORM IV: ATARU

For agile and athletic Jedi, Ataru is a good option. Masters of this form use acrobatic jumps, twirls and twists to drive power into their bold attacks. It's also handy for short Jedi like Yoda who want to add height to their reach. Furthermore, it's useful for confusing and distracting your opponent.

ALSO KNOWN AS: Way of the Hawk-Bat or Aggression Form

ATARU
PRE-JUMP
STANCE

Obi-Wan uses his mastery of Ataru along with the Force to add great power to his lightsaber moves.

FORM V: SHIEN/DJEM SO

The two versions of Form V developed out of Form III to combine aggression with the defensive style. Shien is used for redirecting blaster bolts back at the person who fired them. Djem So is used to push back another lightsaber during a duel. Whichever a Jedi chooses, they must be strong and fit so their deflective moves really pack a punch.

ALSO KNOWN AS: Way of the Krayt Dragon or Perseverance Form

Anakin is very strong and he uses this power to drive aggression into his Djem So attacks.

DJEM SO OPENING STANCE

FORM VI: NIMAN

Niman is about balance and harmony rather than aggressive power. It is a good choice for Jedi who are less experienced in battle because it is less demanding than the other forms. It covers the basic moves, but is too general for some situations so is often used with other Force powers like telekinesis.

ALSO KNOWN AS: Way of the Rancor or Moderation Form

Niman is very popular during the Battle of Geonosis among Jedi like Joclad Danva.

NIMAN OPENING STANCE

VAAPAD OPENING STANCE

Mace is one of the few Jedi strong enough to use dark feelings without falling to the dark side.

FORM VII: JUYO/VAAPAD

If a Jedi is super-energetic, then the big, direct moves of Form VII could be their best option. But this style comes with a warning: Form VII can be dangerous because it taps into powerful emotions that can open a Jedi up to the dark side. Juyo is the original version. Vaapad is a variant developed by the Jedi Master Mace Windu that particularly focuses on a Jedi's state of mind.

ALSO KNOWN AS: Way of Vornskr or Ferocity Form

Mace's hilt is plated with golden electrum metal – a decoration reserved for senior Jedi.

Mace chooses a rare crystal that emits a violet glow.

Anakin Skywalker's Lightsaber

Mace Windu's Lightsaber

Luke Skywalker's Lightsaber

Youngling Lightsaber

This lightsaber is passed from Anakin to Luke. It is lost when Luke fights Darth Vader on Cloud City.

After Luke loses his first lightsaber fighting Darth Vader, he builds a new one using notes left by Obi-Wan.

Younglings practise with safety blades. The power setting is very low to avoid injuries.

"Your lightsaber is ...YOUR LIFE!"

OBI-WAN TO ANAKIN

The Sith Darth Maul chooses a saberstaff, which is double-bladed. These are harder to use, but some Sith favour them because they look more menacing and allow a more aggressive style of combat.

Darth Maul's Lightsaber

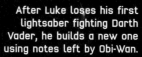

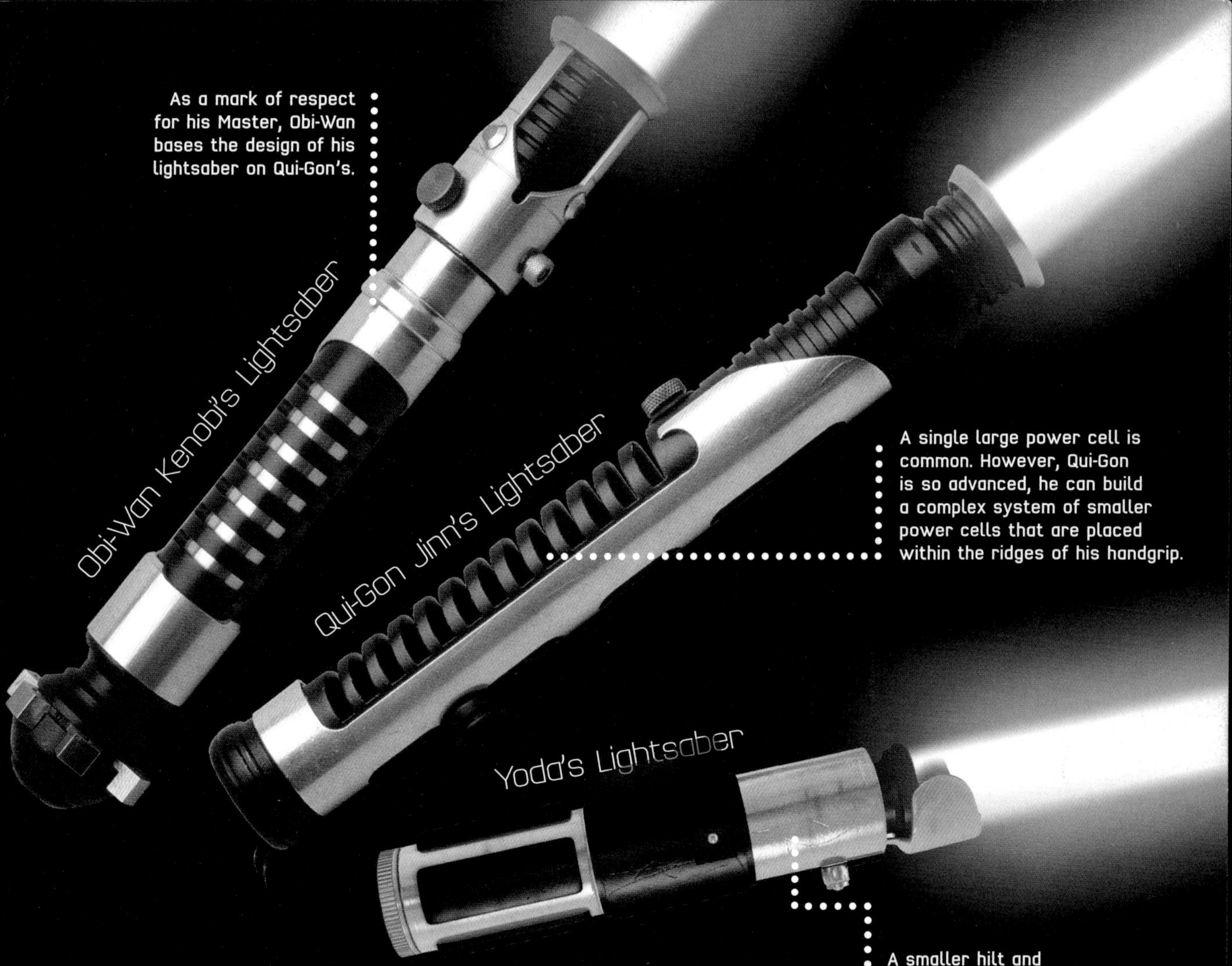

As a mark of respect for his Master, Obi-Wan bases the design of his lightsaber on Qui-Gon's.

Obi-Wan Kenobi's Lightsaber

Qui-Gon Jinn's Lightsaber

A single large power cell is common. However, Qui-Gon is so advanced, he can build a complex system of smaller power cells that are placed within the ridges of his handgrip.

Yoda's Lightsaber

A smaller hilt and shorter blade are perfectly sized for Yoda.

LIGHTSABER SPOTTING

JEDI WISDOM

■ Jedi lightsabers use natural crystals that usually glow blue or green. The Sith use synthetic crystals which glow red; a more menacing colour.

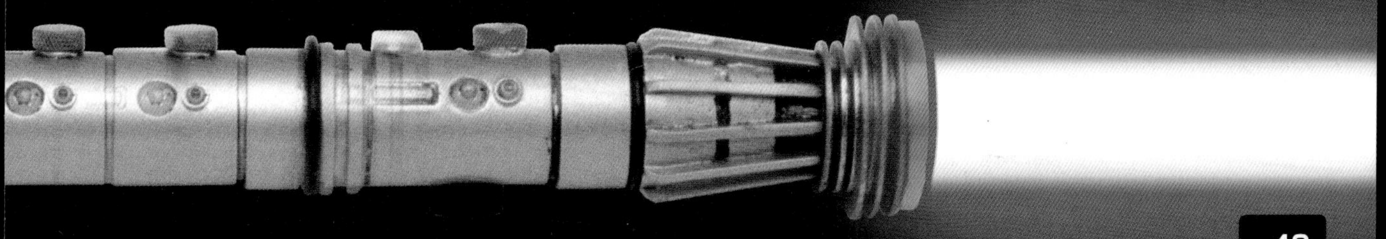

EVERY LIGHTSABER IS handmade by its owner, so there is a dazzling array of variations. A Jedi or Sith can customise the handle, controls, size and colour according to their needs and their tastes.

Aayla SECURA

JEDI STATS
SPECIES: TWI'LEK
HOMEWORLD: RYLOTH
BIRTHDATE: UNKNOWN
HEIGHT: 1.78 M (5 FT 10 IN)
RANK: JEDI MASTER
TRAINED BY: QUINLAN VOS & THOLME
PREFERRED COMBAT STYLE: FORM IV (ATARU) & FORM V (SHIEN/DJEM SO)
TRADEMARK: EMPATHY

BRUSH WITH EVIL

Aayla knows first hand what the temptations of the dark side can be. In her youth, she struggled with dark powers, but this has made her stronger. She is a more determined Jedi as a result.

RUTIAN SKIN COLOUR

LEKKU (HEAD TAILS) CAN EXPRESS EMOTIONS

RESPECTED

Aayla's skill and easy-going nature make her a popular General during the Clone Wars. She soon rises to the rank of Master. However, her career is brought to a swift end when she is killed in the Jedi Purge.

Aayla Secura is a talented Twi'lek Jedi with distinctive blue skin. Her quick thinking has saved many lives. She brings a light-hearted and mischievous approach to the serious business of being a Jedi.

KI-ADI-MUNDI

LARGE BINARY BRAIN

As a Cerean, Ki-Adi-Mundi believes in a simple way of life, and this simplicity serves him well as a Jedi. His large Cerean brain gives him extra thinking power and earns him a well-deserved seat on the Jedi High Council.

BODY HAS TWO HEARTS TO SUPPORT LARGE BRAIN

BRAINY GENERAL

The outbreak of the Clone Wars sees Ki-Adi-Mundi's insightful and logical mind put to work on the battlefield. He leads his troops with honour and survives the conflict, only to die in the Jedi Purge.

JEDI STATS

SPECIES: CEREAN

HOMEWORLD: CEREA

BIRTHDATE: 92 BBY

HEIGHT: 1.98 M (6 FT 6 IN)

RANK: JEDI MASTER

TRAINED BY: YODA

PREFERRED COMBAT STYLE: FORM III (SORESU)

TRADEMARK: INTELLIGENCE

FAMILY MAN

Although Jedi are not allowed to marry or have children, a special exception is made for Ki-Adi-Mundi because the Cereans have a very low birthrate. Nevertheless, he always puts his duties as a Jedi ahead of his feelings, even when his family is killed in the Clone Wars.

THE JEDI TEMPLE TOUR

The Jedi Temple stands out on Coruscant thanks to its unique appearance. One of the oldest and largest buildings on the planet, the 4,000-year-old Temple has a huge, pyramid-like base and five colossal spires. It is the headquarters of the Jedi Order. Come, take the Jedi Temple Tour.

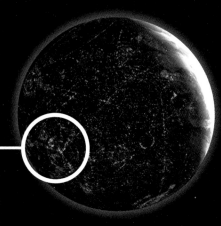

THE PLANET

Welcome to Coruscant – a planet entirely covered by a single city. You are visiting the place that is the most important political hub in the galaxy, thanks to its central location. Coruscant was the capital city of the Republic, home to the Galactic Senate, the office of the Chancellor, and, of course, the Jedi Temple. During the Emperor's reign, the planet was also home to the Imperial Palace. Enjoy your stay!

COUNCIL OF FIRST KNOWLEDGE TOWER

SURFACE LIFE

This planet is a bustling metropolis, full of bright lights and congested skylanes. It is home to over 1 trillion residents, made up of a multitude of races and species. Many areas are built up with beautiful, modern architecture – but be warned! A dangerous underworld lurks in the shadows. Watch out for prowling gangs who make some areas unsafe.

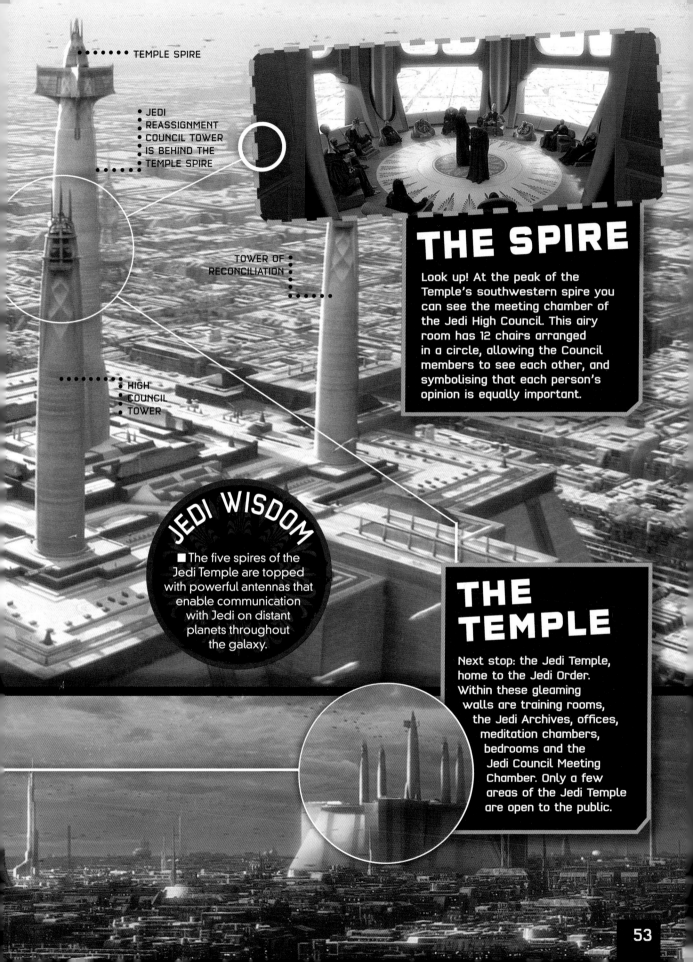

TEMPLE SPIRE

JEDI
REASSIGNMENT
COUNCIL TOWER
IS BEHIND THE
TEMPLE SPIRE

TOWER OF
RECONCILIATION

HIGH
COUNCIL
TOWER

THE SPIRE

Look up! At the peak of the Temple's southwestern spire you can see the meeting chamber of the Jedi High Council. This airy room has 12 chairs arranged in a circle, allowing the Council members to see each other, and symbolising that each person's opinion is equally important.

JEDI WISDOM

■ The five spires of the Jedi Temple are topped with powerful antennas that enable communication with Jedi on distant planets throughout the galaxy.

THE TEMPLE

Next stop: the Jedi Temple, home to the Jedi Order. Within these gleaming walls are training rooms, the Jedi Archives, offices, meditation chambers, bedrooms and the Jedi Council Meeting Chamber. Only a few areas of the Jedi Temple are open to the public.

YADDLE
Yaddle contributes wisdom, compassion and patience to the Council.

SAESEE TIIN
Saesee is particularly valued on the Council for his skill of foresight.

KI-ADI-MUNDI
Ki-Adi-Mundi, Mace and Yoda are the three most senior Council members.

THE JEDI HIGH COUNCIL

EVEN PIELL
Even's seriousness makes him well-suited to important Council business.

OPPO RANCISIS
Oppo believes the Council should focus on traditional ideas, not modern ones.

ADI GALLIA
Adi's intuition and network of informants strengthen the Council.

LATER COUNCIL MEMBERS

ANAKIN SKYWALKER
Chancellor Palpatine chooses Anakin to serve as his personal representative on the Council. Palpatine and the Council each want Anakin to spy on the other.

SHAAK TI
The Sith spare Shaak's life so she can report Palpatine's kidnap to the Council.

OBI-WAN KENOBI
Obi-Wan proves himself worthy of a place on the Council during the challenging Clone Wars.

COLEMAN KCAJ
Coleman follows in the footsteps of many Ongree Jedi who have sat on the Council.

YODA
Yoda is the most respected Jedi and leads the High Council.

MACE WINDU
Mace's wisdom meant he joined the Council at the very young age of only 28.

PLO KOON
Plo thinks his friend Qui-Gon Jinn deserves a seat on the Council, but the others find Qui-Gon too unpredictable.

IF YOU PROVE YOURSELF to be among the most skilled and wise Jedi, then you may be given the highest honour – a seat on the Jedi High Council. As a Council member, you will have a role in organising the Jedi Order. There are always 12 seats and if a member dies or steps down, a new member is selected by the Council to replace them.

DEPA BILLABA
Experiencing the horrors of the Clone Wars causes Depa to turn to the dark side.

YARAEL POOF
Yarael has two brains with which to ponder Council debates.

EETH KOTH
Eeth's intelligence and insight bring clarity to Council discussions.

STASS ALLIE
Before she joined the Council, Stass had a role as an advisor to senior officials in the Republic.

COLEMAN TREBOR
Coleman is media savvy and becomes the spokesperson for the Council.

KIT FISTO
Kit's achievements in the Clone Wars earn him a seat on the Council.

AGEN KOLAR
Agen is very loyal to the Council and, like most Jedi, does not question its decisions.

JEDI WISDOM
■ There are three types of Council membership. Life members commit for life. Long-term members can step down. Limited-term members serve for a fixed period.

JEDI WISDOM

For Jedi, wisdom and knowledge are the keys to success. A mission's outcome can hinge on having the most accurate data available. Gathering information is a never-ending task. Like Obi-Wan, you must ensure your facts are reliable and up-to-date. Here are some tips to guide you on your search.

4. MAKE CONTACTS

Sometimes it's not what you know but who. Some people are happy to talk, but others may want money. You never know who might be useful. When Obi-Wan seeks information about underworld weapons, he goes to his old friend Dexter Jettster.

1. USE THE JEDI ARCHIVES

With its ancient collection of Holocrons and millions of holobooks, the Jedi Archives are the perfect place to start your search for knowledge. Every time a piece of information is learned by the Jedi Order, it is filed and stored in the Archives for future use.

2. DIG DEEP

Always question and analyse your data – don't take anything at face value. Once, Obi-Wan couldn't find the planet Kamino in the Archives' records. Jedi Librarian Jocasta Nu told him that meant Kamino didn't exist. Obi-Wan was not so sure – someone may have tampered with the Archives.

3. GO UNDERCOVER

On the trail of a tricky villain, you might have to improvise. If you can't learn the truth through simple methods, you may have to resort to spying. Obi-Wan tracked Count Dooku to Geonosis where he overheard him discussing his plans for a Death Star.

5. GO THE EXTRA MILE

Sometimes, all the research in the galaxy is not enough. If nobody is willing to talk, you might just have to put in lots of extra effort to get the facts. When Obi-Wan was chasing Zam Wesell for information, he risked his life by speeding through Coruscant's skylanes hanging on to an assassin droid!

Holocrons are mysterious databanks that store the deepest secrets of the Jedi. Unlike simple data files and holobooks, these ancient artefacts can be accessed only by using the Force.

Informatic stations are situated throughout the Jedi Archives. Insert a holobook into the station and it will link up with new data being accessed from all over the galaxy.

Obi-Wan Kenobi is a model Jedi. He is humble, calm and steadfast, but can be combative when the need arises. Tutored by Qui-Gon, he passes his knowledge on to Anakin Skywalker and, later, to Anakin's son, Luke.

Obi-Wan KENOBI

JEDI STATS

SPECIES: HUMAN
HOMEWORLD: STEWJON
BIRTHDATE: 57 BBY
HEIGHT: 1.79 M (5 FT 11 IN)
RANK: JEDI MASTER
TRAINED BY: QUI-GON JINN
WEAPON: BLUE-BLADED LIGHTSABER
PREFERRED COMBAT STYLE: FORM IV (ATARU); LATER FORM III (SORESU)
TRADEMARK: NEGOTIATION

Obi-Wan is an ace with a lightsaber. When he was only a Padawan, he took on Darth Maul and his double-bladed lightsaber – and won.

LAYERED TUNIC

HOODED
ROBE

HIGH HOPES
Obi-Wan sees a little of his former self in his Padawan's arrogance and impatience. This makes him believe that he can influence Anakin to be a better Jedi, as his Master, Qui-Gon, did for him.

THE NEGOTIATOR
Obi-Wan is known for his ability to resolve disputes with words and reason. People listen to him because of his charm and skills as a negotiator, but also thanks to his reputation with a lightsaber. These qualities make him a respected General in the Clone Wars.

STANDING FIRM
Obi-Wan is fiercely loyal to the Jedi Order, democracy and justice. Even when held prisoner by Count Dooku, he refuses to join him. Nothing would make Obi-Wan turn his back on what he believes in.

59

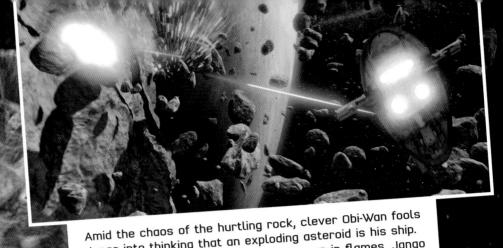

Amid the chaos of the hurtling rock, clever Obi-Wan fools Jango into thinking that an exploding asteroid is his ship. Believing that he has seen Obi-Wan go up in flames, Jango zooms off, not expecting to see Obi-Wan again.

HOW DO YOU OUTWIT A BOUNTY HUNTER?

WHEN A BOUNTY HUNTER is fighting you, he or she will not stop until the job is done and you are captured – or worse. Obi-Wan hates flying at the best of times, but now ruthless Jango Fett is gunning for him. Being a good pilot, and even steering his Delta-7 starfighter into an asteroid belt, is not enough to throw Jango. It requires something much more cunning to outwit him.

DARK SUSPICIONS

Mace has never hit it off with Anakin. Mace's deep connection with the Force means that he can sense Anakin's strong emotional attachments and so he fears for his future. Mace tries to keep Anakin in check, but the more he does this, the more he pushes Anakin away.

Mace never ignores a Jedi in trouble so he is quick to volunteer for the dangerous mission to Geonosis. The daring rescue quickly escalates into full-scale battle, but Mace's skill helps him and his troops to victory.

Mace
WINDU

Across the galaxy, Mace Windu is respected for his wisdom and nobility. As a senior member of the Jedi Council, he has heavy burdens to bear. Mace has a deep knowledge of Jedi history and philosophy. When he talks, people listen.

JEDI STATS

SPECIES: HUMAN

HOMEWORLD: HARUUN KAL

BIRTHDATE: 72 BBY

HEIGHT: 1.88 M (6 FT 2 IN)

RANK: JEDI MASTER

TRAINED BY: UNKNOWN

WEAPON: VIOLET-BLADED LIGHTSABER

PREFERRED COMBAT STYLE: FORM VII (JUYO/VAAPAD)

TRADEMARK: STRENGTH

NO PUSHOVER

For Mace, the Jedi are peacekeepers, not soldiers. He likes to spend his time meditating in the Jedi Temple, but that doesn't mean he's a coward. When events force the Jedi into war, Mace is ready to stand up and fight for the things he believes in – the Republic and the Jedi Order.

RARE VIOLET BLADE

GRIP FOR SWIFT ONE-HANDED STRIKES

JEDI UTILITY POUCH

BETRAYED

As a guardian of the Republic, Mace steps up to arrest Chancellor Palpatine when he learns that he is a Sith Lord. The powerful Jedi is capable of defeating Palpatine. However, Mace's misgivings about Anakin return to haunt him. Anakin steps in and Mace dies.

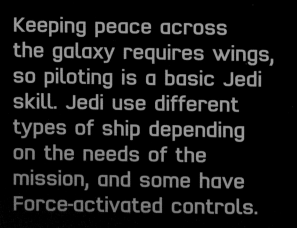

Keeping peace across the galaxy requires wings, so piloting is a basic Jedi skill. Jedi use different types of ship depending on the needs of the mission, and some have Force-activated controls.

PRESSURIZED COCKPIT

DELTA-7 STARFIGHTER

• MAIN USE: SCOUT AND PURSUIT
This small, wedge-shaped ship is sleek and fast – ideal for keeping a low profile during enemy pursuit. Obi-Wan pilots one of these streamlined ships on his scout mission to Kamino, making use of its excellent manoeuvrability when pursuing the bounty hunter Jango Fett.

ANCIENT JEDI SYMBOL

LENGTH: 8 m (26 ft)
HYPERDRIVE RATING: Class 1.0
CAPACITY: 1 person

LENGTH: 5.47 m (18 ft)
HYPERDRIVE RATING: Class 1.0
CAPACITY: 1 person

ETA-2 INTERCEPTOR

• MAIN USE: COMBAT
This compact model is the Jedi ship of choice in the last years of the Republic. Adapted so Jedi pilots could use the Force instead of traditional controls, this lightweight vehicle is fast and agile. It does not have its own internal hyperdrive, so it uses an external booster ring to reach hyperspace.

SECONDARY ION CANNON

WINGS OPEN DURING INTENSE FIGHTING

LONG-BARRELLED LASER CANNON

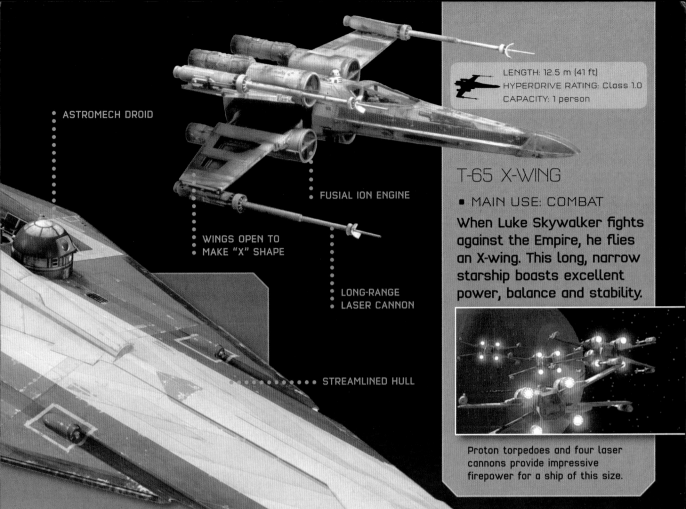

ASTROMECH DROID

FUSIAL ION ENGINE

WINGS OPEN TO
MAKE "X" SHAPE

LONG-RANGE
LASER CANNON

STREAMLINED HULL

LENGTH: 12.5 m (41 ft)
HYPERDRIVE RATING: Class 1.0
CAPACITY: 1 person

T-65 X-WING

- MAIN USE: COMBAT

When Luke Skywalker fights
against the Empire, he flies
an X-wing. This long, narrow
starship boasts excellent
power, balance and stability.

Proton torpedoes and four laser
cannons provide impressive
firepower for a ship of this size.

BORROWED SPEED

Jedi missions are unpredictable and you can't always
expect the perfect vehicle to be ready and waiting.
Sometimes you have to improvise with what's available.

TATOOINE SWOOP BIKE

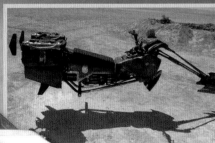

Anakin borrows
Owen Lars's swoop
bike for his search
for his mother.
This utilitarian,
repulsorlift bike is
perfect for the sand
dunes of Tatooine.

HOTH SNOWSPEEDER

On the icy planet of
Hoth, Luke flies a T-47
snowspeeder. These agile
two-seaters are civilian craft
that have been adapted for
battle with dual forward-
facing cannons and a rear
harpoon gun.

CORUSCANT AIRSPEEDER

Anakin's choice for a high-speed chase was a good one.
This open-cockpit, twin turbojet-engine luxury speeder
zips through the busy traffic over Coruscant.

Anakin refuses to abandon his Master. He shunts his ship into Obi-Wan's in the hope of knocking the buzz droids off. They are all dislodged apart from one – which crawls onto Anakin's ship!

WHAT DO YOU DO WHEN BUZZ DROIDS ATTACK?

BUZZ DROIDS ARE BAD NEWS for a pilot. These small, scuttling robots cling to a ship and dismantle it from the outside in. Above Coruscant, Obi-Wan's ETA-2 Interceptor is attacked by buzz droids, which start shutting down its systems. Firing at them is no good, because it risks destroying the ship! The only way to defeat them is teamwork.

Astromech droids are perfectly positioned on the outside of ships to target buzz droids. However, Obi-Wan's astromech droid, R4-P17, is no match for them and he is pulled apart in seconds. Anakin's droid, R2-D2, is made of sterner stuff. He zaps the buzz droid right in its centre eye.

Kit FISTO

Kit Fisto is a popular Jedi Master, respected as much for his fighting skill as for his ready smile. An easygoing Jedi, Kit values friendship as highly as he values the Jedi Code.

SENSORY HEAD TENTACLES

SENSITIVE

Kit is able to breathe in both air and water. He also has tentacles sprouting from his head, which he uses to sense the feelings of those around him. Being able to detect changing emotions enhances Kit's people skills, and gives him an edge on the battlefield.

UNBLINKING, BIG EYES GIVE EXCELLENT NIGHT VISION

LIGHTSABER ADAPTED TO BE WATERPROOF

BRAVE TO THE END

Kit Fisto is not one to stand still when villains are nearby. He joins Mace Windu on his mission to arrest Chancellor Palpatine, but is killed when Palpatine draws his lightsaber and attacks.

JEDI STATS

SPECIES: NAUTOLAN
HOMEWORLD: GLEE ANSELM
BIRTHDATE: UNKNOWN
HEIGHT: 1.96 M (6 FT 5 IN)
RANK: JEDI MASTER
TRAINED BY: UNKNOWN
PREFERRED COMBAT STYLE:
FORM I (SHII-CHO)
TRADEMARK: FRIENDLINESS

Plo KOON

JEDI STATS

SPECIES: KEL DOR

HOMEWORLD: DORIN

BIRTHDATE: UNKNOWN

HEIGHT: 1.88 M (6 FT 2 IN)

RANK: JEDI MASTER

TRAINED BY: UNKNOWN

PREFERRED COMBAT STYLE: FORM V (DJEM SO/SHIEN)

TRADEMARK: DECISIVENESS

Plo Koon is a senior member of the Jedi Council. This stern Jedi Master is known for making fast decisions. Plo's ability to act quickly makes him both a fierce warrior and a fearsome starship pilot.

THICK KEL DOR HIDE

GAS MASK FOR OXYGEN-RICH ATMOSPHERES

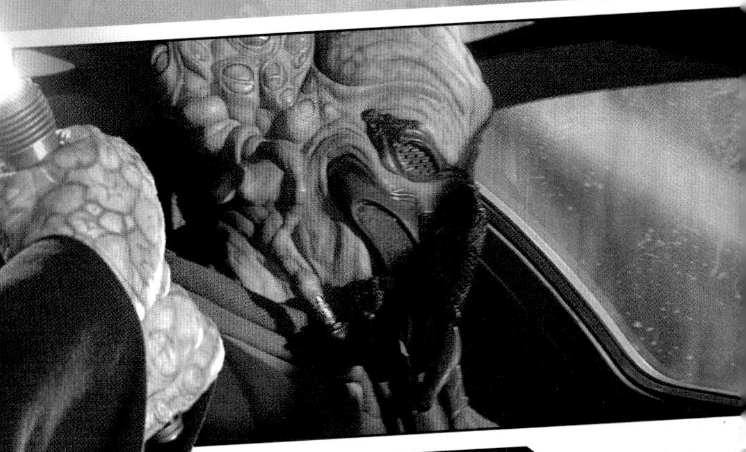

STARFIGHTER HERO

As a Jedi General, Plo was one of the best pilots in the Republic Fleet. The mere sight of his blade-shaped starfighter terrified his enemies. But when his own troops opened fire on his ship during Order 66, Plo could do nothing to save himself.

MAN OF CONVICTION

Plo is motivated by a strict sense of right and wrong. Although he is always focused on hunting down the bad guys, he displays such concern for his troops that he has been known to risk his own life to save theirs.

THE JEDI TEMPLE is full of useful gadgets. Whether you are training a new Padawan, searching for an underwater city, taking on an AT-AT walker or travelling to the Outer Rim, make sure you take along the right tools. You never know when they'll come in handy.

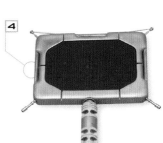

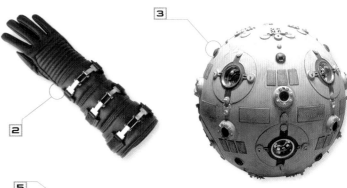

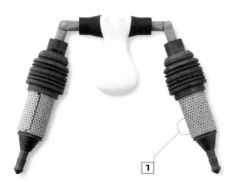

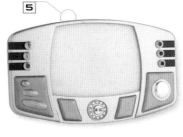

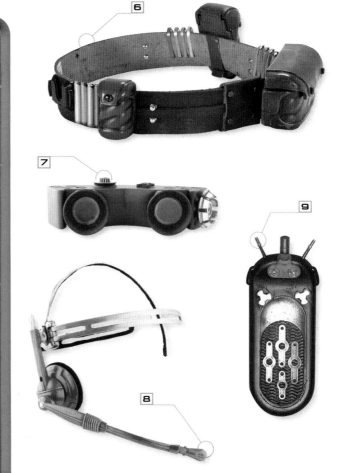

KEY

1. A99 AQUATA BREATHER to enable breathing underwater, in outer space or in a poisonous environment.

2. Auto-seal, close fitting GLOVE to cover and protect artificial limbs.

3. TRAINING REMOTE to fire harmless beams at Padawans during lightsaber training.

4. Force-operated TESTING SCREEN to constantly challenge Padawans.

5. VIEWSCREEN to view incoming communications.

6. UTILITY BELT with storage pouches and food capsules.

7. MACROBINOCULARS for extreme long distance and outer space viewing.

8. HEADSET COMLINK to enable communication when in flight.

9. Security-enhanced COMLINK to send and receive audio messages.

10. CABLE RETRIEVER to retrieve grappling hook line.

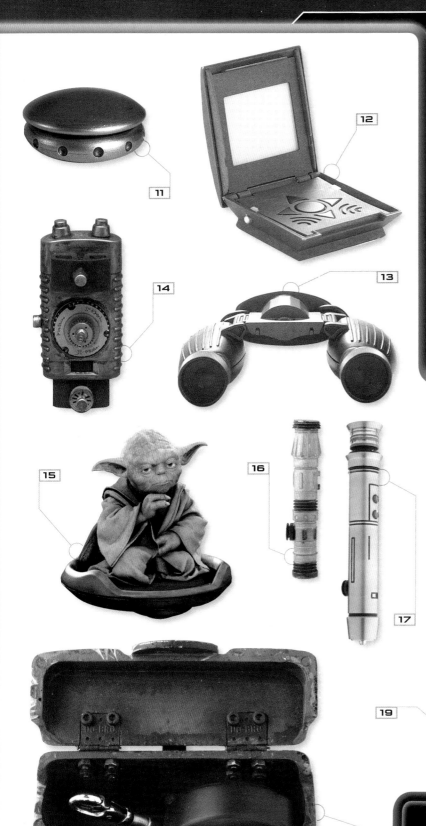

11. TRACER BEACON to track a moving target.

12. SCANNER MONITOR to detect nearby movement, life-forms, metal or communication signals.

13. BINOCULARS to observe long distances.

14. IMAGE ENHANCER for when transmissions are coming from exceptionally long distances.

15. HOVER CHAIR to enable easier transport within Jedi Temple.

16. TRAINING LIGHTSABER for Younglings with reduced-size hilt and low-energy blade.

17. LIGHTSABER for use during battles and duels.

18. HOLOPROJECTOR to send and receive secure, encrypted holotransmissions.

19. GRAPPLING HOOK for leaping extremely high or crossing large chasms.

20. Sturdy UTILITY POUCH with built-in grappling hook and line.

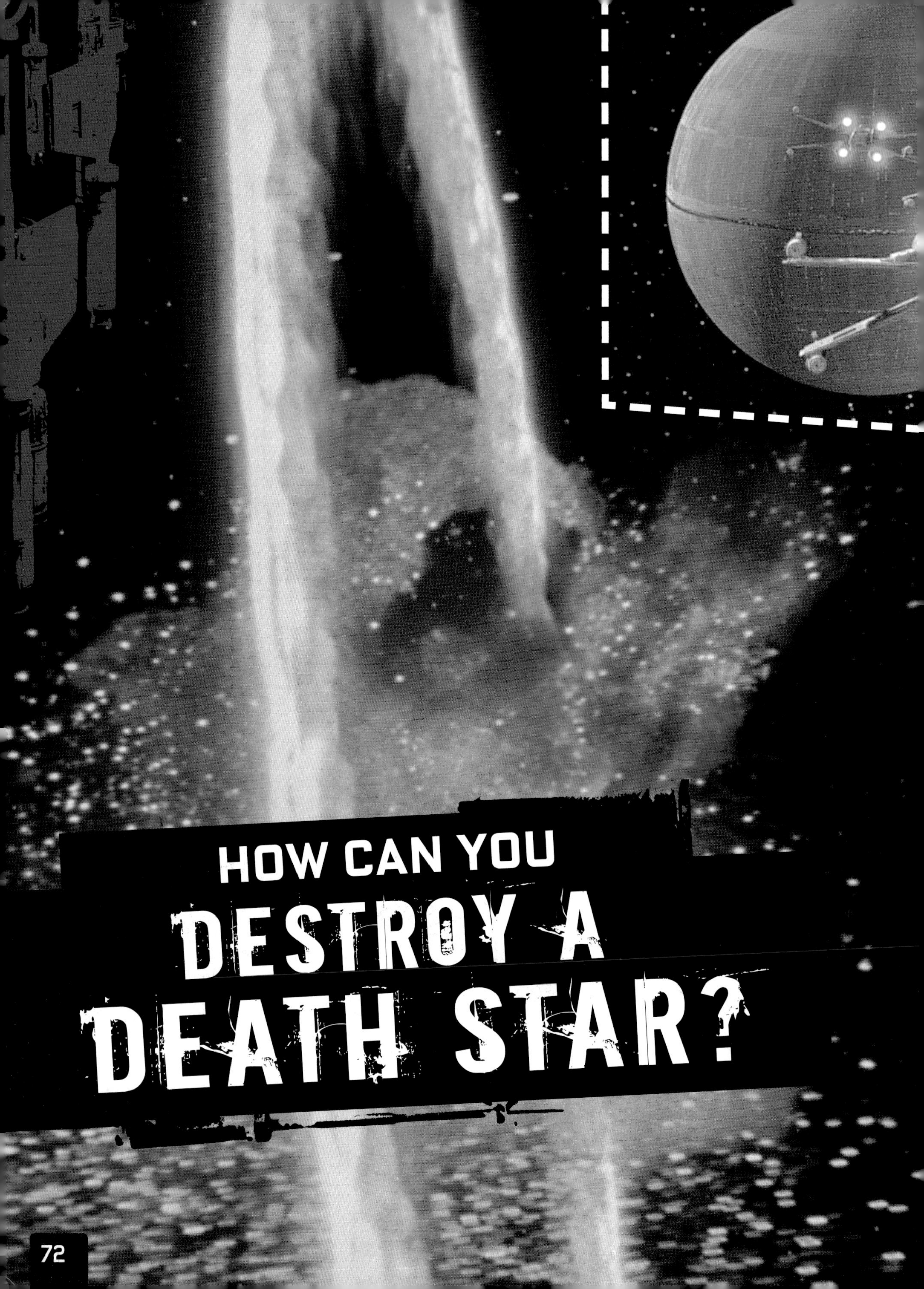

HOW CAN YOU
DESTROY A
DEATH STAR?

All the brave Y-wing pilots of Gold Squadron, except one, are destroyed by Imperial fire. Next, Red Squadron gets to work in their X-wings, but the mission is just too hard. Pilot after pilot is defeated, until only one remains.

The last hope lies with Luke Skywalker. But he is no ordinary pilot: the Force is strong with him. To the horror of the other Rebels, Luke switches off his tracking computer. He hears Obi-Wan telling him that if he trusts in the Force and listens to his feelings, then the Force will guide him.

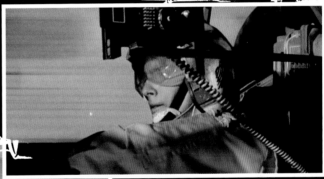

Bullseye! Luke launches the proton torpedo right on target. It begins a chain reaction that causes the whole station to explode. There's just enough time for Luke to get out of there before he is engulfed in flames.

THE GIANT ARMOURED station called the Death Star is like the Empire that created it – huge, powerful and dangerous. It seems impossible to defeat, but the resourceful Rebel Alliance has found its weakness: one direct hit on a small exhaust port opening will reduce the monster to rubble. Getting close to it, however, is no easy task.

JEDI COMRADES

The Jedi Order is made up of beings from every corner of the galaxy. Species, age, height or gender are not important; it matters only that you are attuned to the Force and committed to the Jedi way. Every Jedi has something unique to offer the Order.

STRONG WILLED

SPECIES: THOLOTHIAN
HOMEWORLD: THOLOTH

STASS ALLIE seeks peace, but she believes that sometimes you have to fight in order to achieve it.

FALLEN JEDI

SPECIES: CHALACTAN
HOMEWORLD: CORUSCANT

DEPA BILLABA sees terrible things in the Clone Wars and her troubled emotions lead her to the dark side.

WILL OF STEEL

SPECIES: IRIDONIAN ZABRAK
HOMEWORLD: NAR SHADDAA

EETH KOTH works so hard at disciplining his mind that he can withstand great physical pain.

SUPER-SENSORY

SPECIES: TOGRUTA
HOMEWORLD: SHILI

SHAAK TI's hollow headtails allow her to sense her surroundings ultrasonically or duck blaster fire.

WAR WISDOM

SPECIES: THISSPIASIAN
HOMEWORLD: THISSPIAS

OPPO RANCISIS is a military mastermind and the Republic's secret weapon in the Clone Wars.

ATHLETIC JEDI

SPECIES: HUMAN
HOMEWORLD: KUAT

BULTAR SWAN is a fan of martial arts and this greatly influences the way she swings her lightsaber.

POWERFUL JEDI

SPECIES: UNKNOWN
HOMEWORLD: UNKNOWN

YADDLE has mastered Morichro – the ability to control others' body functions such as their breathing.

INJURED JEDI

SPECIES: LANNIK
HOMEWORLD: LANNIK

EVEN PIELL lost an eye in battle and he wears his scars as a reminder of past troubles.

LONER

SPECIES: IKTOTCHI
HOMEWORLD: IKTOTCH

SAESEE TIIN likes to spend time alone, meditating and honing his skill of foresight.

CUNNING JEDI

SPECIES: QUERMIAN
HOMEWORLD: QUERMIA

YARAEL POOF prefers not to use weapons – he uses his mastery of mind trickery against his enemies.

FAITHFUL JEDI

SPECIES: THOLOTHIAN
HOMEWORLD: CORUSCANT

ADI GALLIA is Stass Allie's cousin. She was inspired to be a Jedi as a child, when Even Piell saved her life.

FIERCE FIGHTER

SPECIES: IRIDONIAN ZABRAK
HOMEWORLD: CORUSCANT

AGEN KOLAR is no diplomat. Instead he prefers to influence people in battle, with his lightsaber.

OPEN-MINDED

SPECIES: ONGREE
HOMEWORLD: SKUSTELL

COLEMAN KCAJ's face shape allows him to see different angles. He can also see many sides to a problem.

LANGUAGE MASTER

SPECIES: VURK
HOMEWORLD: SEMBLA

COLEMAN TREBOR is a skilled communicator. He becomes the spokesperson for the Jedi Order.

BOOKWORM

SPECIES: HUMAN
HOMEWORLD: CORUSCANT

JOCASTA NU is a Consular Jedi. She is an academic, not a soldier, and looks after the Jedi Archives.

THE PATH TO THE...

DEDICATION
Qui-Gon's dying wish is that Obi-Wan train Anakin. Although he is sometimes hot-headed and impatient, Anakin becomes a loyal Padawan.

ANGER
When his mother dies at the hands of Tusken Raiders, Anakin's anger consumes him. He destroys the whole clan.

DEFIANCE
Anakin breaks the Jedi Code by marrying Padmé Amidala in secret. His love makes him so afraid of losing her that he is blinded to all else.

POTENTIAL
As a child, Anakin shows great skill, but also much fear. The Jedi Council is unable to see his future and Anakin is too old, so it refuses to train him.

DARK SIDE

Anakin Skywalker is a great Jedi, but he struggles to control his feelings and greed. If Jedi do not keep their emotions in check, they are open to the temptations of the dark side. Darth Sidious covets Anakin as a Sith Apprentice so he plays with Anakin's emotions until they consume him and draw him over to the dark side.

POWER
During the Clone Wars, Anakin proves himself to be a brave Jedi hero. But he still wants more and feels that the Jedi are holding him back.

HATE
Anakin is goaded by Darth Sidious into killing Count Dooku. It is not the Jedi way to kill an unarmed prisoner, but Anakin gives in to his emotions.

EVIL
Anakin is given the Sith name Darth Vader. After fighting his old Master, Obi-Wan, Vader needs a metal suit to keep him alive. His journey to the dark side is complete.

GREED
Anakin is terrified Padmé will die. Darth Sidious claims he can save her, so Anakin greedily chooses the Sith over his fellow Jedi, and Mace dies.

WHAT HAPPENS WHEN A STUDENT TURNS ON HIS TEACHER?

THE BOND BETWEEN MASTER and Padawan is strong. From the moment Anakin turns to the dark side, a confrontation with his Master Obi-Wan Kenobi becomes inevitable. On Mustafar, Anakin rejects Obi-Wan's attempts to reason with him. Now serving a new master, a Sith master, Anakin isn't about to let any Jedi get in his way – even if that Jedi is one of his oldest friends.

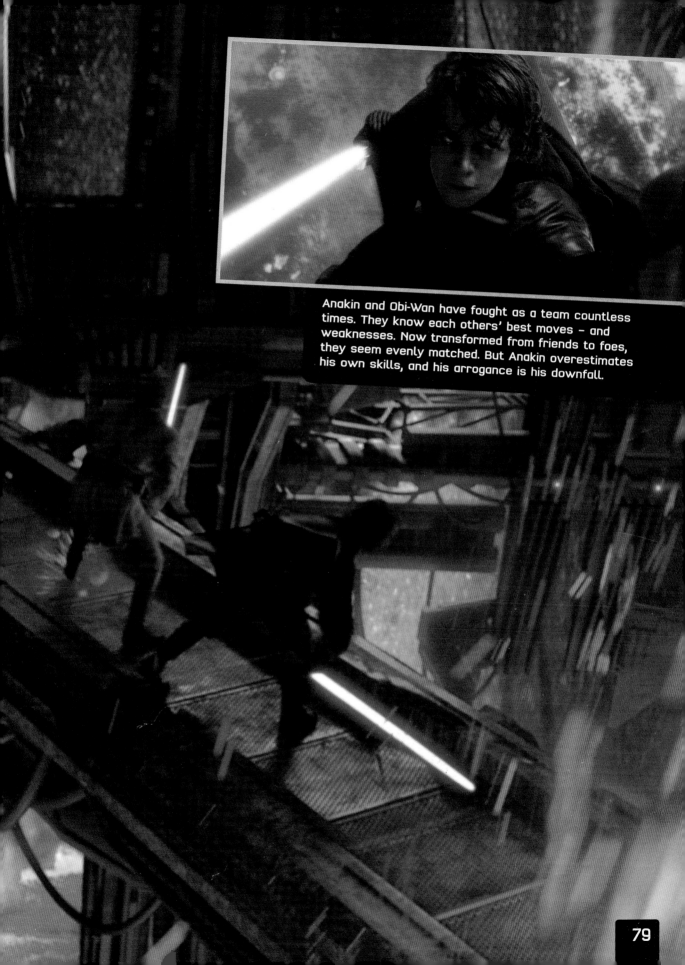

Anakin and Obi-Wan have fought as a team countless times. They know each others' best moves – and weaknesses. Now transformed from friends to foes, they seem evenly matched. But Anakin overestimates his own skills, and his arrogance is his downfall.

DARTH TYRANUS

Long ago Count Dooku rejected the Order
that trained him as a Jedi. When Darth
Maul is killed, Dooku becomes Darth
Sidious's new Apprentice, Darth Tyranus.

DARTH MAUL

A Dathomirian trained
in secret by Darth
Sidious, Darth Maul
is the first Sith to
reveal himself for
1,000 years.

BEWARE THE SITH

FEAR...GREED...HATE...TYRANNY...these are the lifeblood of the
Sith. The Sith are the oldest enemy of the Jedi. They, too, use
the Force, but they have been seduced by the powers of its
dark side. The Sith are driven by their greed for power and
will not let anyone stand in their way – especially the Jedi.

DARTH VADER

Darth Vader is Sidious's final Apprentice. Vader is controlled by his Master and no longer bears any resemblance to the man he once was – Anakin Skywalker. His body is so damaged that he is dependent on a metal suit to keep him alive.

DARTH SIDIOUS

The Dark Lord of the Sith, Darth Sidious is a master of deception. For decades he fools everyone into thinking that he is the kind and peaceful Palpatine. In this guise, he rises to the position of Supreme Chancellor of the Republic and manipulates both sides in the Clone Wars. When the time comes to fulfill his master plan, he destroys the Republic and installs himself as Emperor of a new galactic order.

JEDI WISDOM

■ The Rule of Two states that there can be only two Sith at a time: one Master and one Apprentice. When Darth Sidious wants Anakin as an Apprentice, he manipulates him into killing Darth Tyranus.

ORDER 6

ORDER 66 IS a secret military instruction created by Chancellor Palpatine to help him take over the galaxy. The Clone Army is programmed to follow the orders of the Chancellor, so when he gives Order 66, they have to act. The Clone Army turn on their former allies, the Jedi, with deadly consequences...

BREAKING NEWS: Rumours circulate that the clone troopers of the Republic Army have received executive orders from Chancellor Palpatine...

...UTAPAU: Commander Cody orders an AT-TE clone pilot to fire on Obi-Wan Kenobi...Jedi believed to have escaped...order issued to shoot on sight...

...FELUCIA: Commander Bly and the 327th Star Corps turn on Aayla Secura...Jedi confirmed dead...

...SALEUCAMI: Commander Neyo and CT-3423 fire on Stass Allie...death confirmed...

6

...MYGEETO: Galactic Marines led by Commander Bacara attack and kill Ki-Adi-Mundi...mission complete...

...CATO NEIMOIDIA: Plo Koon's Delta-7 starfighter shot down by Captain Jag...wreckage confirms pilot dead...

...KASHYYYK: 41st Elite Corps trooper and Commander Gree sneak up on Yoda...soldiers killed in counterattack... suspect fled...order issued to shoot on sight...

...CORUSCANT: Anakin Skywalker now loyal to Sith...leads 501st clone trooper legion in raid on Jedi Temple...no survivors...

...THE DARK TIMES BEGIN...

WHAT HAPPENS WHEN OLD ENEMIES MEET?

JEDI WISDOM

■ Some Jedi, like Obi-Wan, can make themselves one with the Force. This means that they can live on after death as part of the Force.

TWENTY YEARS HAVE passed since Darth Vader and Obi-Wan duelled on Mustafar. Aboard the Death Star, the former Jedi Master and his Padawan meet again. There is only hatred and revenge on Vader's mind, but Obi-Wan is serving a more important purpose. While the Rebels attempt to rescue Princess Leia, Obi-Wan engages Vader in a duel.

Although Obi-Wan is still a match for Darth Vader, he allows himself to be killed in the duel, giving Luke and the Rebels precious time to escape. Unlike Vader, who tries to control death, Obi-Wan is willing to submit to it: he passes over to the non-physical to show Luke that his spirit can continue beyond death.

SEPARATED AT BIRTH

When Luke sets off to rescue a princess, he finds more than he bargained for: a twin sister. He is fiercely protective of his sister, Leia, and does everything he can to keep her safe.

Luke always sees the good in people, even someone as cruel as Darth Vader. He never gives up hope that his father will change.

Luke
SKYWALKER

Luke is an adventure-seeking boy from Tatooine who brings new hope to the Rebel Alliance and the few remaining Jedi. He comes to Jedi training late in life, but the Force is strong with him and he is guided by a wiser Obi-Wan and Yoda. Luke faces a daunting task: to defeat Darth Vader and the Emperor.

JEDI STATS

SPECIES: HUMAN

HOMEWORLD: BORN ON POLIS MASSA; RAISED ON TATOOINE

BIRTHDATE: 19 BBY

HEIGHT: 1.72 M (5 FT 8 IN)

RANK: JEDI MASTER

TRAINED BY: OBI-WAN & YODA

WEAPON: BLUE & LATER A GREEN-BLADED LIGHTSABER

PREFERRED COMBAT STYLE: FORM V (SHIEN/DJEM SO)

TRADEMARK: LOYALTY

EXCEPTIONAL CONNECTION WITH THE FORCE

HIS FATHER'S SON?

Luke's father is Anakin Skywalker. Like him, Luke is a good pilot and has a knack for knowing how to fix things, and he can also be impatient and reckless. However, Luke differs from his father in one key way: despite the Emperor's best efforts, Luke refuses to submit to the dark side.

LIGHTSABER ONCE BELONGED TO ANAKIN

FAITHFUL FRIEND
Luke shows great loyalty to his friends, even the droids. To Luke, astromech droid R2-D2 is far more than just a robot, and he wouldn't swap him for the world.

Wampas are deadly ice creatures who aren't fussy about what or whom they eat. A human wouldn't normally stand a chance against these mighty beasts, but Luke has a special weapon – the Force.

HOW CAN YOU ESCAPE FROM A FIERCE WAMPA?

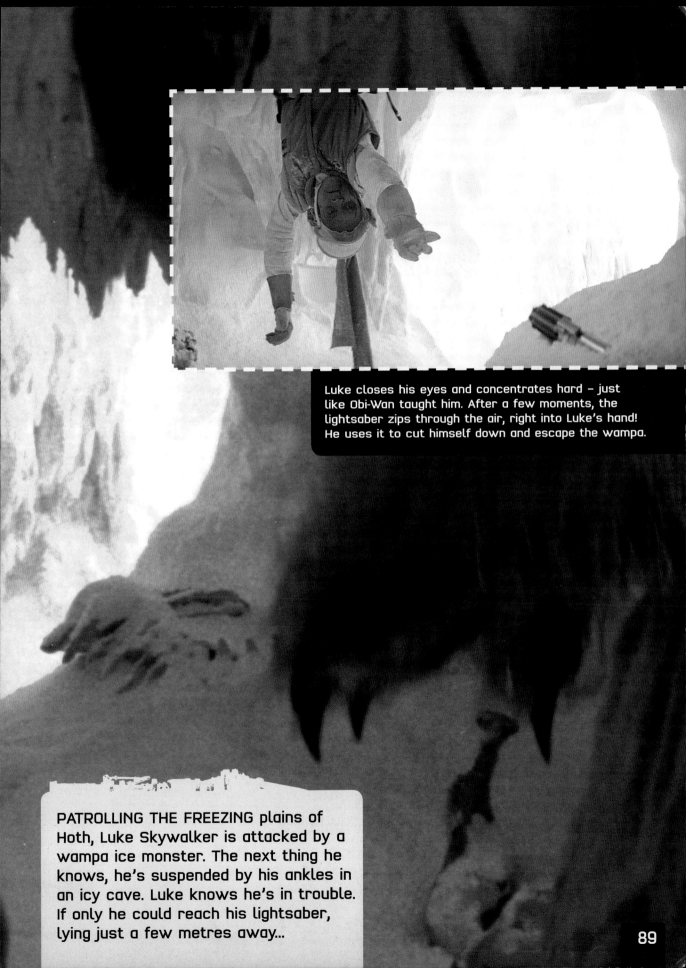

Luke closes his eyes and concentrates hard – just like Obi-Wan taught him. After a few moments, the lightsaber zips through the air, right into Luke's hand! He uses it to cut himself down and escape the wampa.

PATROLLING THE FREEZING plains of Hoth, Luke Skywalker is attacked by a wampa ice monster. The next thing he knows, he's suspended by his ankles in an icy cave. Luke knows he's in trouble. If only he could reach his lightsaber, lying just a few metres away...

HOW CAN THE LIGHT SIDE OF THE FORCE DEFEAT THE DARK SIDE?

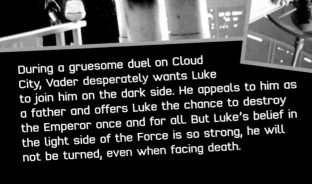

During a gruesome duel on Cloud City, Vader desperately wants Luke to join him on the dark side. He appeals to him as a father and offers Luke the chance to destroy the Emperor once and for all. But Luke's belief in the light side of the Force is so strong, he will not be turned, even when facing death.

Luke resists the dark side again during another duel with his father on the second Death Star. Luke's extreme dedication to the light side shames his father, and when the Emperor attempts to kill Luke, Vader hears Luke's pleas and rescues his son. As he dies, Vader finally finds peace in the light side of the Force.

THE AGE-OLD battle between Jedi and Sith, between the light and dark sides of the Force, has always hinged on temptation. Sith Lords often recruit Jedi with promises of incredible power. However, sometimes the desire for honour and justice can be powerful too.

GLOSSARY

ASTROMECH DROID
- A utility robot that repairs and helps navigate starships.

BATTLE DROID
- A Separatist robot designed for combat.

BATTLE OF GEONOSIS
- Conflict in 22 BBY where the Republic Clone Army attacks the Separatists' battle droid army on the planet Geonosis, marking the start of the Clone Wars.

BATTLE OF NABOO
- Conflict in 32 BBY where the Trade Federation invades the planet Naboo with their battle droid army.

BLOCKADE
- A political strategy that prevents food and resources from reaching a specific destination.

BOUNTY HUNTER
- Someone who tracks down, captures or kills wanted people in exchange for money.

BUREAUCRATIC
- Consisting of lots of time-consuming office work.

BUZZ DROIDS
- Small droids that latch onto and sabotage enemy spacecraft; often used by Separatist forces in space battles.

CEREAN
- A species from the planet Cerea; Cereans are similar to humans but have tall heads to house their double brains.

CHANCELLOR
- The title given to the head of the Galactic Senate and Republic.

CHOSEN ONE
- The subject of an ancient prophecy referring to an individual who will restore balance to the Force and to the universe.

CLONE ARMY
- An army of genetically identical soldiers, all trained to be perfect warriors. They fight for the Republic.

CLONE WARS
- A series of galaxy-wide battles fought between the Republic's Clone Army and the droid army of the Confederacy of Independent Systems, which took place between 22 and 19 BBY.

CORUSCANT
- The capital of the Republic. This planet is home to the Senate Building, the Jedi Temple and the Jedi Council.

CYBORG
- A being that is partly a living organism and partly a robot.

DARK SIDE
- The evil side of the Force that feeds off negative emotions and offers raw power to those who study it.

DEMOCRACY
- A system of government where all senior politicians are elected by the population.

DROIDEKA
- A destroyer droid used in battle by the Separatists.

EMPEROR
- Ruler of the Empire.

EMPIRE
- A tyrannical power that rules the galaxy from 19 BBY to 4 ABY under the leadership of the Emperor, who is a Sith Lord.

FORCE
- The energy that flows through all living things, which can used for either good or evil.

FORCE LIGHTNING
- Deadly rays of blue energy that can be used as a weapon by someone who has embraced the dark side of the Force.

GRAND MASTER
- The leader of the Jedi High Council.

GUNGANS

■ An amphibious species from the planet Naboo.

JEDI

■ A member of the Jedi Order who studies the light side of the Force.

JEDI ARCHIVES

■ The large collection of research and knowledge about the history of the Jedi Order; housed in the Jedi Temple.

JEDI CODE

■ The set of rules that establishes the behavior and lifestyle of members of the Jedi Order.

JEDI HIGH COUNCIL

■ The 12 senior, respected members of the Jedi Order who meet to make important decisions and give advice.

JEDI KNIGHT

■ A member of the Jedi Order who has studied as a Padawan under a Jedi Master and who has passed the Jedi Trials.

JEDI MASTER

■ A rank for Jedi Knights who have performed an exceptional deed or have trained a Jedi Knight.

JEDI ORDER

■ An ancient organisation that promotes peace and justice throughout the galaxy.

JEDI PURGE

■ The attempt by Chancellor Palpatine in 19 BBY to annihilate the entire Jedi Order.

JEDI TEMPLE

■ The headquarters of the Jedi Order, located on the planet Coruscant.

LIGHTSABER

■ A weapon with a blade of pure energy that is used by Jedi and Sith warriors.

LIVING FORCE

■ The view that the Force is present in all living things. Living by this view means relying on instincts, being aware of the people around you and living in the moment.

MENTOR

■ A wise teacher or advisor who gives guidance.

NABOO

■ A beautiful planet near the border of the Outer Rim Territories.

ORDER 66

■ An order given by Chancellor Palpatine that began the Jedi Purge. Every clone trooper in the Clone Army was ordered to kill all members of the Jedi Order.

PADAWAN

■ A Youngling who is chosen to serve an apprenticeship with a Jedi Master.

PODRACING

■ A popular sport, especially on the planet Tatooine, in which competitors race against each other in high-powered Podracers.

REBEL ALLIANCE

■ The organisation that resists and fights against the Empire.

REPUBLIC

■ The democratic government of the galaxy, under leadership of an elected Chancellor.

SENATE

■ Government of the Republic, with representatives from all parts of the galaxy.

SENATOR

■ A person who represents their planet, sector or system in the Senate.

SEPARATISTS

■ An alliance against the Republic. Also known also the Confederacy of Independent Systems.

SITH

■ An ancient sect of Force-sensitives who study the dark side to gain control and succeed in their greedy plans.

TRADE FEDERATION

■ A bureaucratic organisation that controls much of the trade and commerce in the galaxy.

TUSKEN RAIDERS

■ Fearsome savages who live in the desert wastelands of the planet Tatooine; also known as Sand People.

TWI'LEK

■ A species from the planet Ryloth. Twi'leks have colourful skin and a pair of tentacles (lekku) that grow from their heads.

YOUNGLING

■ A Force-sensitive child who joins the Jedi Order to be trained in the Jedi arts.

ZABRAK

■ A species native to the planet Iridonia. Zabraks have small horns on the top of their heads.

INDEX

Characters are listed under their most frequently used common name, for example Luke Skywalker is found under "L" and "Count Dooku" is under "C".

Main entries are in bold.

LONDON, NEW YORK, MELBOURNE,
MUNICH, AND DELHI

For Dorling Kindersley
Editor Shari Last
Senior Editor Elizabeth Dowsett
Designer Toby Truphet
Senior Designer Lynne Moulding
Additional design by Owen Bennett, Nathan Martin,
Rob Perry, Rhys Thomas
Managing Art Editor Ron Stobbart
Publishing Manager Catherine Saunders
Art Director Lisa Lanzarini
Associate Publisher Simon Beecroft
Category Publisher Alex Allan
Production Editor Siu Yin Chan
Production Controller Nick Seston

For Lucasfilm
Executive Editor J. W. Rinzler
Art Director Troy Alders
Keeper of the Holocron Leland Chee
Director of Publishing Carol Roeder

First published in Great Britain in 2011
by Dorling Kindersley Limited
80 Strand, London, WC2R 0RL

4 6 8 10 9 7 5

001-178200—Mar/2011

A CIP catalogue record for this book is
available from the British Library.

ISBN: 978-1-40536-299-3

Colour reproduction by Media Development Printing Ltd
Printed and bound in China by Hung Hing

The publisher would like to thank Chris Trevas and
Chris Reiff for their artwork on pages 42–43 and Julia March
and Victoria Taylor for their editorial work.

Discover more at
www.dk.com
www.starwars.com